INSIDE MAN

INSIDE MAN

The Discipline of Modeling
Human Ways of Being

Mihnea C. Moldoveanu

Stanford Business Books
An Imprint of Stanford University Press
Stanford, California

Stanford University Press
Stanford, California

Special discounts for bulk quantities of Stanford Business Books are available to
corporations, professional associations, and other organizations. For details and
discount information, contact the special sales department of Stanford University
Press. Tel: (650) 736-1782, Fax: (650) 736-1784

Printed in the United States of America on acid-free, archival-quality paper

Library of Congress Cataloging-in-Publication Data

Moldoveanu, Mihnea C.
 Inside man : the discipline of modeling human ways of being /
Mihnea C. Moldoveanu.
  p. cm.
 Includes bibliographical references and index.
 ISBN 978-0-8047-7304-1 (cloth : alk. paper)
1. Human behavior models. 2. Thought and thinking.
3. Psychology—Methodology. I. Title.

BF39.3.M65 2011
150.1′1—dc22

                    2010024489

Designed by Bruce Lundquist
Typeset by Newgen in 10.5/15 Adobe Garamond

*To Ludwig Wittgenstein and Frank Ramsey,
my most attuned thinking partners along the
paths taken herein.*

What can be said at all can be said clearly, and what we cannot talk about we must pass over in silence.

Ludwig Wittgenstein

I have not worked out the mathematical logic of [my procedure] in detail, because this would, I think, be rather like working out to seven places of decimals a result only valid to two.

Frank P. Ramsey

CONTENTS

FIGURES AND TABLES

FIGURES

TABLES

PRELUDE AND AN OUTLINE

Inside Man is a live exercise in modeling human ways of being—thinking, feeling, acting. "Live" means that the book does not merely introduce *models*; it also attempts to teach—impart, imprint—model*ing* and to produce within the reader the abilities, predispositions, and attitudes of the modeler: a *distancing* from the individual whose behavior is modeled, an *engineering* approach to the model-building process, a (self-)critical approach to the process of model testing and elaboration, and a pedagogical and therapeutic approach to communicating and enacting models—to using them to transform the humans whom they model. This book seeks to make the process and the phenomenon of modeling transparent and explicit, and clarifies why modeling human behavior, thought, and feeling should be an interactive process between the modeler and the modeled. As such, it is situated at the intersection of analytical and computational thinking about rationality, reasoning, and choice with the more recent traditions of action science and action research.

Inside Man is a different sort of book from the kind one typically finds on "how to build a model of humans." It introduces the reader not only to the nuts and bolts of *models* but also to the life-world, activities, and mental habits of the *modeler*—and it does so without oversimplifying the logical structures of models themselves. It is different from other books in the field (e.g., Lave and March [1975]; Kreps [1988]; Elster [1989]; Casti [1991]; Gershenfeld [1998]) in that it treats the modeling languages it utilizes as *fundamentally unfinished* and the modeling enterprise as an iteratively and recursively self-correcting activity.

In what follows, the modeler and the modeled are real protagonists—with real wishes, aims, and temptations. The modeled sometimes models the modeler back, and this is something the modeler must keep in mind when building and deploying his models. Here, the modeler's usually privileged epistemic position is never quite secure: Alternative explanations are always possibly and sometimes probably better or more valid than those arising from the model currently being tested. The process of testing a model is not the tidy one whereby "data" supplied by the behavior of the modeled provide dispositive verifications or refutations of hypotheses, but rather one by which the status of data as data must be secured by a process of interaction with the modeled. Moreover, the individual whose behavior or thought is being modeled is available to the modeler for questioning, deliberation, debate, and confrontation; and the modeler will often *need* to avail himself of this opportunity for dialogue.

This is a messy situation. Messy situations can lead to messy outcomes, and it is the métier of the modeler to stare the mess in the face without flinching, averting his gaze, or seeking the comfort of "disciplinary" legitimacy and "foundations." It is just such a "mess" that this book intentionally wades into as a way of highlighting the thoughts, behaviors, and ways of being of the modeler—rather than focusing merely on the cognitive by-products of the modeling activity (i.e., the models themselves).

This does not mean that the models themselves will receive short shrift. They are on prominent display throughout; without them, where would "modeling," as a life form, be? But the models here do not "steal the show" from the activity of modeling, for one *lives out* models of behavior as much as one *knows of*—or can see the world in terms of—such models. It is this "living out" of the models, and of the activity of modeling itself, to which I want to draw the attention of those who can spare it.

I begin by placing the project of this book in the context of the current discursive landscape of normative, descriptive, and prescriptive "science" and of the wider aims of a phenomenology of being-in-the-world (Chapter 1).

My protagonist modeler is heedful of the cleanliness and precision of axiomatic models of choice but is also attuned to both experimental investigations that can be interpreted as placing the validity of the axiomatic bases in peril and to intuitions and insights that arise from his own first-person access to the life-world of the object of his models—another individual—with the result that the modeler will attempt to forge a connected and responsive dialogue among phenomenology and the descriptive, normative approaches to "modeling human behavior."

I then proceed along a path best summarized as "differentiation by parts": Some part of the total function must be kept constant while taking the derivative of the part that is currently in focus. I first consider models of the behavior of a human individual as the outcome of a choice or a set of choices that express or instantiate a set of preferences via more or less complicated deliberation and maximization exercises (Chapter 2). I show how models of behavior as choice can be productively modified and augmented to deal with concerns raised by experimentalists about the putative coherence and invariance of preferences and the consciousness of the chooser. I inquire into ways by which the modeler can justify (to the modeled) the representational choices he makes—his choice of models—and show the importance of the justifiability of a modeler's model to the modeled in situations where the model's object is able to field and respond to reasoned arguments.

I shift the focus of attention next to modeling the epistemic states—or states of mind that are about propositions describing states of the world—and consider probabilistic models of the personal degrees of belief that an individual holds regarding the truth value of various propositions (Chapter 3). The modeler inquires into the epistemic states of the subject of his inquiry by first positing a model for the structure of these states and then offering the subject bets on the truth value of propositions that may be true or false depending on states of the world and ways in which these states are rendered into language. The modeler can justify these models to his subject by positing scenarios in which violating their structure places the subject, with high probability, on the losing side of a bet or a sequence of bets. I show how the modeler can use the basic probabilistic framework for measuring personal degrees of belief to model and inquire into the meaning, kinematics, and dynamics of the epistemic states of his subject and into the dependence of these epistemic states on the subject's visceral and emotional states and the subject's purpose in holding the beliefs that she does.

Chapter 4 introduces models of the processes (e.g., inference) by which the subject of inquiry comes to hold certain beliefs. These models are based on the canonical structure of the problems that a subject can attempt to solve and on a "pico-economics" of thinking, which aims to measure the average, fixed, marginal, and opportunity costs of thinking. The resulting economics of mental behavior allows the modeler to deploy decision-theoretic representations of behavior to represent the dynamics of the subject's "states of mind." The modeler uses this approach to represent the basic processes by which the subject reasons, perceives, and infers (i.e., thinks) and to make inferences and measurements of the states that a thinking subject may be said to undergo, "along the way," while thinking. The model is then extended to include states of being of the subject that, although "intelligent," are nonrepresentational in the following sense: They do not rely on the *explicit* representation by the subject of a specific problem, of the procedures that may be used to solve it, of the objects and entities that together are used to describe the current and desired conditions of the problem solver, or of the space of possible solutions to the problem the subject is attempting to solve.

Although learning can be understood as a problem-directed inferential process, it is treated separately in Chapter 5, wherein the modeler attempts to come to grips with what it means for a subject to "learn" and what it means for the modeler to learn about the ways in which the subject learns. A particular model of learning is proposed—one that navigates between the Scylla of unbounded inductivism and the Charybdis of untethered fallibilism—and is shown to accommodate basic insights and intuitions about learning. This model attempts to salvage both the "betting odds" interpretation of personal degrees of belief and the fallibilist approach to the lawlike generalizations that undergird inference from the known to the unknown.

Because the modeler is in frequent and crucial *dialogue* with the subject of his inquiry, the final chapter (Chapter 6) sets forth a model of dialogical communication that constrains both the modeler and the subject to produce oral behaviors that are coherent, connected, responsive, relevant, and informative contributions to a dialogue. Participation in a true dialogue commits the discussants to certain obligations to justify and explain their utterances

lest the latter should fail to count as "speech acts." This model of communication enjoins participants in a genuine dialogue from transgressing against
a set of constitutive rules about what it means for an exchange of oral noises
to constitute a dialogue—on pain of excluding themselves from the dialogue
and losing their status as communicators.

INSIDE MAN

CHAPTER 1

INTRODUCTION
What Are Models For?

Wherein the aims and goals of ascriptive science—the discipline of making valid ascriptions of mental states to humans on the basis of observing their behavior—are introduced and illuminated against the current intellectual landscape of normative, descriptive, and prescriptive approaches to the human sciences and against the background of strands of hermeneutics, the philosophy of language, and the theory of rational choice inherited from a century and a half of writing and thinking about the subject.

WHAT FOLLOWS is an attempt to build a rigorous science of human action from a repertoire of moves and conceptual structures provided by decision and rational choice theory, classical epistemology, artificial intelligence, the philosophy of language, and the experimental methods and results of cognitive and social psychology. The resulting science expressly and explicitly distances the modeler of human behavior and thought from the subject of his or her models. In building this science I make deliberate and frequent use of mathematical and logical models of thinking, believing, emoting, and behaving, and I use them to the explicit end of helping modelers achieve distance from the behavior being modeled with the aim of increasing the precision with which one can represent what and how humans do, think, and feel.

By abducting the essence of the models away from the often lukewarm and fuzzy innards of common English language usage, I hope to accomplish two objectives. The first is to increase the precision with which we can formulate propositions about thinking and behavior and design tests of those propositions. Mathematical representations and first-order logic help greatly with the project of turning quality into quantity or scale, which is important for ascertaining progress in a field of inquiry—even if not always for progress itself: "Better" is made more precise when it is interpreted as "more accurate" or "more valid." If we want "better" models and can agree on measures of validity and accuracy, then we will be able to know and tell which way we are going when we model. It is one thing to say that John is "poor at reining in his appetite for whipped cream" but quite another to characterize the rate at which he trades off a certain amount of guaranteed whipped cream consumption for other entities he values—including the value he derives from the sustained validity of his self-concept as a being capable of self-control—as a function of various visceral states (such as satiation, hypoglycemia, level of sexual arousal) and of various prototypical social situations in which he finds himself (work-related meeting with bosses, work-related meeting with subordinates, stroll with friends). By showing the payoff that decision science brings to action science in terms of precision, I hope to exculpate the former from the often valid accusation that it is a "toy science"—a banal endeavor that is good enough at making all-things-considered ensemble predictions about the behavior of consumers but that cannot and should not be deployed when things begin to matter: in *this* particular case, in the high-stakes decision scenario, in the one-off interaction that "does one or foredoes one quite." I want, then, to create a *decision-science-for-when-it-matters*.

The second objective is to capitalize on the distancing effect that is produced when we talk about people as agents or decision agents (or TOTREPs, "trade-off-talking rational economic persons" [Kreps, 1988]) and attempt to measure various quantities that are relevant to our models of these agents— just as when, in a study of "animal learning," we would measure the proclivity of a rat in a maze to exhibit a modification of its behavior in response to a repeated set of pain/reward-mediated stimuli. Indeed, the distancing effects that characterize the modeling approach of traditional rational choice theory and the experimental approach of pre– and post–Cognitive Revolution psychology are, I predict, among the most valuable contributions these fields will be deemed by future historians of ideas to have made to the understanding of human behavior. Universal models—such as those provided by rational choice and decision theory—will be used to create an emotional *distoscope*, which functions (conversely to what one would expect of an emotional *micro*scope) to produce emotional distance between the modeler and the "modelee"—a move that is particularly helpful when those we wish to model are either ourselves or other "emotionally close" individuals. Thereby, "action science" will become more science-like even as it remains focused on action.

Achieving these goals hinges delicately on what I mean by "models" and what I intend to do with them; delicately because, if misunderstood, the new action science I am aiming for quickly becomes another "discipline"—which I would consider an unfortunate outcome—rather than "a way of living" for those interested in the competent prediction and intelligent production of behavior. So, on to *models*, then, and their uses.

1. WHAT MODELS ARE FOR: REPRESENTATIONAL AND PERFORMATIVE DIMENSIONS

We have inherited the following picture of models in science: They are representations of "reality," of behavior or thought, that can be used to take us from a set of observable or known quantities or variables (past choices, past measured features of thinking) to a set of predictions of future—or otherwise unobserved, and thus unknown—quantities or variables (future behavior, hidden and private features of thinking). Models embed within them algorithms and formulas for predicting the evolution of observables. Thus, a simple answer can be given to the question of "why model?": *to make inferences about what we do not know on the basis of what we do know.* If I observe Mathilda choose white bread from a bread-stand that offers both white and wheat bread, then I can model Mathilda as an individual who instantiates—through her behavior—a set of preferences (of white over wheat bread, in this example) and use it to infer that she will choose white bread over wheat bread the next time she has a choice between these two options. The *representation* of Mathilda's behavior as the instantiation of a set of preferences (which are hidden to me, the modeler) is critical to the model of Mathilda used to predict her future behavior; and it is the representation that we use to *model* Mathilda that constrains the kinds of questions we can hope to answer by making use of the model. Had we modeled Mathilda as an automaton that reliably produces certain kinds of behavior ("buy a loaf of bread and devour it") in response to a particular stimulus ("abusive behavior by her lover"), then we could make no prediction about Mathilda's selection of one kind of bread over another but we could still make predictions about Mathilda's behavior after certain life events.

The link between the nature and structure of models and the nature of the questions that we can pose on the basis of those models suggests that the representational function of models is incomplete and, in fact, unreasonably *benign*. In particular, the modeler can (A) *create* models that answer certain kinds of questions that she is interested in, (B) *interact* with the objects of her models, and even (C) *force them* into answering certain kinds of questions that are based on a particular representation or (D) induce them to *interpret themselves* through the lens of the proposed model, thereby altering their behavior.

Example of (A).   I am interested in understanding how you act when you are simultaneously faced with (a) an impulse to produce destructive behavior (an unrestrained temper tantrum) in the context of (b) a situation in which acting on such an impulse has a high social cost to you (loss of face and reputation). I create a model of you in which the two conflicting impulses or motives (for self-expression and self-censure) can be co-present and capable of interacting, and I then posit various interaction mechanisms (winner-take-all, compromise, competitive equilibrium) between the impulses that can be used to explain certain kinds of observable behavior (temporary loss of attention or of eloquence, sudden lapses into sullenness) that you may produce when I intentionally (but covertly or deniably) behave so as to irritate you in a public setting that is meaningful to you.

Example of (B).   The question, "Why did you choose to arrive five minutes late to this meeting?" forces upon the subject a particular model of behavior and thought (conscious, knowing, and intentional choice of a set of actions that have led to the tardiness) that has a *lensing* effect: The representation becomes a lens through which behavior is seen for the purpose of the interaction. Of course, the subject may reject the representation of his person and behavior implicit in the question (*Because the elevator took a long time to arrive*), but the lens can often be reestablished (*Why did you* choose *not to leave a few minutes earlier in order to arrive on time, given that you knew or had reason to know there was some uncertainty in the timeliness of the elevator service?*).

In each case, models emerge as interventional devices and not merely representational ones. They are used to *intervene by representing*, and these two functions are closely interconnected. In what follows I will draw on the significant representational power of models generated in various branches of decision theory (from the phenomenological through the economic and the psychological) and focus on the *performative dimension* of these models, comprising that which one does to oneself and to the modeled by the act of modeling. This move commits me to a view of the science of human behavior that is based on an ongoing interaction between modelers and modelees. What does this science look like?

2. THE NEW ACTION SCIENCE OF HUMAN WAYS-OF-BEING: FROM NORMATIVE-DESCRIPTIVE-PRESCRIPTIVE SCIENCE TO ASCRIPTIVE SCIENCE

We are accustomed to following Howard Raiffa's distinctions and to speak about descriptive (what is the case?), normative (what should be the case?), and prescriptive (what should be done, given what we know to be the case?) approaches to the science of behavior and thought. Thus, *descriptive* behavioral science informs us of how people *do* respond to certain stimuli; *normative* rational choice theory tells us about what a logically and informationally omniscient decision maker *would* do *if* she had certain preferences; and *prescriptive* behavioral decision theory tells us how people *should* try to think and act, given what we know or what we think they should know about their own and others' deviations from the model of the ideal decision maker posited by rational choice theory. In each of the three cases, felicitous (and often unwitting) use is made of two elements: the *ideal type* and the *statistical ensemble* (or the "average man," if you believe in turning statistics into probabilities). The ideal type is to normative science what the average man is to descriptive and prescriptive science: a stylized, tractable reduction of the all-important ideal agent that enables simple inferences from the unknown to the known. If Gary models Pauline as the omniscient, coherent ideal type of rational choice theory and deduces Pauline's preferences from her observed choice behavior, then he is on his way to building a model that can be used to predict Pauline's future behavior. If Amelie models Gary as an "average man" whose patterns of thinking and behavior—based on tests performed by Amelie and her friend Dan in their labs—differ from those legislated by the ideal model in reliable ways, then she can produce predictions of Gary's future behavior based on the same kind of inferential device that Gary used to make predictions about Pauline. Thus proceeds the conventional approach to the science of human behavior, which resonates greatly with the representational use of models.

Now enters Chris, who cares not only about understanding what Pauline will do *given* that she is a rational or super-rational being but also about whether or not Pauline (*this* individual *here and now*) *is*, in fact, a super-rational being; and not only what Gary will do given that he is *an average guy* (as defined by Dan and Amelie's tests) but also whether or not Gary *is* actually an average guy in the precise Amelie-and-Dan sense of averageness. Chris is in a position familiar to most humans (including Gary, Amelie, and Dan themselves, when they leave their offices), who must deal with individuals here and now and whose here-and-now predictions matter (and matter a lot) *here* and *now*. Chris no longer has the luxury of being able to "explain away" a particular behavior either as "irrational" (an explanation that is available to normative and prescriptive theorists) or as "noise" (available to descriptive and prescriptive theorists).

In exchange for the additional complication, Chris has the opportunity to *interact* with the subject of his models; thus his science taps into the performative dimension of models. Of course, Chris never quite leaves the representational dimension of models. He starts out with his own models of Pauline (perhaps the same as Gary's) and of Gary (perhaps those of Amelie and Dan). In fact, Chris needs a certain minimal model of Gary just to begin talking to him (for, in talking, he is *saying* and in saying he makes truth claims and in so doing he assumes that Gary understands them, which means that Gary has the sophisticated and never-before-seen-in-the-animal-kingdom capacity called "linguistic understanding," and so forth). Yet Chris understands that the models themselves shape the interaction: They supply or constrain the questions that Chris can ask and also co-opt certain kinds of behavior from Pauline and Gary and, in turn, from Chris himself. The models are causally influential within the interaction and can lead to the production of novel behaviors from all three protagonists.

Such an interaction places Chris's science outside of the usual space spanned by the descriptive, normative, and prescriptive dimensions of the "normal science" of humans. It is a different kind of science, which another Chris (unrelated to our hero) calls "action science" [Argyris, 1993] and I shall call *ascriptive science*—not because I feel the need to be different (as evidenced by my appropriation of this term from Itzhak Gilboa [1991]) but rather because I require a meaning that is different from the one that "action science" has taken on through repeated usage. "Ascriptive" science, as the name suggests, is the science of making valid ascriptions: of ascribing entities (such as rationality and intentionality) to oneself and others on the basis of structured interactions that aim both to discover and to educate.

Understanding ascriptive science is most easily accomplished by asking how it overlaps and interacts with normative, descriptive, and prescriptive science. In order to do this, it is important to understand not only the different kinds of science of behavior but also the predispositions, activities, and dominant concerns of the scientists who practice them. For this purpose I draw on Ian Hacking's [1983] categorization of natural scientists as speculators, calculators, or experimenters. Hacking argues that natural science "comes together" as the result of the conjoint efforts of the activities of three kinds of people: Speculators (e.g., Galileo, Newton, Einstein) generate new distinctions and introduce new concepts that are useful in describing, manipulating, and/or creating phenomena; calculators (Laplace, Penrose, Thorne) use the basic schemata articulated by speculators and perform the necessary logical and computational work that takes us from concepts to testable models and useful algorithms; and experimenters (Kepler, Eddington, Penzias) create effects in the laboratory and the field that are based on distinctions articulated by the speculators and sharpened by the calculators—"effects" that historians of science, as well as philosophers of science bent upon rational reconstructions of scientific activity, then portray as being "tests" of one theory (or model) or another. Seen through this behavioral categorization pattern, normative scientists speculate and calculate (Bayes, Ramsey, de Finetti, Schelling, Nash, Aumann); descriptive scientists calculate and experiment (Allais, Ellsberg, Tversky); and prescriptive scientists do some of each (in addition to pontificating, which is a function that I shall ignore). The ascriptive scientist draws on the core skills of each of the speculators, calculators, and experimenters who have conspired to engage in normative, descriptive, and prescriptive behavioral science. He speculates insofar as he uses and refines the basic distinctions made by normative science (rationality/irrationality, knowledge/belief/ignorance) to put together structured models of behavior and thought, which he uses calculatively to make predictions about a subject's behavior and thinking, which he tests by designing real-time experiments whose results he then uses to modify or fortify his speculative models of the subject's behavior and thought. But unlike the normative, descriptive, or prescriptive scientist, the ascriptive scientist is guided in his inquiry and behavior by pragmatic questions (*How can I induce X to do Y? What will X do or say if I do or say Y?*) that are typical of everyday human interactions and ways-of-being-toward-one-another of humans rather than by the questions that concern typical behavioral scientists vis-à-vis their subjects (*How can effect X be instantiated at level of reliability Y in subject population S given temporal and material budget constraint C?*).

The claim that I shall defend throughout the book is that, in spite of the significant difference in the types of questions that preoccupy ascriptive and "normal" scientists, there is great value to the ascriptive scientist in appropriating both the discipline and the skill sets of the speculators, calculators, and experimenters whose work has produced the normative, descriptive, and prescriptive human sciences. "Shall" entails that this defense is "about to happen," so the reader is asked to withhold judgment on my claim until a substantial part of this "ascriptive" science has been developed.

2.1. *Precursors I: Oneself as Another—Nietzsche's Overman*

Perhaps the earliest precursor of *ascriptive* science appears in the documented thought of Friedrich Nietzsche. In *Also Sprach Zarathustra* [Thus Spake Zarathustra; Nietzsche, 1892/2007] he introduced the concept of the *Übermensch*—the Overman, sometimes inappropriately (notably by Goebbels) translated as the Superman—to represent the individual who can hold himself out as an object of inquiry, analysis, and experimentation. The distinguishing feature of the Overman is the ability to distance himself from his own raw feels, emotions, perceptions, thoughts, intentions, and other first-person internal psychological states to the point where these states (and the attending behaviors) can be beheld *as if they were another's*. What is gained thereby—the argument goes, and I also contend—is a capability for a more accurate representation of one's own states of mind and body and the relationships between internal psychological states and behaviors. If one can model oneself while maintaining the same state of mind as when one models a light switch or a rat in a maze, then one can more accurately and validly see one's own behavior and intervene to ameliorate that behavior—along with the thoughts and feelings associated with it—by using the same representation-guided tinkering used to repair the light switch or to change the path of the rat; and one can also hope to produce both internal states and external behaviors in ways akin to those by which one designs different mazes and reward conditions to influence an experimental rat's behavior. The act (and attendant benefits) of such dispassionate self-beholding is, of course, far more easily recognized than produced, and the intention of ascriptive science is to facilitate the *production* of the states that characterize the Overman. On this view, the Overman is neither a personality type nor a character in the "hardwired" sense of those terms; rather, it is a state of being that can be achieved through training.

Of what could this training consist? The argument I shall develop claims that the basic tool kit of the speculators, experimenters, and calculators that produced the contemporary human sciences circa 2010 CE can be interpreted in a way that provides a valuable set of distancing mechanisms whose value ranges far beyond the purely descriptive use to which they have been put so far. Understanding oneself (or a close friend or coworker) as an agent equipped with a computationally potent (but not omnipotent) reasoning faculty aimed at producing optimal or maximal outcomes based on informationally "scient" (but not omniscient) perceptual inputs allows one to relate the mental and verbal behavior of the "creature" being modeled in a way that is far closer to how one understands a light switch or the behavior of a rat in a maze than to the everyday (fuzzy and forgiving) ways in which humans usually "give accounts" and "produce narratives" about themselves and others.

Understanding oneself or another as a causal nexus of neurophysiological mechanisms acting in consort to produce certain behaviors, including mental behaviors, enables still another powerful set of "distancing maneuvers": Of himself the Overman can now say *It is emoting in ways related to the visceral state of hunger* and—having characterized the influence of this visceral state on his own ways of perceiving, thinking, and feeling—he could proceed to tinker with various visceral states and changes therein for the purpose of producing new and potentially more useful behavioral patterns. Seen in this light, Nietzsche's Overman models a modern scientist who has turned his purely cognitive understanding of a phenomenon into feelings and action. Here, conceptual commitments to various models of individuals will have ceased to be mere ways of talking and will have become ontological commitments that are lived through. For example, viewing the mind as a sequence of states of a digital computer ceases to be a "mere metaphor" that organizes the ways in which cognitive scientists achieve mutual understanding about experimental results for the purpose of publishing papers in legitimate journals; instead it becomes a structuring device for thinking through one's own thinking and for designing pointed changes in the patterns of that thinking.

2.2. *Precursors II: Heidegger and the Distancing/ De-distancing Dialectic of* Dasein

In *Being and Time*, Martin Heidegger [1927/1962] picks up on the relevance of the operation of *distancing* by stating: "*Dasein* [Heidegger's term for the being of a person, translated as "being-there" or, more precisely if less intelligibly, as "there-being"] is a *de-distancing* being"—one whose basic disposition is to reduce or eliminate the distance between itself and the objects that make up its world. One builds implicit mental models of rocks as animated by desires and proclivities, talks about organizations and bureaucracies "wanting to do *X*," and speaks of market economies as "punishing free riders." The anthropomorphization of all or parts of the world is a prototypical de-distancing move insofar as it attempts to understand the world in terms of categories antecedently used to analyze the behaviors and internal psychological states of the self.

The "scientific mindset," which seeks to explain phenomena in terms of covering laws (causal or otherwise) constrained by initial and boundary conditions, can then be understood as the result of a distancing maneuver—albeit one that is neither easily nor intuitively undertaken. It is genuinely distance producing, for instance, to understand a friend's behaviors in terms of a model of her as a decision agent and not in terms of one's own states of mind duly projected upon the friend in question. Using this approach, one can understand the friend's oral noises and other behaviors (including mental ones) from a stance more typical of the way one seeks to understand the behavior of a bread box, a garbage compactor, or a brain immersed in physiological serum and subjected to certain electrical inputs that can be controlled by an observer. This is precisely the stance that the garden-variety descriptive scientist takes toward the "subject," a stance that is based on the dual principles of representationalism and nomothetic explanation and that leads to various kinds of reductionism. A model *represents* behavior and does so in a particular way: as the instantiation of laws and principles that can be parameterized and refined through a process of repeated experimentation.

Ascriptive science recognizes the value of the distancing move that descriptive science unreflectively perpetrates on its practitioners, and it also recognizes that the distancing move entailed by modeling other beings using the language employed to model rats in mazes (or brains in vats) is not without consequences for both the modeler and the modelee. In other words, the mere categories and mere concepts themselves—used by descriptive scientists to represent behavior—become real entities in a way that they cannot be for the untrained layman. Representational tropes become perceptual lenses and experimental levers, and the merely "ontic" plane of scientific activity (wherein objects and concepts are "categories" and "manners of speaking") becomes an ontological plane (wherein objects are the stuff of "what is" and "what is real").

The ascriptive scientist thinks of the subject of her inquiry in a language that is foreign to that subject, a "scientific language" that allows her to distinguish between states of being and kinds of behavior that the layman typically cannot distinguish among and also to make connections and thereby manipulate variables that the layman would not normally contemplate. One can, for instance, examine the relationship between states of sexual arousal or anxiety of the creature being modeled and the creature's proclivity to notice a logical contradiction in its own explanation and attempt to resolve that contradiction while heeding the standard rules of logic, rather than denying one of the logically incompatible propositions and "wishing the contradiction away"; or the relationship between the creature's current blood glucose levels, its brain glucose metabolism in states of intense cognitive processing, and its ability to exercise self-control in the face of standard "potent" temptations (those with high desirability and low observability). Thus, what the ascriptive scientist receives in return for the alienation incurred by seeing other people through the lens of "cold, cruel science" is *insight* and the ability to act more precisely upon the subject of inquiry—in ways akin to those in which the surgeon cuts into the flesh of his subject.

2.3. Precursors III: Wittgenstein's Consequentialism and Hacking's Interventionism

The later Wittgenstein—the Wittgenstein of the *Philosophical Investigations* [1953]—is a direct source of and precursor to the stance of the ascriptive scientist vis-à-vis models of human behavior and thought. For Wittgenstein, the contents of a mind—the images, concepts, and metaphors that make up models—are to be understood in terms of their beholder's comportments or behaviors and not as representational structures that can be analyzed independently of the modeler's identity, context, and ways-of-being. "Meaning is use." Models not only shape, constrain, modulate, and induce behavior, they *are* behavior. Accordingly, they are always-already causally potent; and it is by virtue of these causal powers that models can and should be analyzed.

Understanding a human creature as no more than a collection of neurons, muscles, and viscera connected into a causal nexus is, on this view, properly understood not as an *image* of that person but rather as a collection of behavioral dispositions of the modeler toward the creature and a set of linguistic conventions that shape and constrain what can be said, perceived, or desired of that person. Modeling, then, is *doing* of a particular kind: unto the modelee but also unto the modeler, whose behaviors are shaped by the conventions and rules invoked when using the model correctly (where *correctly* means "engaging in linguistic behaviors around the use of the model that are intelligible to those with whom the modeler communicates").

Relatedly, Hacking's form of realism (as articulated in *Representing and Intervening* [Hacking, 1983]) focuses attention away from the contents of the modeler's mind and toward the kinds of things that the modeler can do (or see herself doing). Thus, in responding to the question "Do the (representational) entities in terms of which we theorize about the world (electrons, photons, etc.) correspond to anything real in nature?" Hacking admonishes us to focus on the kinds of *causal powers* that certain modeling languages confer upon the modeler. If one can speak of "getting electrons to fly off the end of an electrode" and also *produce* behavior (guided by this mini "action map") that reliably yields intersubjectively valid results that two or more people agree to encode by the sentence "electrons are flying off the end of an electrode," then electrons are real in this special sense—and more real than are the "animal spirits" or Zeitgeists invoked to make sense of (i.e., "explain") complex patterns of stock market buying and selling behavior among putatively self-interested, intelligent agents. And the reason why they are more real is that one cannot use Zeitgeist language to produce desirable effects in the same way that one can use "electron" language to produce them.

Models, then, are generating engines for successful action patterns: Their deployment allows the modeler to produce behavior and cause effects upon the modelee. Faced with the radicalness of this approach, the reader should resist the metaphoric appeal of the argument just made and instead consider the *consequences* of focusing on the *consequentiality* of models by engaging in the slightly alienating exercise of thinking about a close friend or relative exclusively in the language of neuropsychology. Thus, "she is afraid" is replaced by "she is in brain state X, corresponding to a hijacking by the amygdala of the inputs to the neocortex"—which in turn creates possibilities for relating to the "she" that did not exist as long as she was viewed as an extension or projection of the "me." Acting on these possibilities and interacting with her brain to produce new behavioral patterns is the essence of modeling, which from this perspective is an activity of constant ontological construction and experimentation guided by the language forms of the various sciences. Modeling science, then, is also the practice of experimental ontology.

2.4. Precursors IV: Frank Ramsey, Paul Samuelson, and the Behavioral Interpretation of Mental Events and States

Idle talk? I would argue not. Wittgenstein's talented and engineering-minded contemporary, Frank Ramsey, took to heart the behavioral interpretation of mental events and states and produced an interpretation of

personal degrees of belief in terms of the betting odds that one is willing
to accept on the truth of a proposition, thus cutting through the Gordian
knot of the "proper interpretation" of the probability measure (as a limiting
relative frequency, as the inverse of the number of alternative possibilities,
or as a measure of the epistemic gain produced by the acquisition of new
information). A personal degree of belief or probability is not merely an
occult, obscure, or indeterminate "state of mind" but rather a specific and
ascertainable *behavioral disposition*—namely, the disposition to accept certain bets.

When Paul Samuelson introduced his "axioms of revealed preference" in
the house journal of the London School of Economics [Samuelson, 1938],
he was pursuing a project—one wholly sympathetic to Ramsey's approach—
which would make it possible to infer, from observations of choice behavior,
a chooser's *preferences*; this, in turn, would enable inferences about subsequent
choice behavior. If option X is (weakly) preferred by a creature to option Y
(the theory goes), then the creature will not choose option Y when option X
is also available. This commonsensical and "innocuous" argument is at the
foundation of modern microeconomic science, much as Ramsey's interpretation of personal probabilities as betting odds is at the foundation of modern
decision theory.

Ascriptive science continues Frank Ramsey's project. It interprets other—
more complicated and subtle—internal states and activities of human creatures in terms of the kinds of behaviors instantiated by creatures in these
states. For example, temptations, itches, pains, thrills, and habits (Chapter 2)
become experimentally "tractable" as proclivities to engage in certain kinds of
temporal discounting of future options. The coherence of personal degrees of
belief can be interpreted as the proclivity to engage in certain kinds of bets
on the truth value of *ensembles* of different propositions (Chapter 3). States
corresponding to different degrees of *certainty*, rather than belief, become interpretable as the proclivity to engage in further computation aimed at reducing the spread, or entropy, of the creature's epistemic states (Chapters 3 and 4).
Different *styles of reasoning* are interpreted as proclivities to engage in the use
of certain kinds of *algorithms*, which are detectable by the rate at which the
creature's thinking produces new information that is useful and relevant to
its predicament. Different modes of learning (Chapter 5) are interpretable

as proclivities to *ask* different kinds of questions regarding the relationship of particulars to universals (and vice versa) and to engage in different kinds of experiments aimed at testing hypotheses about these relationships. Different approaches to interpersonal communication (Chapter 6) are interpretable as proclivities to *answer* certain kinds of queries made by a principled interlocutor.

Ascriptive science is continuous with both Wittgenstein's anti-representationalism and Ramsey's engineering approach to "social science," but it is also *reconstructive* of what a social science is: Unlike the descriptive scientist, who takes for granted the basic modeling language he has inherited from his learned predecessors and "applies" it by "testing hypotheses" against what he calls "data," the ascriptive scientist actively *interacts* with the creature that is the subject of her studies, engaging this creature in dialogue aimed at understanding the limits of a model and often at educating the creature being modeled about the footprint its behaviors leave on the fabric woven by the logic of the model in question.

The ascriptive scientist, then, is closer in spirit to Tom Schelling's understanding of "theory"—in his case [Schelling, 1960], game theory—as a *logic* and far closer to that discipline than to the discipline of classical mechanics (especially as it is conceptualized by social scientists). As John Searle has pointed out, a logic is primarily something one *does* and is only derivatively and after-the-fact something one *knows* [Searle, 2001]. One does not consult a logical truth table in order to make inferences; instead, one makes inferences as a matter of course and then constructs truth tables in order to document how valid inferences are made. Inferences are also needed *in order* to reason from knowledge of a truth table to knowledge of how to make any one particular inference; and, of course, *those* inferences require another truth table, which in turn requires inferences to be made that require still another truth table, which . . . , which is all precisely the point of at least one of *Alice in Wonderland*'s "pedagogical" scenes. In the same way, ascriptive science refers to the modeling that one *does* and only derivatively to the models that one *knows* or *tests*. It is the *doing of thinking* and the *doing of interacting* that are the proper subject matter of this discipline, which has been nascent, and sometimes stillborn, for the past 75 years.

2.5. *Precursors V: Popper, Argyris, and the Prediction and Production of Behavior*

Ascriptive science is indebted to Karl Popper and Chris Argyris for aspects of their thinking that have received less attention than is warranted by their importance: Popper's insistence on the act of making *intersubjectively valid predictions* [Popper, 1959] that function as proper tests of a theory (a conjunction of universal statements and initial conditions); and Argyris's challenge to social scientists that they *produce* the behaviors they claim to understand [Argyris, 1991; Argyris, 1996] as a way of demonstrating that understanding. The *prediction* (and not the mere explanation) and the *production* (and not the mere description or prescription) of behavior are to be understood as cornerstones of this new science of human behavior, which allows the scientist very few places to hide from the disasters that the world wreaks on his theories and models and allows only limited (and auditable) opportunities to fortify or insulate the products of his mental activities—his theories and models—from refutation by experience.

In spite of subsequent reinterpretations of Popper's refutation-oriented logic of scientific discovery (see, e.g., Friedman [1953]) that conflate *explaining* and *predicting* for purposes of validating a theory, Popper's own view on the matter seems not to have changed: Intellectual honesty and the search for truth require that the scientist stick his neck out and make predictions about the phenomena that his theories or models "represent." To argue that "explanation is nothing but prediction in reverse," and therefore that "explaining a phenomenon" has the same epistemic value as making predictions about that phenomenon, is to ignore the decisive impact of the passage of time on one's own states of knowledge. Explaining a phenomenon will always be informed by a prior knowledge of the *what*—of the set of observation statements standing in need of explanation—and so the class of theories and models that ex post are deemed suitable candidates for testing will always be far narrower than the class of theories that one must consider when attempting to make predictions. Seen through this prism, neoclassical economics and its variants appear to more likely conform to Popper's conception of psychoanalysis than to his conception of physics: Like the psychoanalysts who aped Freud's "methods" to the point of exulting in the practical impossibility of refutation, neoclassically trained empiricists find comfort in the confidence that they can "explain anything." And that, according to Popper, "is a bad thing" because it is the mark of pseudo-science for a theory to be irrefutable *no matter what.* From this it follows that the "hardness" of physics, as a science, compared to that of economics as currently practiced is a matter of the predictive focus of theoretical and experimental physicists. Scientists attempt to *predict* the results of experiments, whereas economists attempt to explain, ex post, stylized facts or collections of "data." I therefore predict that the epistemic quality of economic theorizing will not change significantly for the better until the profession of economics changes its practical orientation from a *post-dictive* to a *pre-dictive* one.

However, ascriptive science looks beyond this distinction to the one between the *understanding* and *production* of behavior, which was made by Argyris and is collinear with the *performative* or *engineering* approach to knowledge of Wittgenstein and Ramsey. Of course, one could say (with Hacking) that it is precisely the *pro*-ductive—rather than the merely *pre*-dictive—approach to their craft that distinguishes scientists who are "doing real work" from those who are merely "playing with words." The pathbreaking physicist advances knowledge far more authentically when he engineers an effect than when he explains a phenomenon, not only because *explanation is cheap relative to prediction* but also because *understanding is cheap relative to production.*

Ascriptive science heeds Argyris's injunction to focus on behavioral production in two ways: first, by developing and training a *modeling discipline* in the ascriptive scientist, to include attitudes toward the human phenomena that one models, as well as tools for the *engineering* of models and tests thereof; and second, by examining and designing the *interaction* between the ascriptive scientist/modeler and the object of her science, an interaction that can be used to co-opt, coerce, shape, inform, modify, or transform the behavior of the creature being modeled. *Experimenting, interrogating, training,* and *calling the modelee to task* are all part of the process of *ascribing.* "Help me understand," says the ascriptive scientist to the subject of her models, "why I should *not* interpret your behavior as an instantiation of either a failure of consciousness or of self-control, given what you know I know you know and want." She then proceeds to interpret the answers produced by the modeled creature as *putative* but not decisive corroborations or refutations of the basic model that she has used to structure the interaction that led to her insight. Those familiar with Argyris's structured interventions that aim to produce "double-loop learning" behavior (see, e.g., the collection of essays in Argyris [1993]) will recognize in the foregoing description a basic characteristic of the "action science" that has emerged over the past 30 years; they should similarly recognize in ascriptive science an attempt to sharpen the tools of action science via the analytical techniques developed by normative or descriptive scientists and simultaneously to retain the emphasis of action science on the performative dimension of knowledge and on the indissociable nature of the knowing-being-doing nexus.

3. WHAT ARE MODELS FOR, AGAIN?

We have inherited a basic tenet: "Models are for representing," for picturing the world in symbols. However, having labored through increasingly sophisticated epistemological arguments and discussions over the past century, we can claim with some conviction that "models are for doing," for intervening— in a way that does not exclude their representational function but, to the contrary, makes clear the sense in which representing *is* doing of a particular kind, a doing that has causal import to both the modeler and (in the case of human models) to the creature being modeled. "The mind and the world together make up the mind and the world" as Hilary Putnam [1985] puts it, without the slightest inclination toward pure idealism or solipsism.

The work of the ascriptive scientist starts where the work of the epistemologist ends. Following the examples of Ramsey and Schelling, ascriptive science attempts not only to picture human behavior in symbols but also to shape the interaction between an ascriptive scientist bent on "learning" and a human creature bent on "behaving," "believing," and "emoting." It is this interaction that a model itself shapes—no less than it shapes the contents of the ascriptive scientist's "mind." Indeed, when understood correctly, ascriptive science is as much about interpersonal learning as it is about the kind of piecemeal social engineering that Karl Popper once urged [Popper, 1961].

For this reason, much of the ascriptive science that I *do* in what follows aims to establish foundations not only for the ways in which a scientist can set up clever "test situations" for the creature he wishes to understand but also for the kinds of justifications that the scientist can provide to that creature for deploying certain models (and not others) as basic templates that are "filled in" by data points supplied by the creature's behavior. A good model should enable the ascriptive scientist who deploys it to persuade the creature being modeled of its own validity and value; accordingly, *communication* between creature and scientist is required for the deep and insightful test of any model. At the proverbial "end of the day," a complete description of ascriptive science should provide a normative force that binds the creature to *communicating* with the scientist in ways that are self-revealing and can genuinely advance learning. To be sure, this is a difficult task especially for a science, but I argue that the task is one that must nevertheless be tackled head-on if that science is to count as "human."

CHAPTER 2

DECISIONS AND CHOICES, IMMEDIATE AND PLANNED

Wherein the protagonists of this work, Ask and Creature, are introduced to the reader and to each other, and Ask proceeds directly to apply himself to the work of understanding Creature's behavior through the use of models that represent Creature's behaviors as the outcome of choices, which in turn are taken to express either conscious and coherent preferences or unconscious and less coherent impulses. Ask probes into Creature's incontinent or impulsive behavior by using models that incorporate the dependence of Creature's preferences on time and the temporal evolution of Creature's valuation of its objects of desire. Ask seeks to understand Creature's ways of dealing with its own impulsive and counterproductive impulses and desires via models of self-control and self-command, whose structure and dynamics are also investigated.

RATIONAL CHOICE THEORY (RCT) calls out to a family of models of human behavior that represent observed or observable behaviors as outcomes of choices that are the result of decisions made to fulfill desires given a set of beliefs. Thus, "Adam went to the movies on Thursday night" is understood as: "Adam had several options, one of which was going to the movies; Adam deliberated on the options and decided to go to the movies, as doing so was the best course of action given his preferences and beliefs; and Adam instantiated the behavior 'going to the movies' as a causal consequence of having decided to go to the movies." Call this the RCT explanation of the proposition p, or RCTE(p), where p represents "Adam went to the movies."

Of course, if asked "Why did you go to the movies last Thursday?" Adam might not reproduce—in fact, is likely to *not* reproduce—RCTE(p). He might instead say "I had a date" or "I wanted to see *Black Dahlia*." This does not present the rational choice theorist with a problem, for he can argue as follows. (A) "Adam is not very disciplined, or precise, in representing the internal psychological states and processes that have led him to go to the movies and hence may not see that (i) he could have chosen to do something else altogether and (ii) his desire to see a specific movie, coupled with his belief that this movie is playing at such and such a cinema, are both necessary constitutive elements of the decision that determined his choice." Or (B) "Adam behaved *as if* RCTE(p) were true, but RCTE(p) itself need not be true; it simply has to make predictions about Adam's behavior that are true or at least testable."

Suppose the rational choice theorist argues (A). Then one might hope that, by a meticulous questioning of Adam or by training Adam in RCT, one might get him to describe his choice in the language of RCT and thereby test the explanation RCTE(p) directly against Adam's subsequent and authentic self-reports of his internal psychological processes when he experiences choice-based behavior of the type "going to the movies." In such a case, Adam "just sees" the truth of RCTE(p) and appropriates it. In doing so, he comes to interpret himself by it. Suppose the theorist argues (B). Then one could make predictions about Adam's future behavior ("When will he choose to go to the movies? What movies will he choose to go to?") on the basis of observations of past behavior and a basic predictive mechanism that infers preference from past choices and future choices from preferences.

In either case, the model *attributes* to Adam some internal psychological states. Argument (A) does so directly; (B) does so indirectly but in a way that is still testable. Yet the attribution of internal psychological states is critical in case (B) (no less critical than in case (A)) because without the attribution there are no grounds for making predictions about Adam's future (and unobserved) behavior on the basis of Adam's past (and observed) behavior.

It makes sense for the rational choice theorist to say "I predict Adam will go to the movies when faced with the same menu of options as that facing him last time he chose to go to the movies *because* he prefers going to the movies over the other available options that he has rejected in the past" but not to say "I predict that Adam will go to the movies next Thursday *because* he went to the movies last Thursday." "Because" is critical here: Adam may, in fact, go to the movies every Thursday, but he does not go to the movies *because* it is Thursday. He may, for instance, have a preference for regularity that leads him to go to the movies once a week, and, since the first day he went to the movies was a Thursday, he has just continued going to the movies every Thursday since. But that is a different choice that calls out for a different explanation.

The ascription of even a *minimal* internal set of internal psychological states (in this case, preferences) to Adam is critical for the RCT explanation of his behavior. It is not critical to *every* explanation of his behavior, to be sure. We can produce a stimulus–response model of Adam's behavior wherein Adam goes to the movies automatically in response to it being a rainy day outside, so that we could choose to test "if it rains on day X, then Adam will go to the movies on that day"—or any of a number of regular conjunctions of stimulus and response of the kind. For the moment, though, we are interested in only RCT explanations of the types examined above of Adam's behavior not because they are the only ones that are testable (they are not) but rather because they allow us to self-consistently ask Adam for the reasons for his behavior, rather than for merely its causes. This is a good argument in favor of using explanations of behavior that appeal to such factors as rationality, preference, decision, and choice in an ascriptive science of human behavior. It is a good argument because its negation leads us into trouble when we try to get Adam to account for his actions: When we speak *of* Adam *to* Adam exclusively in terms of the *causes* of Adam's behavior, we commit the fallacy of appealing to a faculty (reasoning and susceptibility to reasons) that Adam must possess in order for him to understand an argument that denies he possesses that very same faculty, which is a performative error even though it is not a logical one. This argument should also lead us to prefer (A)-type RCT explanations to (B)-type RCT explanations as building blocks for a new ascriptive science, since asking Adam to account for his behavior makes far greater sense if we believe that it is generated by consciously willed processes that can be audited and understood than if we believe it is generated by a process that behaves only *as if* it could be audited and understood. Thus, I will henceforth use the RCT model in the sense in which it was deployed to generate the (A)-type explanation of Adam's behavior.

1. THE ACT OF CHOICE IN SLOW MOTION: PHENOMENOLOGICAL MICROSCOPY

It is one thing to will a particular behavior and quite another matter to produce it. Thus, it makes sense to ask: How does Adam make good on his intention to go to the movies, once he has decided to do so? Focus on the trivial but indispensable matters of going to the door, opening the door, closing and locking the door, and so forth—that is, on the sequence of minute behaviors that, when chained together, make the macroscopic description "Adam went to the movies today" true of Adam today—and then ask: What are the necessary conditions for us to be able to ascribe to Adam's production of these requisite behaviors the kind of conscious willfulness that we normally associate with rational choice explanations of behavior? In particular, we want to produce models of Adam's behavior that are psychologically realistic and rationally justifiable so that we can then create valid explanations and predictions of his behavior and also question him about the reasons for having produced that behavior.

Now that the question has been phrased in this way, the following experiment will appear to be relevant.

EXPERIMENT 2.1 [Libet et al., 1979]

Main result: Conscious awareness of intention significantly and reliably lags the formation of the intention.

Specific findings (statistically significant): For subjects that were monitored during the 2 s immediately preceding either a planned or unplanned action, the following sequence of events is invariant relative to the choice of subject.

$T = -1{,}050$ ms: readiness potential (RP) measured for planned intentional movement (PIM)

$T = -550$ ms: readiness potential measured for unplanned intentional movement (UPIM)

$T = -200$ ms: conscious awareness of the will to produce PIM or UPIM registered

$T = 0$ ms: action (movement for either PIM or UPIM)

If Adam were the "average guy" of Experiment 2.1, then we would have some explaining to do about the following sequence of events: "wanting to go to the movies now," "realizing that going to the movies now entails opening the front door," "deciding to open the front door now," "intending to open the front door now," and "opening the front door" in order to walk out of the house. The bug, of course, is that "deciding" to open the front door now comes logically and psychologically *before* "intending" to open the front door now but, if we take the results of Experiment 2.1 at face value, "deciding" comes physiologically *after* "intending" to open the front door. What to do? The expanded repertoire of the ascriptive scientist's interventions and operations comes in handy at this point, for he does not need to hold on to the statistical portrait that behavioral science has painted of Adam.

For one thing, Adam may be "more conscious" than the average subject—and would thus have been labeled "noise" by the behavioral researcher anxious to get the results written up and the ensuing publication out to press.

Alternatively, there may indeed be some behavior along the chain necessary to take Adam to the movies of which Adam is indeed unconscious or not fully conscious—such as opening the door. Adam's unconsciousness may not be behavior-invariant. If Adam were sight-reading a difficult postmodern polyphonic musical piece directly on a keyboard instrument, then this "delayed consciousness" effect may disappear; and it may reappear if he shifts to sight-reading Buxtehude's music. Even so, the ascription to Adam of a conscious, reason-based choice may still hold because he is conscious of enough things enough of the time for him to "qualify": he may be given the benefit of the doubt.

Finally, it is also possible that Adam has—by virtue of having decided to go to the movies and having realized that acting on this decision involves opening the front door—preprogrammed himself to perform the requisite behavior and is now acting out a behavioral program that he has effectively—

and efficiently—delegated to his "subconscious." The delay in his awareness of "opening the door" can be explained by positing that delayed consciousness *in this case* has to do Adam's desire to remember whether or not he has closed and locked the door behind him, rather than his desire to initiate the activity of unlocking and opening the door. Each of these paths opens up avenues of inquiry for the ascriptive scientist, who can design new interventions and tests (on Adam)—not only to refine or refute the resulting model but also to raise Adam's own levels of consciousness, reasonableness, and rationality.

The example is in part meant to illustrate a difficulty with ascribing consciousness to the subject, an ascription that is often performed unconsciously by the normative scientist who deploys RCT-type explanations (especially those of type (B)). It is also meant to illustrate how the *ascriptive* scientist— whom I shall henceforth (for reasons both mnemonic and dramaturgical) refer to as *Ask*—operates. He uses a simple model of intentional behavior (embodied in the will → intention → behavior sequence) that is common to many normative models as an inference engine, but heeds the *descriptive* scientist's cautionary results regarding the tenuousness of the links between conscious will, intention, and behavior and attempts to reach beyond the "mere advice" with which the *prescriptive* scientist is content to a direct attempt to predict or transform the behavior of the subject.

"Heed" does not mean "trust." The result of any one experiment or test performed by Ask is significant but not decisive. Adam's consciousness of his own intentions is placed in question but not assumed away. From the combination of the basic model and the experimental result, Ask generates additional hypotheses and designs and engineers situations aimed at testing these hypotheses. For example, Ask might become interested in characterizing Adam's different perceptual and epistemic "zones" of awareness and oblivion (what he is not aware of and what he is not aware of not being aware of). To this end, Ask can "prime" Adam by using nearly subliminal cues (an innocuous visual irritant, say) and examine the relationship between (a) the cue, (b) Adam's behavioral response (a sudden change of position in an argument), and (c) Adam's account of his behavioral response (some additional information which he had *just remembered* after exposure to the irritant but which, however, bears no "plausible" resemblance or association to the cue). Ask may also become interested in mapping out Adam's various "automatisms"—consisting of Adam's habitual domains, the behaviors that he performs more or less without thinking about them (e.g., a knee-jerk reaction to statements phrased in a particular way, such as "one should always . . ." or "the reality is . . .")—and bringing them to Adam's conscious awareness for the purpose of helping Adam achieve a "reflective equilibrium" between what Adam believes to be the reasons for his behavior and what Ask believes to be the causes of his behavior.

In each case, Ask will find it useful to proceed in a similar fashion to that which led him to pose these questions in the first place: "Import" a well-worked-out model from the realm of normative science to help make sense of the behavior he is about to observe; "heed" experimental work that is relevant to that model (particularly work that seems to invalidate a critical premise of the model); and use the experimentalist's basic approach (work out a hypothesis, specify the conditions under which the hypothesis would turn out to be false, attempt to create these conditions, make an inference from the outcome to the basic model that was used to devise the hypothesis) to validate the "heedful" model that has emerged. In doing so, Ask appropriates more than just the *methods* of the experimentalist (in addition to heeding the results of particular experimentalists): He adopts a particular stance toward his subject—a stance that helps Ask distance himself from the subject. This stance bears further elaboration.

2. THE ASCRIPTIVE SCIENCE OF CHOICE: INTERPERSONAL DISTOSCOPY

Ascriptive science relies simultaneously on phenomenological microscopy and on interpersonal distoscopy. We have seen what sets Ask apart from his normative, descriptive, and prescriptive brethren. But what sets Ask apart from his fellow lay human beings? It is the *distancing* stance that the scientist adopts toward the subject of inquiry. The science of human behavior and thought is "distant science" in that it cares not about the particular and idiosyncratic life history, family background, specific circumstances, particular values, or sociocultural milieu of the subject except in their role as initial conditions or boundary conditions for general statements about the subject of inquiry. Because this science is concerned with models based on the "in-variants of human behavior" (see Simon [1990] for an articulation in terms of what "normal" science *does*, and see Nozick [2001] for an articulation in terms of what science *should* do; both use the notion of invariance), it is wary of both idiosyncrasy and "history." Individual subjects are interesting to the scientific endeavor only insofar as they instantiate a universal principle, rule, or invariant regularity. Its basic models have very limited conceptual "room" for the particular. Killed someone recently? You may be interesting to many people in many ways—to novelists, therapists, and the local police department—but you are of interest to the scientist of human behavior only insofar as there is some connection between a measurable feature of your up-bringing, personality, cognition, genetics, and/or physiology that can be ex-trapolated to other cases. The pursuit of generality and the reliance on maxi-mally universal models makes the behavioral scientist the "pro-creator" of a particular stance that is a recent (late-twentieth-century) addition to the hu-man repertoire of ways of being: the distancing stance.

Ask is an artful user of the distancing stance. He uses the models of the normative scientist and the experimental mindset of the descriptive scientist to create a *distoscope*: an exosomatic instrument that helps Ask achieve a distance from the subject of his inquiry, which in turn aids him in overcoming "natural" inclinations toward cooperation, empathic resonance, justification, and excul-pation that mitigate his ability to make useful distinctions and create experi-mental interventions that yield informative results about the subject of inquiry.

To mark Ask's distancing stance and his use of models and of the experi-mental method to fashion a distoscope for himself, I shall henceforth refer to the subject of Ask's inquiry as *Creature* and increase the distance between him and Creature even further by neutering Creature: Instead of "Adam says" and "he does," I shall write "Creature says" and "it does." The effect of this "change of notation"—and its distoscopic benefit—will be seen by the experi-mentally inclined reader to vary in direct proportion to the affective proxim-ity of the individual to whom it is applied: It will cost little and bring little to refer to perfect stranger Jack as "it, the Creature"; it may cost dearly but will bring much insight to refer to one's lover or oneself as "it, the Creature." With this basic notation in place, we can begin the spadework for an ascrip-tive science of behaviors associated with "choices" and "decisions."

2.1. *The Decision Theoretic Approach to Modeling Choice*

Rational choice theory contributes to Ask's project a family of models of human ways of being that "explain a lot by a little." At its most ambitious, RCT can explain any behavior (including mental behavior—something that its purveyors have underexploited to date) as the outcome of a process of maximization or optimization. A "rational" person is one who chooses the best means to achieve his or her particular ends. It is thus impossible to declare a person "irrational" on the basis of observing that person's behavior without knowing beforehand what the behavior was meant to accomplish and what the person's goals in producing that behavior were. Before declaring Creature rational on the basis of observing its behavior, Ask has to find out what its ends are and how it construes that behavior. This requires much ascribing of internal structures and states to Creature. Rational choice theory provides such a structure, and Ask is happy to employ it; however, being heedful of both his special aims and of the experimental "record" that has been put forth as challenging the basic axioms of RCT, Ask is aware that the basic structure may have to be modified and deployed in new ways.

This ascribed internal structure, which we label DEC, will be used (by Ask) to represent the model of intentional behavior used by RCT. The first difficulty that DEC must solve is that of figuring out what Creature wants—otherwise, it cannot say whether or not what Creature does is a rationally chosen means to Creature's ends. DEC does so by introducing a preference relation that takes one of two possible states (preferred to versus indifferent or not preferred to) and models Creature's desires or volitional states. This relation can be used to *order* any set of options that Creature faces. Consider Creature's choice of recreational narcotics: We say that Creature "prefers" marijuana to mescaline and mescaline to LSD if Creature's preferences order the set {LSD, marijuana, mescaline} into the set {marijuana, mescaline, LSD}. So far, so good. But how do we *know* (or, at least, hope to come to know) that Creature prefers marijuana to mescaline—or, for that matter, prefers anything to anything else?

WARP and Other Revelations.   Normative speculators such as Paul Samuelson [1938] have endowed us with several axioms of revealed preference (ARPs). The one in greatest favor with descriptive scientists (just why this is the case is left as an exercise for Ask) is the *weak axiom of revealed preference*

(WARP), which states that if Creature has been observed to choose marijuana when it could have chosen mescaline, then it does *not* prefer mescaline to marijuana. The relevant implication of the inferred preference relation is that Creature will *not* choose mescaline when marijuana is also available.

The WARP is as powerful as it is seemingly innocuous. It imposes many constraints on our model of Creature. To be useful as modeling tools, Creature's WARP-inferred preferences have to be stable, for otherwise we cannot use them to predict unobserved choices on the basis of observed choices: Creature can choose to try a new behavior for exploratory purposes, learn from the experience, and abandon the behavior in response to the feedback it receives; in such cases, WARP-based interpretations may incorrectly inform Ask that Creature's behavior is in some sense not rational. Creature can also choose differently "this time around" out of sheer boredom and thereby discover new ways of experiencing the outcome of a choice. Ask is aware of this difficulty and is not dogmatic about using the WARP to interpret all of Creature's behaviors in a mechanical fashion. However, he sees something fundamentally useful in the WARP, which is the insistence on *making behavior count* when studying Creature.

Suppose Creature is a general surgeon in the greater Toronto area. As a hospital administrator, Ask is interested in the kinds of things Creature cares about and the order in which Creature cares about them. How would Creature rank the set {higher compensation, better work environment (with "better" specified at a fine enough level of detail), greater opportunity to do research that is internationally recognized}? A surgeon who considers the problem might say "Ask Creature" and, upon registering the answer, proudly proclaim that *Creature holds a better work environment to be more important (to it) than money* because Creature "said so" when asked.

Ask takes a different view of the matter. He *does* ask Creature if the set {compensation, better work environment, greater opportunity to do research that is internationally recognized} captures the entities that Creature might care about in its professional life, but this is where the talk stops and deeds kick in, for he now offers Creature a series of live choices meant to inform a set of conjectures about Creature's preferences. For example: "Will you, Creature, take a 25% cut in annual base salary for these specific improvements in your work environment?" "Please specify the kind of research opportunity improvements for which you would be willing to give up 30% of your net annual compensation." Only upon subsequent observation of Creature's choices in these live situations ("live" because Ask knows that Creature knows its answer will make a difference to Creature) would Ask proceed to create a model of Creature's underlying preference relation.

The case for a *dialogical* interaction between Ask and Creature is an important one. By talking to Creature, Ask can confirm that Creature indeed chooses from the menu of options that Ask had ascribed to it. If, in the earlier example, Adam had gone to the movie theatre because he knows that the way there passes by a tobacco store that he is trying to avoid (on account of having quit smoking)—though he may "drop by" if it can be done innocuously, en route to somewhere else—then Ask's model of Adam's behavior should include this "covert option." Of course, it would not be easy for Ask to get, from Adam, a completely self-aware picture of the roles played by the tobacco store, the movie theatre, and the movie itself in Adam's preference relations. Yet by talking to Adam, Ask can likely at least learn about the existence of the store and Adam's potential intention to visit it; in which case the importance of the tobacco store to Adam's preference relation can be subsequently probed by, for example, informing Adam that the store is closed or has been moved (and observing his subsequent choice) or informing him that the movie he had wanted to see is no longer playing at the cinema conveniently located *à côté* of the store (and observing his subsequent choice). Talk is often cheap, but it *need* not be so and is often of both value and consequence.

Accordingly, Ask's relationship to WARP is not altogether a simple one, because passing from an observation of choice to an ascription of preference is a tricky business. He "trusts but verifies." He leans on the basic idea of a preference relation that underlies choice and on a model that maps behavior onto choice, checks with Creature that the specification of the option set does indeed correspond to the options that Creature considers to be "live" in its deliberations, and then insists on behavioral tests in order to make inferences about the structure of Creature's preferences.

However, as a constraint that DEC places on Ask's models of Creature, WARP pales in comparison to DEC's other requirements on Creature's preference relation. In particular, DEC additionally requires the following of Creature's preferences.

A1: Completeness. Creature's preference relation can order *any* set of options. It may be indifferent between having the Korean soccer team wear red or yellow jerseys at tomorrow's game, or between the kinds of bindings used to hold together the board report for tomorrow's meeting, but it cannot be *undecided*. Why? It is easy to understand why a normative speculator cares for completeness: He will want to use WARP-type devices to interpret individual behaviors in all possible contexts that are represented by menus of options. But why should Creature respond positively to Ask's attempt to hold Creature's preferences up to the standards of completeness? An anecdote sometimes told to justify the completeness axiom is that of the Scottish monk Buridan's ass, which—when faced with a choice between a small stack of green and juicy strands of hay and a larger stack of yellow, dried-up hay—cannot make up its mind and so dies of starvation. In one interpretation, the ass is of "two minds" (i.e., it has two different sets of preferences) but no way to choose between them. From a distance, the green stack looks more attractive than the yellow one. But when it approaches it, the ass begins to pine after the larger stack and, just at the moment when it reaches the green stack, its desire for the larger haystack "peaks" and so it turns back to the yellow haystack, whereupon a similar sequence of internal goings-on conspires to bring it back to face the green stack again. In another interpretation, the ass is prone to regret: Its regret at not eating the green (yellow) stack is at once *caused* by its contemplating eating the yellow (green) stack and outweighs the expected benefit of eating the yellow (green) stack. Both interpretations are suspect, however, in that they hold the ass to be fully innocent of the consequences of delaying indefinitely the act of eating. The story may be an example of the ass's inconsistent preferences, but these preferences are in fact incomplete because they do not include the option corresponding to the most likely outcome (starvation) that the ass faces by its stubborn indecision. (A third scenario is that the ass (a) is aware that it cannot make up its mind, (b) is aware that it needs to make up its mind in order to eat, (c) is aware that it needs to eat to stay alive, and (d) would say "yes" if it could speak and were asked if it wants to stay alive but is *unaware* that the conjunction of (a)–(d) is true. This possibility will be considered in some detail in Chapter 4 as part of a discussion of the relationship between rationality and imbecility or logical sloth.)

Ask is impressed with the basic teaching of the completeness axiom, even though he does not take it to be a fact either that everyone has or that everyone *should* always-already have complete preferences. If Creature is a CEO that oscillates in the fashion of an ass of the Buridan variety between firing a close friend whose behavior is destructive to the business it manages and firing the apparently competent advisors that have been calling for its friend's resignation, Ask finds the benefit of the completeness axiom to be precisely that of being able to point out to Creature the full effects of its oscillatory behavior. "Not deciding" only *looks like* "doing nothing" because of the bizarre ways in which we have come to refer to status quo behavior in everyday language (i.e., as "doing nothing"). Recalling the completeness axiom, Ask would point out that "not deciding" is very much "doing something" (namely, oscillating) and that the effects of this behavior have to be taken into account in Creature's decision problem. Having thus "completed" Creature's preferences, Ask can proceed to observe the choice that Creature makes, a choice that is now over the expanded option set {fire the friend, fire the advisors, continue oscillating}. *Completable* does not entail *complete*. Ask uses the rationale for the latter to get Creature to accept the notion of the former.

DEC also imposes a couple of minimal "consistency" requirements on Creature's preferences, as follows.

A2: Anti-symmetry. If Creature (weakly) prefers option X (say, distributive equity of a pay-for-performance package as represented by payoff distribution pattern, independent of outcome) to option Y (efficiency of the same pay-for-performance package as represented by the tightness of the link between observable and controllable outcome and payoff to the agent whose effort is causally linked to that outcome), then it will not prefer option Y to option X.

Why is anti-symmetry a reasonable thing to ask of a reasonable person? Well, suppose it weren't. Then it would be rational for Creature to simultaneously favor a package designed on the basis of equity *and* a package designed on the basis of efficiency, which entails a commitment to *physically incompatible* states of the world in the future and to *logically inconsistent* statements (describing the respective physical states) right now. If Creature's choice scenario is specified at this level of precision, then anti-symmetry seems to arise from forbidding Creature from sincerely espousing proposition A and proposition not-A at the same time—the basic consistency axiom of first-order logic. If Creature's choice can be interpreted to mean that Creature sincerely espouses a contradiction, then it will have violated a basic axiom. But a basic axiom of *what*?

Ask is impressed with first-order logic as a disciplining mechanism, but he believes that prescriptive purveyors of DEC (and, in particular, of the anti-symmetry axiom) to be too quick in making inferences about Creature's logical consistency on the basis of observing Creature's choice. Thus Ask is concerned, in the case at hand, (a) that Creature understands the relation between the different packages on the table and, perhaps, the principles—equity or efficiency—on which they are based; (b) that Creature does not have strategic or tactical motives or reasons for feigning either indecisiveness or incoherence; and (c) that Creature accepts the link between its putative behavior and the inconsistent set of propositions to which Creature's behavior seems to commit it. Ask, accordingly, must *educate* Creature about Ask's underlying model of Creature and be educated himself about Creature's own model of its choosable options. It is only when the two models—Creature's model of the decision scenario and Ask's model of Creature's model of the decision scenario—"equilibrate" that Ask can make valid inferences from Creature's behavior to its preferences and, subsequently, to its rationality. As part of the equilibrating dialogue, Creature may in turn ask Ask for the reasons why a particular axiom or principle (e.g., "no contradictions") should count in Creature's own deliberations. If we assume classical and not quantum objects of choice, then Ask has a pretty good answer: The two options excluded one another physically or kinematically, and hence they should exclude each other logically as well. But Ask has to ascertain that Creature's use of language is not too far from Ask's own in order to validate the link from "physically incompatible" to "logically inconsistent." To the extent that ascriptive science requires that Ask dialogically persuade Creature of a particular model or schema for interpreting Creature's behavior, ascriptive science will also require Ask to *justify* to Creature the proposed model. Ask is neither mere observer nor mere logician; he is also a pedagogue, which means that he will often have to persuasively respond to potent counterarguments from Creature regarding the models he uses to interpret its behavior.

A3: Acyclicity. DEC forbids Creature from having "cyclical" preferences whereby, for instance, option *A* is preferred to option *B*, *B* is preferred to *C*, and C is preferred to A. The "anecdotal" argument for acyclicity sometimes produced is that, were Creature's preferences cyclical, one could make a "sure profit" off Creature by inducing it to pay in order to move from an aisle seat on an airplane (option B) to a window seat (option A), to pay again in order to move from a window seat to a middle seat (option C), and to pay once again to move from a middle seat to the aisle seat it initially occupied on an airplane. One could in this way create a "money pump" that feeds on Creature's cyclical preferences, which would be destructive of Creature's interests no matter what they may be. As goes this anecdotal argument, so goes the general argument: cyclical preferences enable money pumps to be built against Creature; and these money pumps will deplete its resources without bringing any net gain.

However, suppose there are no observers around either astute or petty enough to build money pumps and that Creature knows this for a fact. Is it *then* the case that Creature is irrational in exhibiting cyclical preferences? Not insofar as they expose Creature to predation by money-pump engineers; but there is still an argument to be made that Creature expends energy (mechanical work, if nothing else) in coming full circle from option A back to option A, and it is only insofar as Creature does not mind the exercise or the time expended in the trip that cyclical preferences can be rationalized. Of course, if Creature actually *enjoys* going around preference circles of the type outlawed by DEC (for reasons that may have to do with the very absurdity of the exercise), then Ask can legitimately say that the preferences he originally ascribed to it are *incomplete* rather than cyclical and that the enjoyment of going around such circles—and perhaps even of the physical exercise of doing so—has to be added to the option set that Creature chooses from.

The predictive benefits of the acyclicity condition are readily apparent. Ask can use the acyclicity requirement of DEC to make inferences about Creature's preference and putative choice between two options (A and C) on the basis of a set of observations of Creature's pairwise choices (between A and B and between B and C). This makes the process of making predictions of Creature's future choices among options it has never chosen among akin to the process of rating two football teams that have never played one another in the past but have each played teams the other team has also faced.

The ascriptive merits of the condition are also significant: Ask can use the "money pump" argument to justify (to Creature) the condition on the acyclicity of preferences and to alert Creature to the pitfalls associated with cyclical choice patterns; and, if Creature nonetheless instantiates a cyclical set of preferences and fails either to give a cogent counterargument to the claim that cyclical preferences are counterproductive or to include a preference for "going around in circles" in its option set, then Ask can advance that Creature is "irrational" in exhibiting cyclical preference patterns of choices and duly inform Creature of this, seeking to "change its mind." Note the amount of work that is required for such a conclusion from Ask as well as the level of interaction between Ask and Creature that such a conclusion requires. It is critical, in particular, that some dialogue with Creature be used to calibrate Ask's expectations formed on the basis of DEC, whose function is to provide the basic distinction between cyclical and acyclical preferences and thus to supply Ask with a basic structure that he can use to design his own interventions upon Creature.

A4: Independence (of irrelevant alternatives). The *independence* requirement that DEC places on Creature's preferences states that an irrelevant alternative will not influence Creature's preferences—and, implicitly, its choices. If Creature prefers spending an hour with Joe to an hour with Joanne over lunch, then, apparently, it will prefer the combination {spend an hour with Joe, go for a run} to the combination {spend an hour with Joanne, go for a run}. The example, of course, was contrived (as are most examples in decision theory texts) so that the third option (going for a run) is, under most plausible descriptions of the event space, in an intuitive sense independent of the activity of spending an hour in a social activity. Making independence vanish is simple enough: Replace "going for a run" with "attending a board meeting" and posit that Creature believes Joanne has information that is useful to Creature in the context of that meeting; then, of course, the pair of options {spend an hour with Joanne, attend the board meeting} are not independent and so the axiom will not apply.

I must also admit to a sleight of hand in *my own* exposition here: The pair of examples (one based on going for a run, one based on the board meeting) was also contrived to suggest that one can tell, without asking Creature or probing further, what is independent from what. For, suppose that Creature must go for a run to "clear its head" before an executive team meeting that requires it to be clear-headed, and suppose further that Creature knows that, although enjoyable under any other conditions, talking to Joe is "draining of its energy" and therefore not conducive to going for a run later on whereas interactions with Joanne, being more superficial, are not draining in the same way. Then "going for a run" is no longer independent of the pair {spend an hour with Joe, spend an hour with Joanne}.

The implication for Ask is that independence should be assumed but also *verified*, either through interaction with Creature or otherwise. Verification may entail precisely understanding *why* Creature wants to go for a run and *what* is the benefit of spending an hour with Joe or Joanne. What is at stake in Ask's applying DEC to understanding Creature is an often unspoken assumption made by those who customarily use DEC to interpret human behavior: *De gustibus non disputandum est* ("of tastes we shall not dispute," more commonly known as "preferences are not discussible"). If Ask is interested in understanding Creature—rather than judging or declaring it to be irrational—then he must be willing to broach precisely the issue of its "tastes" with Creature. It is only on the basis of Creature's answers to such inquiries that the DEC's independence axiom becomes valuable to Ask as an interpretation instrument.

The independence condition seems easy to justify, as it amounts to no more than affirming the apparent tautology that C, if it is logically independent of A and B, is also materially independent of them. I say "apparent" because, as with passing from "raw" behavior to a proposition that describes that behavior, much can go wrong. To unpack precisely what can go wrong requires a set of principles more powerful than that of independence, which I shall class under the catchall name "invariance."

A5: Invariance (of many different kinds). Understanding Creature's behavior through the lens of DEC requires that Ask assume a significant set of invariances of Creature's preferences lest the value of the "preference" concept as an explanation-generating device be lost. Suppose Creature, a CEO, regularly prefers democratic argumentation involving the entire executive team to solitary calculation and deliberation as means of resolving difficult strategic issues—*except* when the deliberations concern issues affecting the firm's chairman, a close friend of his. Creature is conscious of its preference for democratic argumentation as a decision-making process (no matter what the end state of the process is), has created a theory to justify it, and is conscious of the exception but is oblivious to (or denies) its effect on his theory's generality. Ask has understood both Creature's preference and the theory but is unaware of the exception. He will be surprised when his ability to predict Creature's deliberation strategy abruptly breaks down in a situation that involves discussing an issue involving Creature's chairman—but, perhaps, not *shocked* because he is already armed with an experimentalist and playful orientation toward DEC's core axioms, which he treats as informative but not decisive in interpreting Creature's behavior. To be minimally useful as a modeling device, a preference must be invariant to at least *some* changes in circumstances (otherwise, "everything will matter" and the resulting model will fail to pick out observables of interest); it is upon Ask to ascertain precisely *what* these zones of invariance are.

There is a particular kind of invariance that is important to Ask precisely because it can be ascertained through a kind of interaction with Creature that Ask is well suited to initiate, and that is the invariance of Creature's preferences to the *representation* of the option set.

EXPERIMENT 2.2 (adapted from Kahneman and Tversky [1979])
Main result claimed: Subjects' preferences are representation dependent: changing the representation while keeping "the facts" the same can change preferences.
Specific findings (statistically significant): Subjects are told that an outbreak of SARS is expected to kill 600 people in Toronto. They are given a choice between vaccination program A (200 people expected to be saved "for sure") and program B (400 people will be saved with probability 1/3, nobody will be saved with probability 2/3). *Most choose A over B.* Other subjects are given a choice between program C (400 people will die "for sure") and program D (200 will die with probability 1/3, 600 people will die with probability 2/3). *Most choose D over C.* Because A is "materially equivalent" to C and B is "materially equivalent" to D, preferring A to B *and* D to C is held to be inconsistent.

Of course, in this experiment it is not clear that program A is substantially equivalent to program C (or option B to D). To make the options equivalent, one needs additional assumptions about the mapping between the common language of the lay person and the first-order-logic representation of that common language used by the scientist—which this experiment, as reported, does not provide. The situation could be rectified, for instance, by modifying the instruction to assure Creature that the 400 people who will not be saved "for sure" under program A will actually die "for sure" (program C); otherwise, Creature will likely "fill in" its own probabilities, which may make the two situations materially *non*equivalent. Doing so may imperil the "experimental effect," but it would also highlight the importance of the linguistic ambiguity of passing from everyday language to scientific language to everyday decision making and to the interpretation of experimental results concerning it. Let us suppose, however, that we *could* create the right experimental condition and still achieve the result for the statistically average guy or gal. What principle can Ask invoke in order to call Creature to task for behavior such as that instantiated in Experiment 2.2? Any violation of representation invariance of choices among materially equivalent options can be exploited by the mechanism of the money pump, via which Creature could be induced to pay in order to move from program B to program A, be informed that program A is materially equivalent to program C, and then induced to pay again to move from program C to program D. Thus, Ask is armed with both a useful set of distinctions (material equivalence and representational invariance) and with a justification of the axiom that makes use of this distinction; he cannot *from a distance* ascertain whether or not Creature has violated the axiom and must rather seek to understand how Creature itself represents the choice scenario and what Creature's own conception of invariance is.

Gilboa [2009] raises a concern about the putative effect of the very language of DEC and RCT ("options," "payoffs") on Creature's willingness to accept Ask's interpretation of its behaviors. Briefly put, options and payoffs may be acceptable as ways of describing choices among cars but not choices among friends. This is an "invariance" concern, to be sure, but not one that can be resolved by driving—as Ask did above—to a more precise notion of material equivalence, similarity, and independence. But it can be resolved, nonetheless, by going "in the other direction" and modulating the language of RCT to more closely reflect the way Creature thinks and feels without losing the "topological" properties of DEC: "actions," "conditions," and "consequences" may do just as well as "options," "states of the world," and "payoffs." The ingenuity required of Ask is that of designing a description language for understanding Creature's actions and communicating with Creature that does not change Creature's internal states and representations and at the same time remains ably guided by the structural constraints of DEC.

Consciousness, Cognitive Penetrability, and Discussibility. Invariance under changes in X is of paramount importance to Ask's task of modeling, interacting with, and predicting Creature's behavior. This invariance can be understood as a setting of boundary conditions for Ask's model of Creature and therefore either of setting the *bounds of applicability* of various models of Creature ("in all cases except . . .") or of setting up different behavioral domains *within* which different sets of Creature's preferences and ensuing action sequences are coherent (in the sense of DEC) but *across* which they are discontinuous (e.g., "at home" versus "at work" preferences). All of this will not be surprising to hunters and gatherers of behavioral invariances or to astute observers of human behavior. However, focusing on the *kinds* of conditions whose changes produce changes in the structure of Creature's preferences can lead to distinctions that are useful to behavioral scientists and even more useful to Ask. Consider the following thought experiment.

THOUGHT EXPERIMENT 2.1
Creature is the managing director of a large mutual fund. It exhibits the following "curious" decision pattern: a marked and reliable shift toward higher levels of risk in portfolio selection choices when these choices are made in the presence of an attractive person of the opposite sex with whom Creature interacts casually (but to whom Creature need not justify its choices) while making the decision than in cases where Creature makes its decisions by itself.

It is hardly beyond the ingenuity of Ask to posit sexual arousal as a factor that influences a variable considered to be as fundamental (and thus likely invariant) as risk aversion when making decisions in a setting as structured as "portfolio selection," to which most of Creature's explicit previous training presumably applies. However, what is troublesome for Ask is the problem of *intervening* upon Creature for the purpose of producing either deeper understanding of the effect or some behavioral change. To see the difficulty, imagine you are Ask and about to start a dialogue with Creature concerning the pattern you have just observed. There are here, in fact, two difficulties.

The first problem is *cognitive penetrability*. Creature is not aware of the effect of sexual stimulus on its arousal or of the resulting arousal on its behavior, and it is not aware of not being aware of the effect(s), and so forth (it is thus oblivious to the phenomenon) and therefore will not answer a question such as *Are you aware of any changes in your behavior when . . . ?* affirmatively or even with a glint of recognition in its eyes. Creature produces the relevant behavior mechanically, reliably, and unconsciously and does not respond to queries meant to elucidate the causal structure of the effect. Ask uses this problem of the cognitive penetrability of Creature's motivational states to distinguish between visceral and nonvisceral factors affecting Creature's behavior. In particular, cognitively *impenetrable* motivational states correspond to purely *visceral* states that are—by virtue of being cognitively impenetrable—unresponsive to reason-oriented interventions. Ask can intervene upon Creature with the aim of bringing to its consciousness the relevant regularity he has discovered in its behavior. However, this intervention may require the added degree of freedom of manipulating Creature's context—for example, the freedom to induce risk-seeking behavior on Creature's part by manipulating Creature's "sexual decision-making milieu" in order to produce a large-scale event ("failure") that is deemed by Creature to stand in need of a Creature-specific behavioral "explanation," which opens the door to introduction of the regularity in question.

The second difficulty is that of *discussibility*. Even if a behavioral pattern is cognitively penetrable, it may not be discussible for reasons related to Creature's motivation to defend its ego or status. Consider this next thought experiment.

THOUGHT EXPERIMENT 2.2

Creature is a vascular surgeon who exhibits the following pattern of behavior. When in a glucose-deprived state (as measured by blood glucose level, assessed via a simple blood test were it (socially) permissible to administer one), it chalks up end-of-operation small-vessel suture work to "wound structure," leaving large hematomas (internal bleeding) in the wake of its operations. Yet when Creature is in a state of normal or saturated blood glucose, it treats small vessels identically to the way it treats larger vessels for the purpose of suture work and no hematomas are left behind.

In this case—especially given Creature's medical background—it is unlikely that the behavior is not cognitively penetrable by Creature or that Creature will not resonate to Ask's queries. However, its occurrence is not a subject that Ask can easily broach with Creature owing to strong economic and social incentives that shape Creature's behavior: Admitting to such a regularity can be construed as admission of negligence or as powerful status-defensive behaviors (deny the occurrence of any behavioral patterns that cannot be justified as being "for the good of the patient"). Here, Ask must again bring to consciousness Creature's behavioral pattern by extra-communicative means— for example, by gathering and confronting Creature with sufficient data on the basic pattern of Creature's operating-room behaviors ("the pattern is real, or objectively ascertained") and on how the difference in Creature's blood glucose levels affects the recovery of its patients ("the pattern matters")—to make the avoidance of dialogue itself a potentially costly move for Creature.

Achieving Agency: The Ascriptive Maneuver RESP.   To *what end* are the axioms of rational choice theory "deployed" by the rational choice theorist? What does RCT hope to accomplish by the *conjoint* articulation of its axioms? If the question seems awkward, consider that none of the axioms is incontrovertibly justifiable as a universal maxim of behavior, even though each makes sense in a large variety of contexts and facilitates the task of structuring Ask's raw perception of Creature, which could easily be described far less informatively (as, e.g., "a 200-pound mass of bones, muscles, and viscera" or "a space-time hypervolume of itches, pains, addictions, and habits"). Rational choice theorists (see, e.g., Savage [1954] and Kreps [1988]) use these basic "structuration" axioms to prove an innocuous but powerful *existence theorem*: If Creature's preferences satisfy the axioms A1–A4, then there exists a unique objective (or "utility") function that Creature is maximizing by virtue of choosing consistently with its preferences. In conjunction with one ARP or another, the existence theorem allows us to (a) interpret any behavioral sequence of Creature as a set of choices, (b) interpret these choices as being purposefully directed at maximizing an objective function, and therefore (c) interpret any of Creature's behavioral sequences as being purposefully directed at maximizing that objective function. This move leads to a simple interpretive schema for Creature's behavior which Ask can use to produce some far-reaching implications.

What does it mean when we say that Creature "is" maximizing an objective or utility function? The "is" is in question, and the question is very important to Ask. First, what does the schema say about Creature's level of consciousness in producing its objective-maximizing behavior? On its face, nothing: the objective function maximization machine may work at the unconscious or subconscious level for Creature. But since the existence of the objective function is contingent upon conformance of Creature's preferences to a set of conditions of logical consistency (and not upon merely "kinematic," "dynamic," or "physiological" compatibility; see Sen [1993] for the importance of this point), it follows that denying Creature's conscious awareness of its preferences amounts to denying Creature a means of checking the logical consistency of its preferences and thus to denying it part of a necessary mechanism for bringing such consistency about in situations where it is lacking—a tricky position for a modeler of behavior.

One could argue that conscious awareness of locally expressed preferences is not the same as awareness of the objective function that is "expressed" by or "pursued" through the Creature's choices that are governed by those preferences: Performing local consistency checks on sets of choices and the preferences they entail is not the same as performing some global optimization. Creature may, then, be conscious of *immediately accessible exercisable* preferences, *immediately accessible past* choices, and *imminently exercisable* preferences yet not be conscious of the objective function that "generates" these preferences. Creature's instantaneous behavior—its behavior at any one moment in time—may be driven by the overarching objective of climbing to the top of a particular dominance hierarchy, which in turn is constrained by a set of privative rules or proscriptions of the usual type (e.g., "do not deceive unless you believe you will not be caught") but of which Creature is unaware.

In this model, Creature produces behavior according to a local, known preference map that is part of a global, unknown preference map that maps Creature's objective function onto choosable option sets. Here, the model of Creature's preference-based choices is reminiscent of Polanyi's [1958] account of his "fragmented" understanding of the proof of Gödel's theorem, which states that any logical system that is at least as complex as arithmetic is either incomplete or inconsistent. Polanyi understood each of the steps of the proof as well as various sequences of steps, but he could not hold "the entire proof in [his] mind at any one time." In such a case, Ask may say that Creature's global objective function is not cognitively penetrable to Creature.

Let us partition the causes of such cognitive impenetrability into two classes. The first class of causes arises because the cognitive penetration process itself is *computationally* too complex: Creature cannot be reasonably expected to know all of the logical consequents of all of the propositions it does in fact know; and requiring Creature to know "its own mind" to this extent may require that it be logically omniscient, that it know the logical consequences of all that it knows, which Ask can reasonably decline to require. (This problem is dealt with in greater detail in Chapter 4.)

The second class of causes of cognitive impenetrability are unrelated to computational complexity or cognitive prowess; they include self-deception, denial, "plain old ignorance," and distractedness on the part of Creature. In such cases, the objective function instantiated by behavior is unknown but still knowable to Creature: Beholding or discovering this function requires no more cognitive skills or capabilities than Creature already possesses. Under these circumstances, Ask has a powerful "responsibilization" (RESP) role in his interactions with Creature. This role is fulfilled when Ask employs the following maneuver.

> RESP. *Interpret the consequences of Creature's behavior as substantive parts of the goals of Creature's behavior.*

The maneuver may seem harsh, but it is simply the ascriptive science counterpart of the modeling move that descriptive science makes when it applies the WARP to Creature's observed behavioral patterns and then infers Creature's preferences from them. The maneuver is one whereby Ask attempts to establish Creature's "authorship" of its own behaviors. As such, it will be familiar to psychoanalytically trained therapists who attempt to uncover deep (read: "global") motives (read: "objective functions") in seemingly unrelated and disparate (read: "local") behavioral patterns (e.g., the seemingly unconnected set {flirting, biting nails while conversing, repetitive flipping on/off of a light switch}) and to thereby establish ownership of or cognitive jurisdiction over the deep motivation (the global objective function). RESP is the ascriptive science counterpart of the interpretive acts of *analysis* in psychotherapy, of *modeling* in descriptive behavioral science, and of *imputation* in everyday interpersonal interactions.

RESP is a move, but it is not merely a "modeling" move. It is also part of a reasoned attempt by Ask to inscribe within Creature a certain self-interpretation that creates (or restores) agency. As a move, it may be accepted or rejected by Creature "for reasons." But in either case the choice (to accept or reject RESP) is one for which Creature cannot easily shirk responsibility. However, Creature may rationally and reasonably reject responsibility for a *particular* action or choice by arguing that it is not causally connected to a sequence of events that Creature willfully and consciously initiated. Such (unsurprising) countermoves will advance the dialogue between Ask and Creature, moving it to a more precise level of analysis.

2.2. The Ascriptive Approach to the Study of Behavior

We are now in a position to understand the precise ways in which Ask makes use of DEC in his attempts to understand Creature. Ask uses DEC as a starting point, a way and a grammar for structuring his model of Creature; the result is a representation that is susceptible to changes and revisions in view of Creature's actions and its responses to Ask's interpretation thereof. Ask employs the basic (ARP) stipulations that behavioral scientists use to infer preferences from the observed behavior of their subjects, and he employs the basic axioms of RCT to organize his interpretation of Creature's behavior.

Thus far, Ask is proceeding in a fashion familiar to descriptive and prescriptive scientists. Unlike many of his "normal science" counterparts, however, Ask at this point becomes an empiricist about not only the predictions but also the assumptions of DEC, and he tests the fundamental premises on which his model of Creature is based. Because he is a predictive and not a "retrodictive" empiricist, Ask tests DEC's assumptions by using them to make precise point predictions about Creature's behavior in different settings and then assessing the fit between his predictions and the resulting observation statements.

Ask then borrows a page from the repertoire of experimental researchers of human behavior (who use the forced-choice paradigm to design their experiments) and forces Creature into making choices that constitute global tests of his updated DEC-based model of Creature—in contrast with the local tests that merely aim to falsify the point assumptions on which DEC rests. At this stage, Ask breaks with the science-from-a-distance approach of his behavioral scientist counterpart and does what the latter usually considers unthinkable: Ask *intervenes*; he confronts Creature with the results of the forced choice test, and with Ask's interpretation of it, for the purpose of further sharpening his predictive model of Creature.

The protocol for this dialogical confrontation is not structure-free; it will be the subject of a detailed analysis in Chapter 6, where the minimal preconditions for an authentic interaction between Ask and Creature will be articulated by the basic model COM, the communicative counterpart of DEC. However, at this point I am interested in (i) requiring that Ask confront Creature with his "findings" and interpretations of them and (ii) emphasizing that DEC provides a basic template or "code" that structures this interaction: *Why did you choose to produce observed behavior X?* is DEC/RESP-speak for the *Why did you do X?* or *What made you do X?* that we encounter in everyday language. The advantage is that ambiguity in the everyday use of some words (e.g., "why?" can be answered with a statement about *reasons and incentives* or about *causes and stimuli* or both together) is removed in favor of an assumption (conscious will in Creature's production of behavior) that can be tested and that can also be cultivated by the very act of communicating with Creature as if the results of its behavior are its goals.

As Gilboa [1991] envisioned in his own articulation of ascriptive science, Creature is confronted by Ask with an account of its behavior and is asked to respond to Ask's interpretation of it. Creature can respond by changing (or not changing) its behavior—which corresponds to Gilboa's idea of ascriptive science, wherein the subject is asked whether or not it wants to change its choices—or by *arguing* with Ask regarding his interpretation of Creature's behavior, an essential step if misunderstandings between the producer and observer of behavior are to be identified and addressed.

Ask *asks*. He has adopted from the descriptive scientist the questioning stance, but Ask applies this stance uniformly to Creature *and* to the models and experimental findings of normative and descriptive science as well as to the interpretations of these findings by normative and descriptive scientists. The questioning strategy that Ask pursues is guided by DEC and also by the aim of bringing Creature's consciousness in touch with Creature's behavior and observing the outcome. Barring mishaps in communication, Creature's behavior ideally comes to be in "ascriptive equilibrium" with Ask's interpretation of that behavior and, in turn, with a suitably adapted form of DEC.

To gain a sense of how Ask operates in practice, consider (as in the following experiment) the situation in which Creature is an individual whose choices seem to violate the principles that require that choice be independent of irrelevant alternatives.

EXPERIMENT 2.3 [Tversky and Shafir, 1992]

Main result: Subjects are willing to forgo the benefit of making an early decision between two options in the absence of information about an event deemed by the experimenters to be independent of the two options.

Specific findings: The members of one group of subjects were asked to respond to the following scenario. Imagine you have just taken a tough qualifying examination. It is the end of the fall quarter, you feel tired and run-down, and you are not sure you passed the exam. If you failed, then you must take the exam again in a couple of months—after the Christmas holidays. You now have an opportunity to buy an attractive five-day Christmas vacation package to Hawaii at an exceptionally low price. The special offer expires tomorrow, but the exam grade will not be available until the following day. Would you:

1. Buy the vacation package? (32% of respondents agreed)
2. Not buy the vacation package? (7%)
3. Pay a nonrefundable $5 fee to retain the right to buy the package at the same exceptional price *after* finding out whether you passed the exam? (61%)

Members of a second and third group were asked instead to respond to the following scenario. Imagine that you have just taken a tough qualifying exam. It is the end of the semester, you feel tired and run-down, and you've just found out that you passed the exam (or failed the exam and will have to take it again in a few months). You now have an opportunity to buy an attractive five-day Christmas vacation package to Hawaii at an exceptionally low price, but the special offer expires tomorrow. Would you:

1. Buy the vacation package? (54% of the "pass" group and 57% of the "fail" group agreed)
2. Not buy the vacation package? (16% of the "pass" group and 12% of the "fail" group)
3. Pay a nonrefundable $5 fee to retain the right to buy the vacation package at the same exceptionally low price the day after tomorrow? (30% of the "pass" group and 31% of the "fail" group)

Tversky and Shafir want to use the results to highlight a problem with the descriptive use of the sure-thing principle: If the experimental subjects in group 2 ("passed the exam") and group 3 ("failed the exam") behave identically to one another, then choosing the trip is deemed to be independent of passing or failing the exam; therefore, the (majority of) subjects in group 1, who are unaware of whether they passed or failed the exam, seem to be acting in violation of the independence axiom—an effect attributed by the experimenters to "loss of acuity in the presence of uncertainty."

What could be meant by "acuity" in this case? For subjects in group 1, acuity might be defined as the ability and propensity to engage in the two thought experiments corresponding to the experimental conditions for groups 2 and 3 ("suppose I failed" and "suppose I passed"); make choices in those thought experiments corresponding to those of the majorities (and eventually take the trip no matter what the exam's result); realize, on account of these thought experiments, that the trip is independent of the results on the exam; and therefore choose to buy and book the trip right away. There is no lacuna of acuity for those subjects who genuinely would want to take the trip only if they had passed (or only if they had failed) the exam and not otherwise; these subjects therefore *rationally* choose to forgo $5 for the right to choose later.

However, it is possible that a so-called acuity-deficient Creature who chose in apparent contravention of the sure-thing principle did so because: (a) it recognized the cost of making a decision, which it might later regret, in its present state of fatigue and uncertainly; (b) it estimated these costs to be more than $5; and so (c) it chose to invest $5 for the option to decide at a time of lesser uncertainty. We would not explain such a subject's choice by "loss of acuity" but rather by some kind of circumspective rationality or wisdom that functions synergetically with the coherence axioms of RCT to produce better outcomes for the decision maker in various conditions that RCT had not contemplated. It is possible that, if Creature attaches a positive and significant value to the *process* by which it makes decisions (e.g., "they must be carried out only while I am in certain physiological conditions"), then Ask may find it difficult to determine whether or not the subject has violated a norm of RCT—unless Ask has written down a complete model of Creature's decision process.

This is the kind of ambiguity that Ask is interested in resolving. If Creature chooses to give up a sum of money to retain the rights to make a decision *after* an upcoming event that seems irrelevant to the decision (this can be ascertained by running the Tversky–Shafir experiment on Creature and "assigning" to Creature the conditions corresponding to groups 1, 2, and 3), then Ask will confront Creature with the results of the experiment and seek an explanation that illuminates what "independent" means to Creature. Creature's explanation may be: "I erred (and will not do so again)." This is completely consistent with the way in which Savage [1954] intended his statistical decision theory—as a normative tool and template for studying and guiding choice. When confronted by Maurice Allais with the fact that his own choices in a decision scenario had become known as the "Allais paradox," Savage reportedly changed his answer from the "intuitive" one he had given previously to the "normative" one implied by his own theory and said, "I made a mistake" [Sen, private comm.].

Creature's explanation of its own behavior may, alternatively, be that the decision was circumspectively rational and took into account the full set of costs and benefits entailed in the decision scenario (including physiological ones). In any one of these cases, Ask can revise the basic model he has used and proceed to retest. If Creature admits that it "made an error," then its implicit commitment to heed the independence axiom henceforth can be readily tested with a Tversky–Shafir-like construction. By invoking some form of circumspective rationality, Creature makes an (implicit) commitment to a level of awareness about its own (psychological and physiological) states surrounding a decision that can also be tested. Ask could induce a state of disconcertedness and "ontological insecurity" in Creature by, for example, producing nonconcordant combinations of a message's substance ("I bring you terrible news") and the tone in which it is delivered (animated glee) and then immediately asking Creature to make decisions of significant consequence and registering the results. The dialogue remains anchored both in what Creature says and in what it does, with an uneasy but productive tension maintained between the conscious and nonconscious facets of "behavior."

3. FLIPS OF THE WILL: TEMPORAL DYNAMICS OF THE SUBJECTIVE EXPERIENCE OF VALUE

RESP will strike many as being too severe and limiting—even as a starting point for further inquiry—for at least two sets of reasons. The first is that even a simple introspective exercise reveals many previously unforeseen consequences of action that have been willfully initiated by us, along with at least a "flickering" awareness of their unforeseeability. Creature flips a switch in a dark room with the intention of turning on a light. The flip is attached by a string to a guillotine that falls and severs the head of a woman. Should Creature be held responsible for the woman's death? RESP clearly suggests that Creature *is* responsible, but common sense rebels against this verdict so long as Creature did not know (and had no reason to know) about the connection between the light switch and the death machine. Ask, however, has an easy way out of this difficulty, for ascriptive science does not posit the same barrier between Ask and Creature as the one we encounter in the descriptive sciences. Ask can *confront* Creature with the results of applying RESP to his observations of Creature's behavior and ask: "Is this right? Is there anything you want to add to or change about this interpretation before we agree to use it in order to interpret your subsequent action?" Note the difference between this and Gilboa's [1991] version of ascriptive science. Gilboa posits an ascriptive scientist who asks Creature: "Here is an analysis of how you acted: Is there anything you want to change about your behavior?" This question assumes that the scientist's interpretation of the behavior is correct and makes it hard for Creature to disagree with the scientist's model *or* for the scientist to make further progress if Creature (having murdered its best friend, for instance, despite previous declarations of affection) declares itself to be "quite happy" with the way it acted. Note also the similarity between my version of ascriptive science and Argyris's "action-science" interventions, wherein the scientist approaches Creature with a query of this form: "Help me make sense of the behavior that you have produced as it is experienced and related by myself and others around you." The difference between the two versions is the *model-based* nature of Ask's interventions, which make explicit use of an a priori grammar (such as DEC) or modeling principle (such as RESP).

The second set of reasons for judging RESP to be unreasonable is that Creature can experience what can plausibly seem to Ask to be preference *flips* or reversals: Creature may say that it prefers X to Y and may indeed prefer X to Y from afar (i.e., when X and Y are both far enough in the future); however, when the opportunity to choose Y approaches, Creature may *flip* and produce behavior that can well be interpreted by Ask as a choice of Y over X. To make matters worse, when asked it may not even acknowledge that it "really" prefers Y to X; instead, Creature can feel "embarrassed" by this lapse and attempt to hide, ignore, rationalize, or excuse it. This *akrasia*, or what some have called "weakness of the will," will be a genuine problem for Ask's quest to produce a model of "what Creature (really) wants" that can be "trained" on data provided by Creature's verbal and nonverbal behavior.

Some descriptive calculators and experimenters in economics [Laibson, 1997], psychology [Green and Myerson, 2004], and psychiatry [Ainslie, 2001] have attempted to explain flips of the will by introducing models in which Creature discounts the value of future outcomes or options ("lotteries") hyperbolically rather than exponentially. Let V_L denote the value that Creature subjectively experiences upon securing a "larger-later" payoff that occurs at time t_l in the future (e.g., the subjective satisfaction of having run a well-reasoned and detached public deliberation on an important topic), and let V_S denote Creature's subjective value associated with a "smaller-sooner" payoff that occurs at time t_s in the future (say, cathartic pleasure in the venomous public tongue-lashing of an irritating participant in that same gathering); here, true to the definitions, $t_l > t_s$ and $V_L > V_S$. Assuming that

Creature's personal discount rate for value in time is constant and equal to some positive constant k, we can describe the temporal behavior of Creature's "subjective value function" in one of at least two ways.

1. *Exponential discounting.* The temporal behavior of Creature's subjective experience of the instantaneous value of its two future options is given by $v_S(t) = V_S e^{-k(t_s - t)}$ and $v_L(t) = V_L e^{-k(t_l - t)}$, respectively. The descriptive scientist searches for flips of Creature's will by looking for the (crossover) point(s) $\{t_c\}$ at which $v_S(t) = V_S e^{-k(t_s - t_c)} = v_L(t) = V_L e^{-k(t_l - t_c)}$. Solving for t_c yields $t_l - t_s = [\ln(V_L) - \ln(V_S)]/k$, entailing that if Creature applies the same discount rate k to the two values then there is no preference flip.

Human problems with impulse control, by contrast, are supposed to be captured by the following mathematical contraption.

2. *Hyperbolic discounting.* The temporal behavior of Creature's subjective experience of the instantaneous value of its two future options is given by

$$v_s(t) = \frac{V_S}{1 + k(t_s - t)}, \quad v_l(t) = \frac{V_L}{1 + k(t_l - t)},$$

and the search for crossover points between the two curves yields the equation

$$v_s(t) = \frac{V_S}{1 + k(t_s - t_c)} = v_l(t) = \frac{V_L}{1 + k(t_l - t_c)},$$

which has the solution

$$t_c = \frac{1}{k} + \frac{V_S t_l - V_L t_s}{V_S - V_L}.$$

This equation points to a flip of the will for $0 < t_c < t_s$.

Hyperbolic discounting functions are not the only ones that can be used to model flips of the will. Some modelers (see, e.g., Rachlin [2000] and Bénabou and Tirole [2002]) have shown it is possible for exponential discounters to experience a flip of the will—albeit by a different underlying mechanism than that implied by hyperbolic discounting. Creature will experience flips of the will if it exponentially discounts V_S and V_L at *different* rates k_s and k_l, respectively, such that $v_S(t) = V_S e^{-k_s(t_s - t)}$ and $v_L(t) = V_L e^{-k_l(t_l - t)}$. Equating these expressions yields $v_S(t) = V_S e^{-k_s(t_s - t_c)} = v_L(t) = V_L e^{-k_l(t_l - t_c)}$, which has the following solution for the crossover point of the two curves:

$$t_c = \frac{\ln(V_L) - \ln(V_S) + k_s t_s - k_l t_l}{k_l - k_s}.$$

This point will index a flip of the will for $0 < t_c < t_s$ in the model.

From Ask's perspective, the descriptive scientist and his normative brethren attach to the choice of functional form for the discounting function more importance than is warranted by the goal of arriving at a predictively successful model of Creature. If models are useful only insofar as they generate algorithms for the prediction of the evolution of observables (a reasonable description of the aim of descriptive science and of "positive economics"), then why should we care about precise functional forms and precise mechanisms when, in fact, no model will be claimed to have any "ontological weight"? Agreeing on one functional form for the discounting function may be more relevant, in the context of descriptive science, to a concern for achieving interresearcher *reliability* (i.e., consistency in the ways papers are written, theories are articulated, and tenure cases debated), but that is of no concern here.

Ask, however, has additional goals to that of producing algorithms for the prediction of the evolution of Creature's observable behaviors. Ask wants the model to be adaptive to his interaction with *this* Creature at this instant, to make it possible for him to cohesively query Creature and thus to exhibit the combination of robustness, intuitiveness, and flexibility that together make adaptation possible. Ask is also interested in the *performative* value of the model—in other words, he wants to use the model to design probes into Creature's behavior and subsequently motivate Creature to attempt remedial behaviors that enhance Creature's capability for self-control and self-command.

Ask is, in particular, interested in the immediately *testable* implications of each of the alternative models and in the ways he can use the models to design experiments on Creature that will result in sharper, more detailed information about Creature. Toward this end, there are two sets of effects that are relevant to Ask.

(1) Marginal Analysis of the Effects on t_c of Changes. The crossover-point analysis above yielded the result that *both* hyperbolic and exponential

TABLE 2.1. Marginal Analysis of Dependence on Crossover Time t_c on Decision Parameters

	Hyperbolic discounters	Exponential discounters
$\dfrac{\partial t_c}{\partial k}$	$-\dfrac{1}{k^2}$	
$\dfrac{\partial t_c}{\partial k_s}$		$\dfrac{\ln\left(\dfrac{V_L}{V_S}\right) + k_l t_s - k_l t_l}{\left(k_l - k_s\right)^2}$
$\dfrac{\partial t_c}{\partial k_l}$		$\dfrac{\ln\left(\dfrac{V_S}{V_L}\right) + k_s t_l - k_s t_s}{\left(k_l - k_s\right)^2}$
$\dfrac{\partial t_c}{\partial V_s}$	$\dfrac{V_L t_s - V_L t_l}{\left(V_S - V_L\right)^2}$	$\dfrac{V_S}{k_l - k_s}$
$\dfrac{\partial t_c}{\partial V_L}$	$\dfrac{V_S t_l - V_S t_s - V_L t_s}{\left(V_S - V_L\right)^2}$	$\dfrac{V_L}{k_l - k_s}$
$\dfrac{\partial t_c}{\partial t_s}$	$-V_L$	$\dfrac{k_s}{k_l - k_s}$
$\dfrac{\partial t_c}{\partial t_l}$	V_S	$\dfrac{k_l}{k_s - k_l}$

discounting models can give rise to flips of Creature's will to choose in a particular way. However, it is significant that the precise algebraic expression for the crossover point at which such flips can occur differs for the two kinds of discounting regimes. As Table 2.1 indicates, the rates at which t_c varies with V_S, V_L, k, k_s, k_l, t_s, and t_l differ in the two cases. This makes it possible for Ask to design experiments (suggested by the table) that will help him distinguish between a "hyperbolic Creature" and an "exponential Creature" on the basis of altering the values of the larger-later and smaller-sooner rewards and the times at which Creature expects these rewards to materialize. These experiments will require that Ask present Creature with choices that entail numerous combinations (of V_S, V_L, t_s, and t_l) that will allow Ask to make inferences about t_c—provided Ask cares to do so. But why would he?

(2) Dependence and Manipulation of Will-Flipping Behavior. The most important reason for Ask to design such experiments is that the shape of

the discounting function and the magnitude of the discounting factor may function at different levels, at different times, in different milieus—and understanding what kind of discounter Creature is allows Ask to ask sharper questions about systematic variations in Creature's discount modes and rates. Suppose that the shape of the discounting curve is a stable, traitlike predisposition of Creature (i.e., Creature is either an exponential or a hyperbolic discounter but not both) whereas the discount factor that Creature applies to different future options is a function of its internal psychological and visceral states. For instance, Creature may discount future values far more sharply in states of irrepressible rage or deep hypoglycemia than in states of emotional restfulness or detachment. In this case, Ask can further increase his understanding of Creature's behavior by eliciting bids from Creature on options with payoffs of different sizes that materialize at different times in the future (i.e., V_S, V_L, t_s, and t_l) with the aim of extracting—from the data that Creature's behavior generates—estimates of the discount factors that Creature applies to its future options. Ask cannot do this unambiguously until he has figured out the general functional form of Creature's discounting function. Ask's resulting comprehension of Creature's discounting factor is conditioned by his choice of a discounting model.

A second reason why Ask can seek to distinguish between the functional forms of Creature's value discounting function is that he wants to be able to estimate the time window in which his interventions will make a difference, which is related to the crossover time t_c. If this window is different for hyperbolic and exponential discounters, then Ask infers that the shape of the curve is one of the differences in representation that make a difference to praxis.

Ask will have realized, by now, that modeling Creature's "wish-states" (and the behavioral propensities that follow from these wish-states) requires a principle of behavioral interpretation, or ascription, that is more nimble than RESP—for instance, something that runs as follows.

INT. *Action is pulled by incentives (rather than pushed by causes or stimuli). Understanding behavior minimally requires understanding the (micro-) incentives that motivate Creature's actions and that make Creature's behaviors intentional.*

INT is the basic principle behind Ainslie's [1992] "pico-economic" approach to explaining human behavior. It does not require an a priori commitment to a particular functional form (exponential or hyperbolic) of Creature's discounting function. This model will shape Ask's future inquiry.

It is easy for Ask to demonstrate to Creature that its flips of the will are counternormative, from Creature's own standpoint, by using the same logic Ask used to demonstrate that Creature's preference function (whatever it may be) should be complete and in some cases "invariant." If an observer of Creature's actions learns the precise points at which Creature's preferences flip, then that observer could construct a "utility pump" that would reliably extract a positive payoff from Creature by first offering it a bundle of options that includes slightly more of the option with value V_L (larger-later) and slightly less of the option with value V_S (shorter-sooner) just *before* the preference flip in exchange for some positive sum X and then, *after* the preference flip, returning to offer Creature a bundle of options that includes slightly less of the option with value V_L and slightly more of the option with value V_S for some positive sum Y, yielding a sure profit of $(X + Y)$.

If Creature's actions were responsive to such reasons for being consistent over time, then one would expect that its actions would also be responsive to a conscious pursuit of the overall maximization of value that has Creature choose option L (valued at V_L) over option S (valued at $V_S < V_L$). The *reductio* that Ask offers Creature as a reason for consistency would serve, in this case, the purpose of making Creature conscious of an optimization exercise that underlies its choice of V_L in the first place. And if making Creature conscious of its impulsiveness were sufficient to negate the impulse, then this simple maneuver will have turned out to be a highly efficient way to increase Creature's level of self-control. But Creature is not likely to be responsive to this kind of reasoning, in part because of the "blinding" effect of a powerfully felt impulse; so Ask could not reasonably expect it to respond positively if called to task for leaving itself open to the implementation of a money pump at its expense.

We are dealing, then, with behaviors produced by a Creature that is *incorrigible* in the special sense that it is usually not *penetrable* by corrective cognitive processes. These behaviors are part of what INT is designed to capture and what makes it different from RESP. Seen through the prism of INT, Creature is still *causally* connected to the behaviors it produces but is not immediately *consciously* responsible for them. Creature cannot usually give coherent reasons for its flip of the will, so it cannot rationalize the (last-minute) flip in response to Ask's queries. (RESP can "kick in" after Ask and Creature agree that Creature has acted and is prone to act impulsively, that it has the means to rein in its impulses, and that it is therefore responsible for the consequences of not using these means to "control itself.")

Nonetheless, Creature can ex post rationalize any apparently counterproductive choice (e.g., heavy and persistent heroin use). It can posit long-run goals (hedonistic enjoyment of alternate realities, come what may) that are consistent with heavy drug use right now. It just cannot rationalize flips from a completely specified option set with a "larger-later" reward structure to one with a "smaller-sooner" reward structure that is logically incompatible with the "larger-later" option. Thus, whatever the "rationality" that Ask can ascribe to Creature, the ascription cannot be based on observations of single choices; rather, it has to involve judgments made about choice *patterns* (temporal sequences or cross-sectional sequences) whose identification will require Ask to confront Creature with the "data" that Ask has collected about it.

Creature can also seek to rationalize a pattern of behaviors that seems to Ask to display counterproductive preference reversals (plausibly explained by Creature's hyperbolic discounting of value) by positing that its world is "hazardous" and that therefore any reward V will be realized only with probability $p(t)$ within some period of time between the present moment and time t: $V(t) = V_L \, p(t)$. Creature thus incurs a risk $r(t)dt$ that a reward V that is available at time t will be lost at time $t + dt$, which can be expressed in terms of the probability $p(t)$ that reward V will survive time period t via $r(t) = -1/p(t)(dp/dt)$ [Sozou, 1998]. If the hazard rate $r(t)$ is constant, then $p(t) = e^{-Kt}$ and Creature's value discount function will be exponential: $V(t) = V_L \, e^{-Kt}$. However, if the hazard rate is unknown then Creature may well model its parameter k via some prior distribution $f(K)$. If Creature chooses this distribution to be the exponential distribution (i.e., $f(K) = e^{-K/k}/k$), then the cumulative probability at the present time that Creature will realize the value V at time t will be given by

$$\int_0^\infty \frac{e^{-Kt-k/K}}{k} \, dk = \frac{1}{1+kT},$$

which is precisely the hyperbolic discounting profile that Ask had ascribed to Creature. In light of this explanation, then, hyperbolic discounting appears to result from risk-neutral present-value calculation in the face of a reasonable distribution for the parameters of a hazard rate. Ask can, of course, turn this self-explanation into a test by asking Creature to make choices between smaller-sooner and larger-later choices in the context of a scenario in which the hazard rates are either (a) constant or (b) changing in ways determined by an underlying exponential distribution. If Creature's self-explanation is valid, then Ask should observe that Creature's now-versus-later trade-off function tracks changes in the underlying hazard rate. If Creature's self-explanation is valid and if Ask does indeed find that Creature is a hyperbolic discounter only in situations characterized by certain hazard rates, then Ask can still note that there is something incoherent in Creature's positing long-term goals and objectives that it already knows it will forgo in the presence of immediate temptations—and that this inconsistency is actually exacerbated if Creature has a valid model for why this should be so.

4. THE REALM OF INT

Ask is now in a position to model behaviors that are produced by Creature intentionally but are not rationalizable—for example, Creature's propensity to attend to sharp physical pain, to scratch an itch, or to engage in some habitual behavior that is not in Creature's all-things-considered best interest (by Creature's own standards of "best").

The value of precisely modeling such behaviors has been explicitly recognized by thinkers writing in various economics traditions [Thaler and Sheffrin, 1981; Jensen and Meckling, 1994; Laibson, 1997; Rubinstein, 2001; Bénabou and Tirole, 2002] and by applied behavioral scientists [Ainslie, 2001], but some of them have used a *privative* description of behavior that hides what Creature actually *does* when it produces "aversive behaviors" and focuses instead on behaviors that Creature *does not produce* even though it has good reason to produce them. The most telling example is furnished by Jensen's pain-avoidance model of human behavior [Jensen and Meckling, 1994], wherein Creature:

1. knows it should do X rather than Y on the basis of a cost–benefit calculation that assigns a greater value to the outcome of doing X than to the outcome of doing Y;

2. decides to do *X* by virtue of this calculation, yet

3. does not do *X* because the cost (pain) of doing *X* must be incurred before receiving the benefit of doing *X*; and therefore

4. produces the suboptimal behavior *Y*.

For example: Creature reasonably and coolly *decides* that pointing out to its boss an instance of self-deception on the latter's part (*X*) is better, all things considered, than "playing along" and pretending to ignore her defensive pro-clivities (*Y*), but then Creature realizes ("at the last moment") that it cannot suffer through the moment at which it broaches a topic that is not part of any script followed by previous Creature–boss conversations and that will trigger aversive reactions in its boss; hence Creature forgoes the opportunity to pro-duce a potentially cathartic and illuminating conversation, settling instead for the usual "update" or "briefing" on some legitimate topic.

Recognizing that the kinds of phenomena referred to by such pain-avoidance models are highly relevant to understanding the way humans pro-duce behavior, Ask asks: "What, specifically, does Creature *do* when it *does not do X*, having previously *decided* to do *X* upon consideration of sound rea-sons?" A chronic smoker who decides to quit—and hence to "not smoke"—*does something when she does not have* the next cigarette: She may put on a nicotine patch, go for a walk, take a number of deep breaths, or drink a glass of water. A slouch who makes an internal commitment to go to the gym every morning *does something* the morning he ends up not going to the gym. Ainslie's analysis supplies Ask with a modeling maneuver that helps cut through the privative veil of "pain-avoidance-type" descriptions: Look at be-havior as being pulled by (micro- or pico-) incentives, not as being repelled by (micro- or pico-) disincentives. This insight leads Ask to the following modeling heuristic.

POS. *Model the positive content of behavior; that is, focus the modeling "eye" on what Creature does, not on what Creature does not do.*

Although seemingly harmless, POS cuts deeply into the fabric of the activity of theorizing in the study of humans: The heuristic makes it pos-sible to look closely at Creature as it produces the suboptimal (or "aversive") behavior that precludes the production of optimal behavior. "Nature, to be commanded, must be obeyed"—Bacon's dictum—can then be amplified by: "Behavior, to be understood, must be made visible." POS, in association with INT, does for behavior what stains do for bacterial cultures.

Thus, Ainslie argues that pain, to function as pain, must present Creature with a reward structure that micro-locally motivates Creature to *attend* to it in the first place (see Figure 2.1). Even if the interval $(t_p - t_e)$ is very short, it nevertheless must correspond to a burst of intense "positive utility" or pleasure provoked by attending to the physiological signal *pain*; otherwise, Creature would never attend to it in the first place. In the figure, Region B corresponds to the true "experience" of pain, which is causally linked to Creature's choice to attend to pain in the first place: "no attention, no experience," and therefore no pain. Creature seeks, of course, to end the aversive experience of Region B, but its attempts to do so need not end in attenuation (settling pain) or stabilization (constant pain); they could result in amplification (growing pain) as Creature continually seeks out the pleasurable but transient sensation associated with attending to the pain. Thus, an accurate "portrait" (in motivational space) of the pain experience looks more like Figure 2.2:

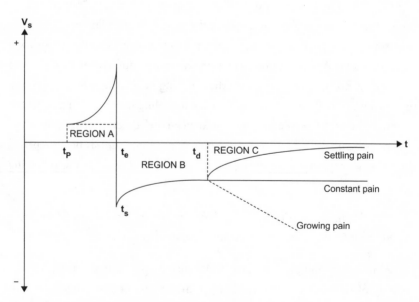

FIGURE 2.1. The motivational landscape of *pain*.

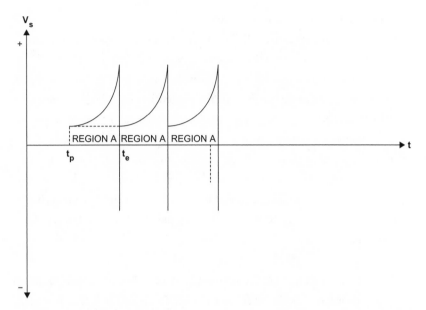

FIGURE 2.2. The pleasure(s) of pain.

Creature "keeps attending" to the physiological pain signal on account of the sharp pleasure that accompanies the act of attending to the pain, but in the process it causally triggers the utility troughs that constitute the experience commonly referred to as "pain."

Pain, then, can be understood as a sequence of alternating highs and lows, which from afar look like (and are felt by Creature as) something that resembles the micro-motivational landscape of Figure 2.2. Thus it is not surprising that manuals put together by the U.S. Central Intelligence Agency—to train agents of South American police states to extract information in interrogation sessions—advise that the infliction of physical pain is "useless" as a means of breaking a prisoner's will to withhold information: The "high" associated with even prolonged experiences of pain works against the purpose of interrogation.

But is attending to pain a real, live option for Creature in the sense that it could choose *not* to attend to pain? In this context, the following experimental finding is relevant.

EXPERIMENT 2.4 [deCharms et al., 2005]

Specific findings (statistically significant): Subjects were equipped to monitor real-time functional magnetic resonance imaging (RTfMRI) scans of a region of their brain (the rostral anterior cingulated cortex, rACC) believed to be involved in the perception of pain; they were then given the task of "controlling their experience of pain" using a set of heuristics (attention control, quantization and categorization of the experienced pain) and the goal of "minimizing the level of instantaneous rACC activation on the RTfMRI scan," which they were given the means to observe in real time. Subjects were successful in reducing both the reported experience of pain and the level of rACC activation.

The experiment suggests that attending to pain is "a choosable option"; its findings indicate that both the subjective experience and objective biological markers of pain are controllable once they have been made in some sense cognitively penetrable. The cognitive penetrability of pain was accomplished by making its instantaneous markers directly observable to the subject through real-time feedback of the fMRI data. (The ability of subjects to witness themselves as "brains in a machine" may also have contributed to the main effect via production of the "distance from oneself" that Ask himself seeks to produce in Creature.) Subjects' controllability of their experiences of pain was enhanced by the availability of heuristics ("attention control"). The successful result is more startling for providing impartial evidence for something "we already intuited" than for uncovering something we did not, but the reliable production of the main effect in Experiment 2.4 suggests that pain-behavior is not a counterexample to INT and perhaps not even to RESP in the form of a cause that necessarily pushes behavior. Attending to pain is a behavior that is plausibly pulled by micro-incentives that can be uncovered by a sufficiently precise phenomenological microscope.

What are the tangible and material implications of this analysis for Ask? The temporal behavior of $V_S(t)$ in Region A ($t_p < t < t_e$) can be described either by a (high-discount-factor) exponential curve or by a hyperbolic curve. Ask attempts to modify Creature's pain response by using the micro-motivational landscape of Figure 2.2. Two examples should suffice, although more could be constructed by a careful application of the marginal value analysis of Table 2.1. (In what follows, Ask assumes that Creature has been ascertained to be a hyperbolic discounter and that the pain is pure physical pain.)

Example 1: Dueling pains. Ask can request Creature to focus on some activity that produces a larger-later reward and whose pursuit requires Creature's full attention; subject Creature to a painful stimulus; and then induce a second physical pain (in a different part of Creature's body) that competes with the first pain stimulus for Creature's attention. The effects should be that (a) the pleasure spike that accompanies attending to *either* of the two pains decreases in value (because attending to one pain will be decreased by the opportunity cost of not attending to the other pain) and (b) Creature becomes better at focusing on the larger-later reward-producing activity.

Example 2: For hyperbolic discounters, the rate of change of the "cross-over time" t_c with respect to the time constant t_s (on which the pleasure that accompanies attending to the pain operates) is in direct negative proportion to the value of the larger-later reward (i.e., $-V_L$). Thus, V_L functions as an attenuator of the effects of changes in t_s (the time constant of pain-induced pleasure) on t_c, the time at which the discounting curves for the larger-later and smaller-sooner rewards cross. Therefore, decreasing V_L (to 0, for instance) should make t_c insensitive to changes in t_s, whereas sharply increasing V_L should make t_c highly sensitive to (negative) changes in t_s. This suggests the following "algorithm" for increasing Creature's ability to cope with pain.

Step 1. Set V_L high to allow for an amplification of negative changes in t_s on t_c.

Step 2. Decrease t_s by inducing a high-anxiety or high-excitability state in Creature; this will have the effect of *increasing t_c*.

Step 3. Repeat until $t_c > t_s$ (i.e., until there is no crossover of the discounting curves for the larger-later and smaller-sooner rewards).

Ask can also use the same marginal effects analysis to guide him and attempt to push t_c over the "threshold" value t_s by assigning a large and negative value to V_L (i.e., by making it a punishment rather than a reward) and then increasing t_s, which can be accomplished by having Creature monitor its own reactions on a clock that (unbeknownst to Creature) has been slowed down so that 1 s on that clock equals 1.5 s on an unmodified clock—a maneuver that is known to slow down Creature's objectively measured internal responses.

"Attending to pain" is a behavior that typically occurs on subsecond time scales and so will be maximally taxing both for Ask's phenomenological microscope (for obvious reasons) and for his emotional distoscope. It will be challenging for the emotional distoscope because (as Experiment 2.4 suggests) some measure of cognitive penetrability is required for Creature to become able to "choose to not attend to its pain," and cognitive penetration takes time. However, as we move upward in time scales, Creature's "unintentionally intentional" behaviors come into sharper focus and are more intuitively handled by a temporal discounting framework. To wit: Compared to the behavior "attending to a (physical) pain," the behavior "scratching an (actual) itch" seems downright deliberate. In particular (see Figure 2.3), the extent of all-important Region A for an itch-scratching Creature will be significantly longer than for the case of pain; this is causally related to the fact that the pleasure accompanying an itch is far easier to conceptualize (by Creature and Ask alike) than is the pleasure accompanying the initial bite of the

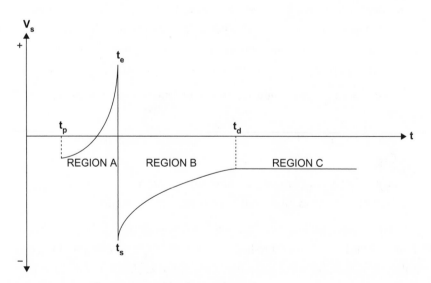

FIGURE 2.3. The motivational landscape of an *itch*.

awareness of being in pain. From Ask's perspective, this represents a significant difference because it suggests that the act of scratching an itch is more
cognitively penetrable for Creature than is the act of attending to pain. Ask
can easily and intelligibly ask Creature to "not scratch an itch" but not as easily and intelligibly to "not attend to a pain."

More generally, then: Any behavior produced by Creature is said to be
pain-like if the smaller-sooner reward is one to which Creature is oblivious
(and thus cannot reasonably talk about without prior training or preparation);
behavior is said to be *itch-like* if the smaller-sooner reward can be conceptualized and talked about without external help. In particular, a counterproductive
habit that Creature instantiates (see Figure 2.4) can be understood as being
either more pain-like (e.g., lashing out unrestrainedly and destructively at a
peer under the blanket justification that "sharp upbraiding produces optimal
learning") or more itch-like (e.g., producing a self-exculpating justification

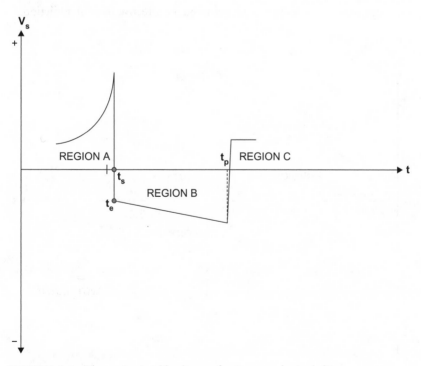

FIGURE 2.4. The motivational landscape of a *counterproductive habit*.

for an apparent error even though no significant punishment is expected to result from admitting to the error) as a function of the cognitive penetrability and accessibility of the smaller-sooner reward that pulls the behavior. In turn, cognitive penetrability is facilitated by a sufficiently large Region A (i.e., when consciousness is slow), which allows Creature to become aware of the utility spike that peaks at t_e.

Addictions and addictive behavior are no more difficult for Ask to model than are counterproductive habits. An addiction is habit and itch-like insofar as the act of engaging in the addictive behavior is not experienced as being involuntary (as it is with pain). An addiction is pain-like in that the withdrawal phase (which Creature would have to endure if it decided to break the addiction) has the motivational characteristics of "pure pain": Creature is "forced" (on micro-local time scales) to attend to the strongly aversive state of withdrawal (Region E in Figure 2.5). This suggests that new addiction treatment mechanisms could meaningfully seek to increase Creature's ability to deal with pain-like states and focus on ulterior goals rather than on decreasing the "urge" that is normally considered to be the affective basis of addiction.

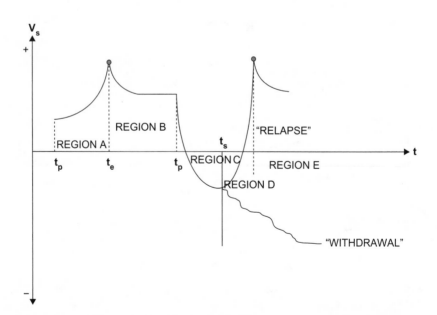

FIGURE 2.5. The motivational landscape of *addiction*.

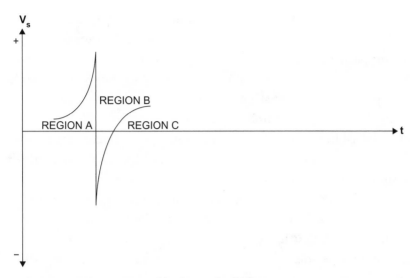

FIGURE 2.6. The motivational landscape of a *thrill*.

Ask will want to distinguish between addictions and other pleasure-center-recruiting behaviors such as the pursuit of thrills. Intense sexual or other non-chemically induced "orgiastic" experiences and activities with very low (but nonzero) risk of serious harm to Creature have micro-motivational portraits of the type shown in Figure 2.6.

What distinguishes the "micro-behavioral engineering" of a thrill state from that of indulging an addiction is absence of the compulsive force of the sharply dysphoric state (Region E in Figure 2.5) of withdrawing from the "high" of an addictive state, which in the case of thrills is replaced by a state (Region C in Figure 2.6) that is not dysphoric. The peak of the thrill (the tail end of Region A) may correspond to a "cathartic" neurological and psychological state (as in an orgasm or the first few hundred milliseconds of the experience of free fall) followed by an aversive state that rapidly returns to a weakly positive motivational "ground state." What makes the thrill thrilling is not only the peak itself but also the foreknowledge of the return to a positively valued end state at the time of the motivational spike that corresponds to the thrill itself. Thrills can become addictive if the motivational ground state (Region C) is negatively valued (as with the case of ennui or metaphysical boredom), creating micro-incentives for Creature to seek a hedonistic escape from the "dysphoria of its everydayness."

On the basis of this model, Ask can intervene and attempt to turn a thrill into an addiction—for instance, by persuading Creature that the systematic pursuit of the thrill (perhaps at progressively higher levels of visceral intensity or probabilities of fatal injury) is part of Creature's identity, of its concept of what it essentially is, which could turn periods in which Creature is not pursuing the thrill into dysphoric periods that are withdrawal-like. Guided by the model, Ask can also attempt to produce the opposite effect, of transforming addictive behavior into behavior that is merely thrill-seeking) by getting Creature to "cognitively revalue" the dysphoric state associated with withdrawal—for instance, by convincing Creature to view that state as being *generative* for certain kinds of artifacts: works of music or poetry, say, that are accessible only from a particular mood that characterizes the aftermath of an episode of the addictive behavior (which has now become more "thrill-like").

Now we can appreciate the relevance and impact of Ask's maneuver to focus his modeling activities on the positive content of Creature's behavior instead of on what Creature does *not* do (as in pain-avoidance models of behavior or models in which Creature does not exercise self-control in a causally successful way). Recall for this purpose our example of the Creature that, at the last moment, loses the nerve required to tell its boss: "You are self-deceived on topic C, as evidenced by your behavior X at time t." (This is a "cleaned-up" description of what happened between Creature and its boss at the time of the former's lapse of will.) Self-control theorists focus on exactly how Creature failed to produce within itself the conditions that would cause the confrontational words to come out at the right time. In contrast, pain-avoidance theorists focus on explaining what Creature did *not* do in terms of the expected value of the pain that Creature knew would immediately follow its production of the (all things considered) correct behavior. There is something useful in both explanations, but neither focuses on what is typically the only thing that Ask can observe: what Creature actually *does* (and not what it does *not* do). So what does Creature do in this case? It engages in a more or less scripted (and therefore habit-like) conversation with its boss, which has a micro-motivational portrait similar to that of Figure 2.4—and is counterproductive because it cannot lead to the better state that Creature wishes to bring about via cathartic intervention. Armed with this knowledge, Ask can intervene and aim to make t_c fall outside of the critical interval $0 < t < t_s$.

5. ACHIEVEMENT OF A SELF:
CONTROL AND COMMAND

Ask is interested in the "science of self-control" [Heatherton and Baumeister, 1996; Rachlin, 2000; Ainslie, 2001; Bénabou and Tirole, 2002] not as a way of issuing prescriptive injunctions to a suboptimal discounter (hyperbolic or exponential) but rather as a modeling and intervention technology that allows him to "cut Creature's behavior at the joints" more precisely and influentially and with the most causally efficacious interpretive schema. The idea is to use various posited mechanisms for achieving better self-control and more continent behavior in the face of temptation as ways of interpreting Creature's everyday behaviors. Not all Creatures cheerfully yield to temptations that can be represented as choices between larger-later and smaller-sooner rewards, and any one Creature will not reliably yield to such temptations in all situations. There are Creatures that invest in and successfully implement personal transformation programs and techniques; who develop compulsive, "addictive" or habitual patterns of behavior that help them navigate the motivational landscapes of pains, itches, and addictions; who develop privative rules and principles ("thou shalt not . . .") as a way of curbing appetites that, all things considered, have counterproductive consequences; or who manage to understand and manipulate their own emotional landscapes in order to produce what they perceive to be "rational" behavior in the face of temptations to do otherwise. Ask is interested in the normative and prescriptive models of the "science of self-control and self-regulation" *qua* tools for designing interventions and experiments that further his understanding of Creature and for making Creature a more successful designer of its own behavior.

The basic "self-control" modeling situation is as follows. Ask observes Creature's behavior in situations that are likely to trigger pain-like, itch-like, or addiction-like behavior from Creature and then uses models of self-management (or *ego-nomic* models, as in Schelling [1984]) in order to pose such questions as this: "Under what conditions will Creature's attempt to produce a behavior in the face of a putative temptation yield the desired

results?" As a student of human behavior, Ask admits that Creature may itself
be a self-modeler and that the models of itself that Creature produces may
be intended to function as self-control devices and tropes. Ask is interested
in describing Creature's actions as "intendedly but boundedly" rational solutions to its problems of self-control. Ascriptive science is open with regard to
the mechanisms of self-control and self-regulation that it allows as modeling
devices. It makes use of these mechanisms to create more precise and accurate
models of behavioral adaptations to a set of problems that Creature generates
internally as a way to deal with temptations. For instance, consider the following example.

"Raw" Exercise of the Will.   Creature uses sheer willpower to curb its proclivity to choose a smaller-sooner reward at the expense of its ability to pursue
a larger-later reward. Ask can follow Heatherton and Baumeister [1996] and
model the *will* of Creature as a muscle. This metaphor buys Ask an interpretive schema that allows it to conduct experiments that yield further insight
into Creature's will mechanisms. A muscle's causally interesting properties include that it can be depleted by exertion and built up by exercise.

Suppose Creature uses willpower to contain its proclivity to flirt with a col-
league. Then the "depletion" mechanism—together with the notion that the
will is connected to some executive function that allows Creature to adaptively
plan and optimize its mental and physical behavior—suggests that Creature's
engagement in *another* activity that intensively tasks its executive function
(e.g., responding to a complex argument that seems to contradict Creature's
own assertions) should weaken its ability to control its primary and untethered
urge. Thus, for instance, Creature should yield much more readily to the urge
to flirt "against its own will" in an environment of high cognitive stress.

On the other hand, the "build-up" mechanism suggests that inducing
Creature to practice self-control of the "raw will" type on a regular basis will
increase its capacity to deal with temptation, even in the face of competing
tasks that stress its executive function. As a test, Ask could persuade Creature
to make the exercise of its will a daily pattern—say, by systematically refusing to pursue primary micro-motivations (e.g., slouching or snacking) on an
hourly basis. In this regime, Creature is to do anything *except* eat when it feels
hungry, drink when it feels thirsty, and sleep when it feels tired. It may be

difficult to produce such "anti-behavior," in part because the privative injunction is content-free: It tells Creature what not to do, rather than what to do. Ask can easily address this problem by giving positive content to the injunction "do anything except," persuading Creature to drink when it feels hungry, to eat when it feels thirsty, and to run when it feels tired. Ask's predictions, based on the will-as-a-muscle metaphor, are (i) that Creature's ability to exercise willpower-based self-control will increase after a prolonged period of such "will enhancement exercises" and (ii) that Creature's will should be increasingly robust to competitive interferences from other executive-intensive tasks as a function of the length and intensity (i.e., the number of self-denying behaviors per unit of time) of the willpower training program.

Privative Rules and Principles. Ainslie [2001] argues that humans have developed principles (especially principles of the privative kind) as adaptations to the problem of self-control and self-regulation. He argues that, for a hyperbolic discounter, a *principle* or rule "lumps together" a large number of aversive sell-outs to hyperbolically discounted smaller-sooner rewards and ends up with a temporal discounting function that does not exhibit the preference reversal patterns typical of hyperbolic discounters. Thus, a compulsive gambler who adopts the privative principle "never gamble" as a method of self-control essentially chooses, at each time, between the option "always gamble henceforth" and the option "never gamble again" rather than between the option "gamble now" and the option "do not gamble now" (or the option "do something else now" that is not compatible with gambling now). As Ainslie points out, self-control mechanisms based on such privative rules and principles are "constitutively" relapse-friendly: Even a single transgression of the rule or principle is likely to trigger a collapse of Creature's power to control its behavior around the focal temptation.

This effect can be supported in some cases by the following pseudo-logical argument from Creature: "I have just gambled and therefore violated the principle 'never gamble,' which means that I have de facto chosen 'always gamble' over 'never gamble' because the logical complement of 'never gamble' (in the space of options from which I am choosing) is 'always gamble' rather than 'gamble once and never thereafter' or 'gamble with frequency no greater than f_g.'" For Ask, figuring out whether Creature uses a principle-based self-control mechanism reduces to performing the negative test of (i) inducing a Creature that seems to behave "rationally" in the presence of a putative temptation (e.g., rage-induced lashing out against employee who has triggered Creature's "rage" motivational system) to "lose it" and engage in the behavior it is trying to inhibit and then (ii) observing Creature's *subsequent* proclivity to engage in the same behavior in a similar situation. If Creature's privative rule for controlling its rage behavior is one that leads to sharp relapse, then the frequency of ensuing tantrums will grow significantly *and rapidly* relative to the baseline state.

Personal Routines and Habits.   Creature's self-control techniques can include the development of habits and routines that *practically* (and often implicitly) exclude or preclude the behavior that Creature is trying to control. Creature may plan its shopping trips along a path that prevents visits to any place (say, a tobacco shop) whose environment is known to Creature to trigger the smaller-sooner behavioral pattern (smoking) it is trying to control (quit). Similarly, Creature may engage in certain tics (hair pulling, nail biting) in order to avert its inner gaze from pain-producing stimuli (worrisome thoughts, spontaneously amplified physical pains). It may design its at-home behavior (lifestyle habits) in ways that reduce the chances of having a temper tantrum during an encounter with its spouse, children, or lover. Creature may also follow certain social interaction scripts ("small talk") in order to avoid exposing itself to various temptations to engage in incontinent social behavior (e.g., broaching taboo topics, speaking its mind in a vehement and incisive fashion). It may pattern its "mental behavior" around solving certain kinds of problems via routines ("methods," "search routines for solution spaces," and sets of questions to be asked) that minimize the chances it will be caught in mental traps such as daydreaming or counterproductive rumination about difficult memories.

When seen through the lens of an ongoing and ever-present problem of impulse control, habits and routines present Ask with a palette of mental objects for working out a behavioral model of Creature and with a battery of tests aimed at elucidating the function of Creature's habits and routines within Creature's own life. Breaking Creature's habit of acting out a routine meant to curb the primary temptation should also break down Creature's ability to curb the temptation. As in the case of privative principles and norms, Ask can attempt to figure out whether or not Creature uses routine-based self-control mechanisms by impeding or retarding the routine that enables Creature to avoid the primary temptation and then observing the consequences. A rage-prone Creature that engages in some sort of "mantric" mental activity in order to resist destructively acting out its rage can be "interrupted" from its mantric activity—with the predicted consequence that Creature's ability to control its rage will diminish when the mantric routine is disrupted.

Attention Control. Creature may seek to exercise control over its impulses not only through outwardly behavioral measures alone: It may implement cognitive or perceptual routines that are meant to direct its attention *away* from the shorter-sooner reward option that it is trying to avoid. Some [Wegner, 1994] have argued that it is impossible (or extremely difficult) for a Creature to purposefully *avoid* thinking about X. An injunction such as "do not think of a white bear" often has the counterproductive effect of inducing more thoughts about white bears than does the absence of the injunction. The mechanism posited for this counterintentional relapse of unwanted thoughts is that the process of keeping thought X out of one's mind requires monitoring the mind for instances of X (so they can be deleted), which in turn self-defeatingly forces the mind to consider X while figuring out whether it is indeed thinking of X at any particular time [Wegner, 1994]. However, "not thinking of X" can be implemented by forcing oneself to "think of not-X" (e.g., an absorbing image Y that is neither semantically nor associationally related to X) and then enacting the positive monitoring function of figuring out whether or not one *is* indeed thinking of Y—rather than the negative monitoring function of figuring out whether one is *not* thinking of X. If Creature interprets "try not to think of a white bear" as "think of a dark-colored BMW" then, the argument goes, the task of mind control is more easily (albeit covertly) accomplished. Thus, Creature can reasonably expect to be able to curb its temptation-seeking behavior by implementing a mind-control routine of the type "think of Y" (and not of the type "do not think of X").

For Ask, Creature's mind-control strategies provide a ground for disruptive interventions aimed at discovering just what kind of self-control technique Creature is attempting, strategies that are based on the now-familiar principle of *distractive disruption* of a particular kind. The kinds of disruptions that test for mind-control strategies are different from those that test for willpower-based strategies. For the latter, it is ideal to use a *competitive* distraction that taxes the executive function; when testing for self-control techniques that are based on mind control, it may be more useful to use a *synergistic* distraction that brings the tempting image to the fore of Creature's consciousness.

Sunk Costs and Manipulation of One's Own Affective Landscapes.   Suppose that Creature becomes familiar with the kinds of emotional landscapes that shape its behavior in the spatio-temporal neighborhood of temptations. Armed with this knowledge and bent on intervening in its own motivational landscape, Creature may try to manipulate *its own* costs and benefits by intentionally decreasing the value of the smaller-sooner reward and increasing the value of the larger-later reward—for example, by making a public commitment to avoid the smaller-sooner option, which means that any transgression of the announced commitment incurs the loss of face and credibility.

For Ask, such self-manipulation may be inferable from the kinds of behaviors in which Creature engages (e.g., a public announcement that "I will start paying my bills on time"). The causal efficacy and robustness of these self-manipulations can be tested by observing the effects on Creature's behavior of interventions like the following. Ask can persuade Creature that the costs it has "built into" its motivational landscape are either lower than Creature had anticipated (e.g., that it is socially acceptable *not* to pay your bills on time) or that Creature's obligation to pay these costs can be strategically manipulated to allow Creature to "have its cake and eat it, too" by investing in techniques for *simulating* honorable behavior that allow Creature to engage in the pursuit of the smaller-sooner option and *also* to reap the benefits normally bestowed only upon those who forgo the smaller-sooner option. If the causal efficacy of Creature's commitments as self-control devices depends on Creature's ability to deceive itself about how real these costs are, then exposing the deception may well lead to a weakening of Creature's will.

Detachment.   Several traditions hail the state associated with the passive observations of one's own micro-motivational states as precursors to or signs of states of enlightenment. Such states are to be achieved either through the mantric path of inward recollection and withdrawal from the world or through the tantric path of wholeheartedly and even recklessly pursuing worldly temptation until experience of the "forbidden fruit" loses its appeal and motivational force. Understanding detachment as a self-control technology—rather than as a "way of being" pursued for its own sake—suggests to Ask that Creature's ability to detach, as well as its propensity to engage in activities that cultivate and nurture that ability, could be motivated by a history of self-regulative failures or suboptimal outcomes that can be probed further with the aim of understanding the true domain and bounds of Creature's detachment. Then, just *what* Creature can detach from becomes a search topic for Ask, who will construct situations aimed at triggering automatic pain-like or itch-like behaviors from Creature and then will (provisionally) conclude that Creature can detach (or not) from its own micro-motivational landscape in certain types of situations. Understanding detachment as a personal technology of self-control gives it both positive empirical content and pragmatic appeal, regardless of the tradition from which it has originated.

Hierarchical Decomposition of Creature. Armed with the *précis de decomposition* supplied by the preceding analysis and inspired by the hydraulic metaphor that Freud used to describe (within the architecture and dynamics of the subconscious and the unconscious) interactions between Superego and Id, Ask can proceed to build a very different portrait of Creature than that supplied by the use (even the recursive use) of DEC or INT. In particular, Ask can use the following principle.

CONT. *Interpret Creature's behaviors on time scale t_1 as outcomes of implementing a self-control strategy S_C aimed at controlling counterproductive impulses and temptations or aversive behaviors that function on time scales $t_2 < t_1$.*

CONT can encode either "control" or "containment," and it is meant to indicate the *purpose* of the technique or strategy used by Creature to "control its self." The hierarchical nature of the resulting decomposition arises from the ordering of the time scales on which temptations and containment techniques operate. If, for instance, "attending to a pain" is a behavior that occurs on time scales of hundreds of milliseconds, then the attention control used by Creatures subject to the experimental intervention of Experiment 2.4 to "control their pain"—by shifting attention to a part of their body other than the part subjected to the painful stimulus—will cause effects experienced over periods of seconds or even minutes (this is, coincidentally, the current upper bound on the temporal resolution of most fMRI scans), which may include *not* attending to a new pain caused in a different part of the body by a new stimulus. If Creature uses the compelling force of a public commitment to keep itself from scratching an itch, a temptation that occurs on a time scale of seconds or tens of seconds, then that commitment may induce Creature to seek out increased social contact as a way of "keeping itself from cheating" on the commitment, on time scales of minutes to hours. If Creature controls its urge for tobacco, which operates on time scales of minutes to hours, by holding fast to "hardwired" routines (such as strictly following a path home that avoids tobacco stores and so prevents Creature from buying cigarettes), then the effects of that routine—including opportunity costs of the overly zealous automatization of Creature's behaviors and incremental optimization costs of taking the new set of constraints into account when designing its trips— may be felt over a period of days or weeks. The basic interpretive "pattern" is that control mechanisms aimed at containing impulses occurring on shorter time scales supply explanatory models for behavior occurring on longer time scales.

Ask can use CONT to devise an interpretation schema for his observations of Creature's behaviors that interpolates smoothly between the "rationality" of DEC and the "irrationality" of INT. Seen through the lens of CONT, the space-time object "Creature" is a sequence of behaviors intentionally but often suboptimally aimed at reining in self-destructive impulses. Thus CONT can be understood as a "Freudian" lens insofar as it views Creature as using other people (via not always explicit commitments), rules, habits, routines, and mantric or tantric activities to contain its aversive preferences and resulting behaviors.

Seen through the CONT schema, Creature can also be an *instrumental* user of its own feelings of guilt (aversion to transgressing a privative rule), shame (aversion to shirking on a public commitment), and regret (aversion to abandoning a routine simply to pursue a temptation), feelings whose "technological" (pragmatic) value to Creature increases as a result of this use. These feelings are the levers by which a self-control strategy exercises causally powerful effects on Creature. Armed with this understanding, Ask can look at Creature's tendency to feel guilt, shame, and regret as useful markers of CONT's validity as an interpretive schema. He may interpret the relative scarcity (or absence) of such feelings on Creature's emotional landscape—or its ability to detach itself from these feelings—as a sign that Creature is capable of the level of self-command that is always-already embedded in DEC *or* as a sign of the animalistic self-indulgence characteristic of a purely impulse-guided existence.

CONT allows that, over time, some self-control strategies can themselves acquire the characteristics of counterproductive habits and temptations. Long after it has broken its smoking habit, Creature may still follow intricate paths from work to its home, paths that it has grown accustomed to and so still follows even though they have outlived their original purpose. Suppose that, when asked, Creature acknowledges the suboptimality and costliness of the outdated route home, concedes that it is now a counterproductive habit, and vows to break it. But how? Absent an adaptive capacity for instantaneous self-command, Creature must choose from the usual menu of personal control technologies. Each, however, will entail both implementation costs and opportunity costs. A commitment to systematically "vary the path home" means that Creature must now endogenously generate variation. The adoption of a new routine aimed at breaking the old routine leaves Creature, at best, only marginally better-off. A privative rule (e.g., "never follow the same path home more than n times in a row") places costly constraints on the "path design problem" and decreases Creature's adaptiveness to changes in its predicament.

Thus, CONT entails no "higher level plan" that Creature could use (a) to control its impulses, (b) to control the techniques it uses to control its impulses, or (c) to optimize (in terms of their relative costs and benefits) the set of control, meta-control, meta-meta-control, . . . techniques that it uses. CONT is a schema that endows Creature with some intelligence, which falls far short of logical omniscience, and with sufficient reflectiveness to understand the narrow ends of its own behavior but that falls far short of the wisdom to rise above its own predicament. Nevertheless, CONT is a serviceable tool, which Ask can use to generate dynamical models of Creature's behavior—as recursive concatenations of temptations, control techniques, and meta-control techniques—or to produce local interventions aimed at heightening Creature's understanding of the causal consequences of its own impulse-control "footprint."

Flips as Dips: Trade-offs between Reward Types.   Thus far, Ask has assumed that Creature cannot or does not trade off between smaller-sooner ("temptations") and larger-later rewards. The value of this assumption is the sharp focus that it places on Creature's temptation-driven behavior and resulting self-control tactics and strategies. However, this is a strong assumption and one that both introspection and observation may signal to Ask as being frequently unwarranted. Creature could decide, all things considered, that it will indulge in smoking three cigarettes a day because the long-run risk to its health is tolerable and also because "three cigarettes a day doth not a smoker make." More reasonably, Creature may decide to share a cigarette with a friend on (infrequent) social occasions without forgoing any appreciable long-run health benefits—*provided*, of course, that this "social" smoke does not lead Creature down the slippery slope that ends in a pack-a-day consumption pattern. Hence it would be useful for Ask to develop a more fine-grained tool for examining Creature's temptation regimes and, in particular, those situations in which Creature is "rationally incontinent" (i.e., engages in behavior that allows it to "have its cake and eat it, too").

Studies of self-control and dynamic preferences [Gul and Pesendorfer, 2001; Gul and Pesendorfer, 2004] have often attempted to incorporate a "preference for self-control" into an expected utility maximization framework of the von Neumann–Morgenstern type [von Neumann and Morgenstern, 1947] via a *betweenness axiom* that constrains Creature's choices in the following way. If Creature prefers an option from set A (the larger-later set) to an option from set B (the smaller-sooner set), then Creature will prefer an option from A to an option from the union of set A and set B, which in turn will be preferred to an option from set B: $A \succ B \to A \succ (A \cup B) \succ B$. In conjunction with axioms that specify completeness and transitivity conditions to hold on Creature's preferences, this axiom is shown to be instrumental in proving the existence of a "self-control-adjusted" utility function that

Creature may be said to maximize when behaving in a "self-restrained" or self-control-oriented fashion. Understanding what the axiom states is simple enough. If Creature knows that having one cigarette (option from set B) will lead down the path to becoming a smoker, then it will reasonably choose to have no cigarette at all (option from set A), and thereby safeguard its long-run health, over the tempting alternative to have "both one cigarette now and clean lungs later." Just how tempting a temptation is, in this framework, is captured by the betweenness axiom—and by Creature's use of this axiom (consciously or otherwise) to guide its behavior in the temporal neighborhood of temptations.

Although this approach is attractive as a means of devising a threshold test of the aversiveness of a preference, Ask will be cautious in using it without further analysis. The first reason is that the axiomatic foundation of the Gul–Pesendorfer model assumes the kind of encompassing rationality (completeness, transitivity) that Creature will likely *fail* to exemplify in the throes of temptation, which induces precisely the kind of fragmentation of its being and faculty of reason that adherence to these axioms requires. Second, whether or not a temptation is truly "aversive" should depend on how the larger-later reward and the smaller-sooner reward are related in Creature's specific case (e.g., whether or not Creature is an addictive type) and on whether or not Creature "knows itself" in the minimal sense of knowing how much more tempting a second cigarette will be after it has just smoked its "one only" cigarette.

To make sense of Creature's behavior in situations where the smaller-sooner reward and the larger-later reward vary in different ways, Ask needs to introduce some additional modeling distinctions (i.e., differences that make a difference), as follows.

Cataclysmic temptations: $dV_L / dV_S = -\infty$. In this case there is no feasible trade-off between the larger-later and smaller-sooner rewards, and engaging in just one instance of the smaller-sooner reward completely annuls the larger-later reward. For example, a single episode of rage-induced temper (smaller-sooner) in a public setting is enough to tarnish Creature's reputation as an executive to the extent that its career (larger-later) is essentially over.

Explosive temptations: $dV_L/dV_S = -kV_S$. Here the value of the larger-later reward decreases sharply in the value of the smaller-sooner reward. One possible mechanism for this is that Creature's propensity to choose smaller-sooner rewards grows quickly as a function of the frequency with which it has done so in the past, and each additional aversive choice decreases the value of the larger-later reward. It might be beneficial for Creature to engage in heroin or cocaine use once or twice a year in order to sample "alternate realities" and "blow off steam" (so to speak), but two heroin shots a year is not a sustainable consumption pattern for it. The probability that Creature will inject itself tomorrow given that it has done so today is many orders of magnitude greater than the probability that Creature will inject itself tomorrow given that it has not done so today, and Creature's brain function—and possibly its ability to exercise restraint—also deteriorates rapidly in response to repeated heroin use.

Degenerative temptations: $dV_L/dV_S = -K$. In this case the value of the larger-later reward decreases smoothly (linearly in this case) in the value of the smaller-sooner reward, so that Creature experiences a relatively smooth "downward path" in its welfare as a function of the intensity of its incontinent behavior. For instance, cardiovascular health declines in relatively linear fashion with the intake of calories above a threshold. This makes it easy to rationalize indulging in fatty foods on a "limited and local" basis but also difficult to design and implement a self-control strategy that induces Creature to eat more healthily. The opportunity cost of indulging an impulse is just not high enough to warrant the implementation of a costly self-control technique.

Stable temptations: $dV_L/dV_S = 0$. Stable temptations are not aversive choices, although from a social perspective they may look like aversive choices. The larger-later reward value does not decrease with the smaller-sooner reward value, though it may appear to do so when seen from afar or through the lens of certain social norms and heuristics. If Creature were actually able to limit its tobacco use to three cigarettes a day, then it is doubtful (though the scarcity of data on this topic corroborates the difficulty of sustaining this regime) that it would experience the long deterioration of its health empirically associated with "being a smoker."

Regenerative temptations: $dV_L/dV_S > 0$. Like stable temptations, regenerative temptations are neither self-defeating nor counterproductive—although they, too, may look that way given their family resemblance to their malignant counterparts or seen through the flattening influence of socially acceptable ways of looking at behavior. In these cases, the larger-later reward *increases* with the smaller-sooner reward because of the way in which the smaller-sooner reward is experienced by Creature. Smoking three cigarettes a day, for instance, may provide Creature with 21 minutes (7 per cigarette) of unconstrained "reflection space" in which it engages with its own life-world—in a way that is unmediated by a "project," "meeting," or other task—with the net effects of decreasing (not increasing) its level of stress and increasing (not decreasing) its cardiovascular health.

Armed with these additional modeling distinctions, Ask can now proceed to examine Creature's behavior around temptations in a manner that is textured by an understanding of "what a temptation means to Creature" and also of "how a temptation functions" in the space of Creature's longer-range goals. *How much Creature itself understands* the structure and nature of its own temptations is, of course, a key modeling variable. Imperfect foresight and imperfect recall are both potential pitfalls for Creature. Under imperfect recall, Creature may forget that it has already smoked three cigarettes today and unwittingly cross into the realm of degenerative or even explosive temptations. Under imperfect foresight, Creature may not realize the massive serial correlation between instances of heroin use and so misguidedly insist it is "trying heroin just this once." Accordingly, Ask will be ever alert to Creature's level of self-knowledge, which will depend in part on Creature's recall and foresight and, more generally, on Creature's ability to make valid connections and distinctions on the basis of rapidly generated perceptions. These topics are important enough to warrant a separate discussion, which is provided in Chapter 4.

6. SAPIENT OPTIMIZATION AND SUPER-RATIONALITY

Lurking amidst all of these possible "dynamics of the self" and the complications they entail—for both Ask and Creature—is a relatively implausible scenario in which Creature "knows all of this stuff already" and optimizes its entire schedule of choices accordingly. In particular, Creature knows that it possesses "aversive preferences" and can make counterproductive choices, knows that it can exercise a large number of self-control techniques to rein such tendencies in, knows the relative danger and addictiveness of various patterns of behavior (and the potential addictiveness of the self-control techniques themselves), and knows the costs—both implementation costs and opportunity costs—associated with each instance of incontinent consumption and each instance of self-control. Moreover, Creature has "perfect recall," and so remembers the choices it has already made, as well as sufficient foresight to predict the evolution of its own preferences over a time period long enough to cover most of the possible dynamics that ensue. Ask may be skeptical about the possibility of so sapient and far-sighted a Creature, but doubtfulness does not entail impossibility. The question is: How would Ask *model* the behavior of such a Creature so as to be able to say how far the actual behavior of Creature really is from this state of super-rationality or wisdom?

One of the attractions of the temporal discounting framework developed here is the ease with which such a model can be put together by considering a few elements:

1. the set of temptations, or smaller-sooner (V_S) and larger-later (V_L) rewards that Creature sees itself as choosing among;

2. the functional form of $V_L(V_S)$;

3. the set $\{S_C\}$ of self-control technologies and strategies that Creature uses to keep itself from pursuing the smaller-sooner reward when doing so is deleterious to its all-things-considered best interests;

4. the implementation costs $c_i(S_C)$ of using each of the self-control strategies at its disposal to maximize the present value of trading off the larger-later against the smaller-sooner reward;

5. a time horizon T_H within which the entire spectacle unfolds and that bounds from above Creature's temporal visibility and "radius of care" in the literal sense that it cares only about options that materialize within $t \leq T_H$; and

6. a time-sampling period t_s, the smallest unit of time over which Creature "optimizes" its self-control behavior (ranging from hundreds of milliseconds for pains to months and years for habits and addictions), which entails that the number of rounds in the optimization game is $N = T_H/t_s$.

Creature may then engage in an optimization problem that has the following structure:

$$\max_{\{S_C\}}\left\{\sum_{k=0}^{N} P(Y_k/X_k,S_C)V(Y_k)\delta^k - C_k(S_C^k/Y_k,X_k)\delta^k\right\}$$

If Creature knows the functional form of each $V_L(V_S)$—or of each $V_S(V_L)$—then it may be able to design a behavioral footprint that is based on a principle of "optimal addiction": Creature will tailor its decisions to resist or give in to temptation on the basis of the all-things-considered costs and benefits of doing so. If all of the possible lives that Creature might have as a function of all of the choices it could make were laid out before Creature's eyes like a landscape before a painter, and Creature possessed the computational and informational prowess to plot its optimal course through that life, then the model would not be an altogether far-fetched one.

It will seem unrealistic to Ask that Creature will at any moment in time know the results of all of its self-control technologies—let alone of all of the temptations it may or will face—and be able to choose an optimal policy (i.e., a sequence of applied self-control techniques) aimed at maximizing its discounted net present value over all possible smaller-sooner–larger-later payoff pairs. A more realistic model for Creature's problem of self-control is one that takes the form of an optimal adaptive control problem [Bellman, 1957]. Suppose that Creature, when it is in state X, can implement a self-control technology S_C that with probability $P(Y/S_C, X)$ takes Creature from the undesired state X (obsessing on a pain, scratching an itch, injecting a drug, indulging a counterproductive habit) to the desired state Y (escaping the temptation altogether *or* optimally trading off between the temptation reward and the larger-later reward, depending on the shape of $V_L(V_S)$). Then

Ask can model Creature's self-control problem as a Bellman-type problem of adaptive optimal control, wherein Creature maximizes its expected value over all possible self-control moves and maneuvers:

$$\max_{\{S_C\}} \sum_{k=0}^{N} P(Y_k / X_k, S_C^k) V(Y_k) \delta^k$$

in other words, Creature maximizes the discounted expected value, over N discrete and contiguous periods of time, of implementing the self-control maneuver at time k (where $k = 0$ denotes the present) that takes it from state X to state Y with probability $P(Y/X, S_C)$. The problem's time horizon N captures Creature's degree of foresight, $P(Y/X, S_C)$ captures the degree of efficacy of Creature's self-control technologies, and Creature's *knowledge* of $P(Y/X, S_C)$ represents its degree of self-knowledge or self-awareness. If Creature knows the true propensity of a self-control technique to take it from a suboptimal to an optimal state, then Creature will be found by Ask to be "self-aware," or conscious. The model relies on the sequence of Creature's states being representable by a Markov process, in which the probability that a self-control maneuver will change Creature's current state to a desired state depends only on the current state and the self-control technique used. This assumption is reasonable for most "visceral" states, but cognitively richer "affective" states may require more complex probabilistic models of state transitions that incorporate more complicated patterns of path dependence. Armed with this representation of a self-aware Creature that is prone to temptation and "lapse" but is capable of self-control, Ask can proceed to examine each of the behavioral assumptions embedded in the dynamic programming model he has pieced together.

Ask is also aware that Creature may use its own behaviors for exploratory purposes and not just for the purposes of "securing utility" and "controlling its predispositions to engage in self-defeating behavior." Creature can, for instance, "try out" certain self-control technologies in order to determine whether they work or what the probability of their working is. (Creature can also try out certain temptations—such as addictive substances and activities—to gauge the value it derives from them.) If Ask suspects that a desire to explore is lurking within Creature, then he can preserve his dynamic optimization model and augment it with a parameterizable preference for the exploration of possible self-control techniques applied to the state space of Creature's internal states—in which case Creature's broader maximization problem becomes

$$\max_{\{S_C\}} \left\{ \sum_{k=1}^{N} P(Y_k/X_k, S_C^k)[V(Y_k) - C_k(S_C^k/Y_k, X_k)]\delta^k \right.$$
$$\left. + \alpha P(Y_k/X_k, S_C^k)\log_2 P(Y_k/X_k, S_C^k)\delta^k \right\}$$

where $P(Y_k/X_k, S_C^k)\log_2 P(Y_k/X_k, S_C^k)$ is the *entropy* of Creature's probabilistic mixture of options and self-control technologies and α is some positive constant that measures the relative strength of Creature's exploratory motivation. As before, the new model creates a "path of discovery" regarding Creature's behavior, a path that Ask can pursue experimentally or dialogically. However, Ask will generally be reluctant to "add complexity" to a model that already burdens Creature's optimization resources: for $t_s = 100$ ms and $T_H = 5$ yr, there are $N = 1.5768 \times 10^9$ "optimization periods" to consider. For Creature, reoptimization would be a computationally highly demanding task. Determining whether or not Creature can and does engage in such a task requires a separate set of models, which Ask will set himself to building shortly.

Ask can also extend the model of Creature's self-control blueprint by breaking up the space-time pattern "Creature" into a sequence of successive selves (impulsive and reflective, planner and doer), each endowed with sufficient intelligence to try to outsmart the other. He can then write down models for the evolution of Creature's behavior as the equilibrium of a repeated set of games played by Creature's successive selves. Aside from the unrealistic computational demands this would place on Creature, Ask is reluctant to pursue such a model because it endows Creature's impulsive self with too much calculative intelligence—when it seems to Ask that it is precisely a *lack* of foresight and calculative capacity that characterizes

Creature's pain-like and itch-like states. Ask can nevertheless treat this insight as a hypothesis rather than an axiom and can attempt to figure out just how computationally potent Creature is while in the throes of an addictive relapse or a powerful but all-things-considered counterproductive impulse. By now, Ask possesses the tools and the frame of mind to pursue this project by himself.

CHAPTER 3

BELIEFS AND BELIEVING

Wherein Ask inquires into the structure and dynamics of Creature's beliefs by deploying a simple model of Creature's epistemic states that helps Ask decode what Creature believes from its willingness to lay bets on the truth value of various propositions. Ask uses the model to interpret Creature's behavior in a way that sheds light on its beliefs and educates or informs Creature about the consequences of betting on the truth value of propositions on the basis of beliefs and belief sets that transgress certain rules and conditions. Ask uses the model to figure out what Creature's utterances might mean and then explores the limits of probing into the meaning of Creature's utterances on the basis of observing Creature's behavior. Finally, Ask uses the model to examine the ways in which Creature's beliefs might, do, and should change as a function of its all-things-considered objectives and emotional and visceral states.

WHATEVER DIFFICULTIES may by now have become apparent in ascribing preferences, intentionality, conscious will, and self-awareness to Creature on the basis of observing its behaviors will compound when Ask tries to figure out what is in Creature's mind on the basis of observing its actions. Knowledge of another's mind is difficult to come by precisely because of the

number and texture of possible "states of mind" that Ask can generate on
the basis of simple introspection. In particular, consider the possible states of
mind of Creature with regard to some statement, denoted by S.

Knowledge: Creature *knows* S in the sense that (a) it believes S is true for a
valid reason R and (b) S is, in fact, true. As a prototype, Creature may know
$S = today \ is \ Tuesday$ on account of reason R (e.g., a trusted friend of Creature
said so when asked).

Certainty: Creature is *certain of* S if (a) it believes S and (b) it can prove S
by a set of self-evident inferential steps starting from a set $\{p\}$ of valid premises
or reasons. As a prototype, Creature may be certain of $S = the \ sum \ of \ the \ angles$
of a triangle lying in a plane is equal to 180 degrees on account of being able
to prove S from Euclid's axioms. Note that Creature may not be certain of
these axioms—and, if it knows something about Riemann's or Lobachevsky's
geometry, then it may not be certain of them *for a reason*. Because logic functions as a transmission mechanism for truth, Creature may then not be certain of S, either. However, it *can* in such a case be certain of $S' = the \ sum \ of \ the$
angles of a triangle lying in a Euclidean plane is equal to 180 degrees.

Self-evidence: S is *self-evident to* Creature if Creature knows S and S does
not stand in need of either immediate or intermediate justification or proof.
Prototypically, $S = here \ is \ a \ hand$ (said by someone holding up a hand) is self-
evident to Creature if Creature does not need prior justification for holding
S to be true. Of course, Creature does have the option of proceeding down
the skeptical path of *requiring* justification for S. For instance, Creature may
argue that it is justified in believing S only if it is antecedently justified in
believing that it is not dreaming, and without this antecedent justification it
is impossible for Creature to feel justified in believing S. However, this entire
"alternate path" turns on the initial (cognitive) choice that Creature makes to
seek justification for $S = here \ is \ a \ hand$.

Risky belief: Creature believes that S is true with probability $P(S)$, which
Creature can state upon request. Prototypically, Creature believes (in this
risky sense) $S = the \ next \ toss \ of \ this \ fair \ coin \ will \ produce \ the \ outcome \ Heads$
with $P(S) = 0.5$.

Uncertain belief: Creature believes that S is true with some probability
$P(S)$ but cannot assign a precise numerical value to $P(S)$. Prototypically,
Creature believes (in this uncertain sense) $S = the \ initial \ public \ offering \ of \ the$
firm's equity will be priced at $2 per share but will not, when asked, be willing

and able (or either) to assign a unique probability to S. Higher-level variants of uncertainty are also possible. If Creature believes that S is true just in case some event e occurs and if that event is generated by a probabilistic causal process that is *evolving*, so that the underlying probability distribution function for e—and hence for the truth value of S—changes as a function of time (i.e., if the process that generates e is nonstationary), then Creature faces a higher-level uncertainty problem of estimating not only the probability of S being true but also the second-level probability that the probability of S being true has changed. Ask realizes that he may need to incorporate up to N levels of uncertainty when accounting for Creature's "uncertain" epistemic states.

Ambiguity: Creature believes that it understands S and nods when asked "Do you understand S?" and may be able to provide a translation of S that explicates its understanding. But Creature is not able to assign *truth conditions* to S by describing the conditions under which S would be true. Typically, if Creature is not a trained physicist, then S = *tachyons (energy-bearing signals that travel faster than light) exist* will be an ambiguous proposition because Creature will not be able to imagine an experimental apparatus that could be used to answer the question: "Is S true?"

Radical ambiguity, or "fog": We say that Creature merely "registers" S if it grasps the physical (phonetic, acoustic, expressive) symbols associated with an utterance or inscription of S but does not believe that it understands S and, a fortiori, cannot assign truth conditions to S. Taken out of context—as it was by Rudolf Carnap—Martin Heidegger's proposition S = *the Nothing nothings itself* will be radically ambiguous to a Creature uninformed of that context. Similarly, and more commonly, S = *a 55y-o wm pres/ w/ ascites* (from a medical report written in shorthand by a resident physician) will be radically ambiguous to a Creature that is not trained in the code of medical shorthand; it will be unable to decode S in order to recover: "a 55-year-old white male presenting himself at manual examination with fluid in the abdominal cavity."

Awareness of level N: Creature can also exhibit higher-order mental states (epistemic states) regarding S. These are beliefs *about* its beliefs about S. Creature is *level-N-aware of S* if it knows (or believes) S, knows (or believes) that it knows S, knows (or believes) that it knows that it knows S, and so forth up to N levels. Prototypically ($N = 2$), Creature (an MBA with a concentration of courses in finance theory) not only *knows S* = *the Black–Scholes formula can be used to compute the efficient price for a European call option on an equity with a known volatility* but also—as part of its identity as a "finance major" that it more or less unconsciously reiterates to itself—*knows that it knows S* and is therefore (at least) level-2-aware of S.

Oblivion: If Creature does not know S, does not know that it does not know S, and so forth ad infinitum, then Creature can be said to be *oblivious to S*. The behaviorally important characteristic of oblivion is that it does not even cross Creature's mind to inquire about the truth value of S—because Creature does not know that it does not know S. Prototypically, if $S = there is a green mark on Creature's nose$ (and in the absence or disregard of any reflecting objects facing Creature), then it may be said that Creature is oblivious to S. Oblivion need not be an "innocent" epistemic state: If $S = Creature is self-deceived about the sexual fidelity of its spouse$, then Creature is oblivious to S in a way that is causally related to the truth value of S: If $S were$ true, then Creature would choose to avoid ways of finding this out.

Unconsciousness: This is a colloquial case of $N = 1$ awareness (knowledge) with no $N = 2$ (higher-level) awareness. Creature is *unconscious of S* if (a) it knows S but (b) it does not know that it knows S. Perhaps Creature has temporarily forgotten it; in any case, S "does not come to its mind" unless Creature is prompted by Ask with a question like "Do you know S?" Prototypically, Creature knows that $S = Harold regularly distorts his facial expressions to produce intended effects in conversations$ is a true statement, but Creature does not take S into account when interpreting Harold's obsequiously flattering behavior at their previous meeting.

Of course, *states* of mind are not all that matters when one is trying to build a model of Creature: Mental *processes* may also be relevant. Consider the following two examples.

Obsession: Creature is *obsessed with S* if (a) it believes S, (b) it repetitively and frantically repeats S to itself, and (c) it designs and produces behaviors intended to confirm (or to disconfirm) S. Prototypically, if $S = I am loved for what I (intrinsically) am, rather than for my status$, then Creature may be said to be obsessed with S if S repetitively flashes in its mind and if Creature comes to structure interactions with others so as to produce confirmations of S.

Rumination: Creature *ruminates* on S if it frequently and intensely alternates between states of knowing S and knowing not-S (or some T that is logically incompatible with S) or between states of believing that S is more likely than not-S (or T) to be true and states of believing that not-S is more likely to be true than S (or T). Prototypically, $S =$ *he is intrinsically trustworthy* and $T =$ *he is building up my trust only to betray me at an opportune moment* are extremes of a ruminative pendulum of Creature's states of mind, contradictory statements that may be equally supported by the "evidence" supplied by the individual in question. Rumination is said to be *self-sustaining* if each of the ruminative extremes induces in Creature a desire to believe or explore the opposite extremum—that is, if believing S puts Creature in an emotional state in which it begins to think about T (and vice versa) in a way reminiscent of the predicament of Buridan's ass.

Finally (though hardly exhaustively), the modeler will also be interested in states of mind that Creature has relative to *other minds*—perhaps most interestingly to the modeler Ask's mind. Consider the related concepts of almost-common knowledge (or belief), common knowledge, and mutual knowledge.

Almost-common knowledge (or belief), mutual knowledge, and common knowledge: We say that S is *almost-common knowledge of level N* between Creature and Ask if Creature knows (or believes) S, Ask knows S, Creature knows Ask knows S, Ask knows Creature knows S, Creature knows Ask knows Creature knows S, and so on up to N levels. As N increases without bound, almost-common knowledge becomes common knowledge; and *mutual knowledge* corresponds to $N = 2$. If $S = I$ *believe you are lying*, then the level-2 almost-common knowledge (mutual knowledge) of S by Ask and Creature yields $S_1 = I$ *believe you believe I am lying* for Ask and $S_2 = I$ *believe you believe I believe you are lying* for Creature.

Faced with this palette of mental states and processes, Ask perceives an immediate difficulty in his attempts to model Creature's "ways of knowing" in ways that enable him to interpret Creature's behaviors in real time: There are too many possible ways of explaining any particular set of observed behaviors of Creature in terms of its mental states and processes that the vocabulary enables. For example, if Creature asserts S then Ask must choose from a large set of options: Does Creature know or believe S to be true or does Creature simply *find it a good idea* to assert S, perhaps in order to confuse Ask or to make conversation or to display its ability to make S-like statements? If

Creature does *not* assert *S*, then what is to be made of this? Is Creature oblivious to *S*? Will Creature be able to remember *S* at the opportune moment?

Suppose we bar game-playing on Creature's part. If it does assert S, we need to know *how* Creature believes *S*. Does Creature believe *S* in a risky, uncertain, or ambiguous way? How can we distinguish among these ways? Does Creature understand *S* in the sense of being able to state conditions that must be satisfied for *S* to be true? Is Creature aware of the problems implicit in assigning truth values to *S* and thus (by at least one theory of meaning—Davidson's [2005]) in rendering *S* a "meaningful" proposition?

More generally: Does Creature explicitly or even implicitly make all of the distinctions made by Ask when assigning states of mind to Creature? Would Creature, in other words, agree that it partitions states of mind into the categories posited by Ask? What are the minimal preconditions for Ask and Creature to unambiguously understand each other about the meaning of a word or phrase that appears in *S*?

Even more generally: What are the *communicative conventions* that govern Creature's speech acts and distinguish them from mere oral "noises"? Are these conventions different from the *inferential conventions* by which Creature structures its thoughts and uses the contents of its working memory?

And pragmatically: How can Ask distinguish, among the mental processes (obsession, rumination, etc.) that may accompany states of Creature's mind, which are actually *about S*? These questions arise (perhaps in slightly different form) only if Ask puts them to Creature in asking for more clarity about its assertion of *S*, which leads to well-known problems of infinite regress that are much feared by modelers of other humans. *What to do?*

The decision theorist—in both her speculator and calculator embodiments—cuts through to a pragmatic and reductive answer: Focus on first-order epistemic states, such as "knowledge" and "belief," and then create a measure of belief ("probability") that unambiguously attaches values (distributed between 0 and 1) to beliefs that Creature might hold. Thus, if Creature is ambivalent (or "evenly undecided") regarding the truth value of *S*, then denote this mental state of Creature relative to *S* with the probabilities $P(S) = 0.5$ and $P(\text{not-}S) = 0.5$. This measure turns "quality into quantity"—arguably a desirable feature for a model—albeit at the cost of losing some of the descriptive richness of the epistemic description language that Ask has built from introspection. Within this framework, "knowledge" ($P(S) = 1$) and "risky belief" ($0 < P(S) < 1$) become tractable and the ignorance associated with uncertainty becomes measurable (as the information that Creature *would* need if it were to assign a positive probability to S). More subtle epistemic states may be lost as a result of the precision that the reductive model requires.

In spite of the great representational power and parsimony of the probability measure associated with S, there are still significant ambiguities to be resolved by the modeler. Let S = *the die will come up 6 on the next throw*, and let us ask Creature: "What probability do you assign to S?" If Creature understands the mathematical or logical properties of a probability measure, then it can *calculate* the probability of S being true in several different ways, which are related as follows to Creature's interpretation of a "probability measure."

Mathematical probability: Because it is a cube, a die has six sides. The end state of a throw wherein the die lands on a flat surface corresponds to a potential energy minimum ("equilibrium") of the cube. There are six such possible states corresponding to the six sides of the die, any one of which could end up landing on the flat surface. (Of course, when one side of a cube faces down, the opposite side of the cube must face up.) The end state of a throw is that the die lies with one of its six sides facing up, so on these a priori grounds there is a 1-in-6 probability that the side facing up at the end of the roll of the die is a 6. This reasoning is usually predicated on one of two assumptions: that all possible end states of the throw are equally probable because of the underlying physics of the toss; or that Creature does not have sufficient time or resources to do the experiments or calculations that would allow it to figure out which one of the six sides is more likely to turn up on a given throw.

Statistical probability: $P(S)$ can be interpreted as a statistical probability, one that is associated with the limiting (as time increases without bound) frequency with which S is true or false of an event that is part of an independently and identically distributed sequence of events generated by an underlying process. $P(S)$ can be interpreted in two distinct ways. As an *epistemic* probability, $P(S)$ ranges between 0 and 1 because we do not have sufficient information about the process generating the event that S encodes to assign it definitive truth (1) or falsity (0). In the case of our die, if Creature could measure the initial conditions of the die throw with sufficient and perhaps arbitrary precision (height of throw, angular velocity, vertical velocity, drag coefficient of die, elasticity of collision with surface), then—when armed with knowledge of the (deterministic) laws that map initial conditions to outcomes—on this interpretation Creature could make an exact calculation of the final resting state of the die and there would be no need for a probabilistic description of its epistemic states relative to S. In contrast, under an *ontological* interpretation of statistical probabilities, there is no way to generate a deterministic prediction of the outcome of the process because the mechanism that produces the end state is stochastic. On one interpretation of this state of affairs, quantum states of a particle can only be modeled probabilistically because the underlying mechanism that generates the states is itself probabilistic. In this case, for a proposition about a state being true, a probability of less than 1 does not represent a lack of information regarding that state but rather an *objective fact* about the process that generates the event to which the proposition refers. Thus, there are important distinctions to be made—and resulting ambiguities to be resolved—even if Creature informs Ask that it is using a statistical definition of probability as its measure of degree of belief. With either definition, of course, Creature must invoke an inductive principle in order to reason from the finite sequence of events used to define its probability and the infinite sequence that the definition of a probability requires before it is applied to a single event. Thus Creature has to make such an inductive jump from the finite, observed sequence of throws of the die to the infinite, unobserved (and unobservable) set on which the probability of the next outcome is defined. Knowing this, Ask's model of Creature's mental contents must include the specification of a (potentially unjustified) belief that Creature holds regarding some principle of induction.

Subjective probability: Creature can choose to define its degrees of belief neither in terms of logical or mathematical possibilities nor in terms of limiting frequencies but rather as a "personal" or "subjective" degree of belief. Suppose Creature is asked: "What is the probability that your sales team in Latin America will sell more than $10 million of product this quarter at a 50% gross margin?" Creature may reply with an answer that can be boiled down to "the probability is 0.3 that we sell more than $10 million of product in Latin America at a 50% gross margin," but it will be difficult for Ask to come up with either a "mathematical probability" or a "statistical probability" interpretation for Creature's response. The reason is that there is neither a well-defined sequence of events that can be used to calculate a statistical probability estimate nor an unambiguously defined set of allowable "possible worlds" that can be used to calculate a mathematical probability estimate. Therefore, "0.3" is the *reduction of a hunch to a number*, where the hunch may be more or less informed by data that is more or less processed by Creature.

It is possible that Creature arrives at the probability estimate by comparing its degrees of belief about propositions describing various revenue estimates (e.g., $0–$10 million in $500,000 increments) with its degrees of belief about propositions that can be more easily interpreted in statistical or mathematical terms. For example, Creature can compare its degree of belief in S with its belief that the toss of a fair coin will come up Heads (and find that $P(S) < 0.5$) or compare $P(S)$ with its degree of belief that the first two outcomes of a fair coin will each be Heads ($P = 0.25$ if the outcomes are independent) and find that $P(S) > 0.25$. However, Creature's personal degree of belief will not in itself contain any information about the *process* by which this probability was computed. Hence Ask cannot—from knowledge of $P(S)$ alone—glean any knowledge about the kinds of intrapsychic processes that led Creature to $P(S)$ and thus cannot make any more detailed inference about Creature's epistemic state vis-à-vis the proposition "the probability of S is $P(S)$."

Algorithmic probability: Creature can also define its degrees of belief in terms of the semantic and syntactic properties of S itself *without* basing this probability on "data" specifically regarding the truth value of S. Creature can do this by a simple procedure that has come to be known as "Shannon coding" [Cover and Thomas, 1991]. Suppose that Creature must assign probabilities to each of four sentences ($S_1, \ldots, S_4$) constructed such that S_1 has one clause, S_2 has two clauses, S_3 has three clauses, and S_4 has four clauses, where all clauses are conjunctively linked. It then might reason as follows. "Longer sentences—those with more clauses—should prima facie be *less* likely to be true because *a sentence is a code for a state of affairs* and, if the code were efficiently designed, then it should assign shorter codewords (sentences) to states that are more frequently observed and assign longer codewords to states that are less frequently observed. Therefore, shorter (resp., longer) sentences should have higher (resp., lower) probabilities of being true." So far, so good; but Ask wants to know: "How *much* of a difference will length make, and how do you define *long*?" This is where a well-known result due to Shannon (and Weaver [1949]) is useful. Shannon posits that an efficient code will assign codewords to states of affairs such that the length of a codeword is inversely proportional to the probability of observing the state of affairs to which the codeword refers. Mathematically speaking, we have $P(S) = |D|^{-L(S)}$, where D is the alphabet from which the codewords are built, $|D|$ is the size of D (and equals 26 if the letters of the English alphabet are considered or tens of thousands if all English words are considered), and $L(S)$ is the codeword length expressed in the alphabet's basic units (i.e., number of letters or words). On this interpretation, Creature uses the properties of the language in which sentences are expressed—along with the assumption that the target language was designed as an efficient coder–decoder—to assign "personal" probabilities to the truth value of S.

1. INTERPRETING BELIEF AND BEHAVIOR
IN TERMS OF BETTING ODDS

To these difficulties, the modeler may bravely reply: "So what? After all, not every difference (say, in the way in which Creature comes up with $P(S)$) *makes* a difference (to Creature's behavior)." The craft of modeling is precisely that of identifying which of many potential differences and distinctions in descriptions of the object of the model do make a difference—with the aim of producing a "tuned" predictive and interpretive instrument for its behavior, an exosomatic machine that maps observed variables onto unobserved but observable ones.

Ramsey [1931] proposed a way of arriving at estimates of personal degrees of belief that enabled the experimental study of decisions among risky or uncertain option sets ("lotteries") by cutting through the knots and ambiguities inherent in any attempt to reduce a phenomenologically precise account of epistemic states to a unidimensional measure ("probability"). To do so, Ramsey interpreted personal probability in terms of a *bet* that Creature is willing to make on the truth of a proposition S. In modeling this bet, Ramsey made use of two lotteries: L_1 has a payoff of U_1 that one gets "for sure"; L_2 has a payoff $U_2 = U_t$ if S turns out to be true and $U_f = 0$ if S turns out to be false. Given this set-up, Creature is asked how much it would pay to play L_2 given that $U_1 = 0$; in other words, how much Creature is willing to *bet* on S being true. Let B represent the amount of the bet (Creature's "stake") on L_2. Assume that Creature assigns a probability of $P(S)$ to S being true and a probability of $1 - P(S)$ to S being false. Then, at the point where Creature is indifferent between L_1 and L_2, Ask solves for $P(S)$ as follows. Since $U(a) = 0$ by definition, it follows that $P(S)U_t + (1 - P(S))(-B) = 0$ (by the indifference principle) and therefore $P(S)(U_t + B) - B = 0$ (by algebraic manipulation), which gives $P(S) = B/(U_t + B)$.

Armed with this personal probability extraction device, Ask is ready to interact with Creature in a way that will inform him about Creature's personal degree of belief about S. Now the question *What is your estimate of the probability that the deal will close tomorrow or sooner?* is replaced by the question *How much are you willing to bet now in order to win U_t if the deal closes tomorrow or sooner?* Ask then uses Creature's answer ($\$B$) to solve for Creature's implied $P(S)$ via the previously derived $P(S) = B/(U_t + B)$. This procedure is the basis for a modeling move, which is parallel to RESP, that we call BET.

> BET. *Interpret Creature's epistemic states in terms of its personal degrees of belief, interpret personal degrees of belief as probability measures, and use Creature's choices among lotteries to recover personal degrees of belief from the bets that Creature is willing to accept.*

Let us consider the mechanics of Ramsey's maneuver. The probability estimate ($P(S)$) that it yields depends solely on Creature's observed behavior. Ask need not "delve into Creature's mind" in order to recover and make sense of the processes by which it has computed $P(S)$—or such is the claim. However, this claim is not accurate because, to use the device, Ask must either force Creature into a bet or secure sufficient grounds for interpreting Creature's actions as instances of bets that Creature is willing to make.

Even if Creature (a vice-president of sales in this example) states $S = I$ *am sure that the deal will close by tomorrow at 5 p.m.*, it may not be willing to stake $5,000 on a lottery that pays $1,000 if S indeed holds (i.e., yields Creature a profit of $1,000 net of its bet) or pays nothing otherwise. There could be several reasons for Creature's reluctance to bet in this way in this case. First, Creature may be risk-averse, in which case the personal probability implied by its betting behavior will be significantly lower than the probability Creature is willing to assert if a bet is not required. Second, Creature's degrees of belief may not satisfy the finite additivity axiom that governs probability measures and therefore $P(S) + P(\text{not-}S) < 1$. This means that our calculation of the personal degree of belief should be amended to read $P(S) = aB/(U_t + aB)$, where $P(S) + P(\text{not-}S) = a < 1$, entailing that a bet B' from Creature on the truth value of S must be interpreted as a "real" bet of $B = (B'/a)$. Third, there is a "credibility risk" that Creature associates with making too precise a prediction about the timing of the contract's closing, and this potential credibility loss must be included in Creature's calculations that aim to maximize expected value when choosing whether or not to accept the bet.

Ask takes these observations seriously, but he does not view them as insurmountable obstacles to the application of BET to help recover Creature's personal degrees of belief. In particular, the application of BET accommodates the existence of effects that influence the informativeness of the measured $P(S)$ relative to Creature's stated $P(S)$, but BET solves the problems such effects raise by stipulating that Creature's personal degree of belief is as measured by the pattern of bets that Creature is willing to accept. In other words, Ask stipulates that the $P(S)$ entailed by Creature's bet already incorporates effects such as risk aversion and fear of credibility loss. Separate estimates of these effects can be derived by experimental manipulations that test for each effect separately. Creature's risk aversion, for instance, can be measured by reconstructing the shape of Creature's indifference curve between lotteries offering a certain payoff of X ($P(X) = 1$) and lotteries offering a risky payoff of Y with varying probabilities $P(Y)$ but with the same expected value as the risk-free lottery—that is, between pairs of lotteries $(X, 1; Y, P(Y))$ for which $X = YP(Y)$. The shape of curves can then be factored into the design of the Ramsey betting mechanism to achieve an estimate of $P(S)$ that is corrected for Creature's risk aversion.

There are several ways to interpret Ramsey's maneuver as a way of probing Creature's epistemic states. In one interpretation, the maneuver is an *assimilative* one: Creature's more subtle epistemic states (ambiguity, radical ambiguity, oblivion, awareness) are all "subsumed" into its betting odds, which are set to equal its personal degrees of belief in the truth of a well-formed sentence. In another interpretation, the maneuver is an *eliminative* one: It focuses only on Creature's first-order beliefs and leaves open the possibility that other beliefs may matter—including, for instance, Creature's beliefs about the hidden motives of the person who is offering the bet and its higher-level uncertainties about the situation "taken as a whole." In yet another interpretation, the maneuver is a *reductive* one: It attempts a systematic reduction of all epistemic states to personal degrees of belief, and consequently to betting odds, via a sequence of well-specified logical steps. Ask is well advised to be precise and internally consistent about the interpretation it chooses, but Ramsey's maneuver is valuable under any of these interpretations.

The difficulty of getting Creature to place a bet on its beliefs signals, however, a deeper problem with the application of BET. If Creature is resistant to making bets that vouchsafe its use of language ("It is likely that . . . ," "I believe *S* with probability . . . ," etc.), then the very mechanism for eliciting behavior that can inform Ask about Creature's personal degrees of belief is in question. This difficulty creates the need for making a further distinction in the application of BET, which will be signaled by introducing the following two variants.

> BET* (Walk the Talk). *Interpret epistemic states as personal degrees of belief, interpret personal degrees of belief as probability measures, and force Creature to choose among lotteries designed to recover personal degrees of belief from the bets that Creature is willing to accept in order to recover its personal degrees of belief from the betting odds it is willing to accept.*

This "manipulative" variant of BET has Ask using the Ramsey procedure as a (partly) interventional device that forces Creature to "walk its talk." Using BET* may require Ask to structure Creature's payoffs in such a way that the costs of *refusing* to place bets—or to specify its beliefs at a level of precision that allows Ask to turn them into bets—equal or exceed the costs of risking its credibility by making a precise statement backed by a bet.

> BET** (Talk the Walk). *Interpret epistemic states as personal degrees of belief, interpret personal degrees of belief as probability measures, and explicitly and publicly interpret Creature's behaviors as choices among lotteries in order to recover personal degrees of belief from the bets that Creature is willing to accept.*

Unlike BET*, BET** is a "pedagogical" version of BET. Here Creature is not *forced to make* a bet; rather, its behaviors are *interpreted as* bets and this interpretation is made public as a way of getting Creature to "internalize" it. Hence BET** makes use of the following counterfactuals.

C1: If Creature risked $\$B$ to get $\$U_t$ in case S is true, then it could not have estimated the probability of S as being *greater* than $P(S) = B/(U_t + B)$.

C2: If Creature risked $\$B$ to get $\$U_r$ in case S is true, then it could not have estimated the probability of S as being *less* than $P(S) = B/(U_t + B)$.

If Creature (in this case, a large shareholder in a private firm) refuses to give in to a joint threat by its executive team to resign en masse by time t if the option pool allocated to them is not increased by an aggregate of 20%, then—assuming Creature values the negative consequence of mass resignation at $-\$V$ and the dilutive cost of additional options at $-\$C$—Ask may deduce that Creature is not willing to bet C in order to get V should the statement $S =$ *executive team will resign* hold true and hence that it does not think $P(S)$ to be greater than $C/(V + C)$.

This "pedagogical" version of BET is necessarily weaker as a modeling tool than its "manipulative" counterpart because, with BET**, Ask does not control as many of the variables required to measure Creature's $P(S)$ as when he uses BET*. For example, suppose that the large shareholder in question does not possess the cognitive skills to calculate the expected value of the loss of the executive team or the dilutive cost of issuing additional options on the firm's equity. Then the probability estimate that BET** yields will be misleading to Ask for reasons that have nothing to do with either the situational constraints or the shareholder's actual beliefs. Thus it turns out that deeper insight into Creature's mind may be needed to validate and calibrate the decision model, and a model of "the way Creature's mind works" should be something Ask still worries about.

2. WHY BE EPISTEMICALLY RATIONAL?

What kinds of constraints must Creature's degrees of personal belief satisfy in order for them to be representable *qua* probability measures? The question is significant in part because Creature, in producing behavior, should not be viewed as a priori bound by the normative axioms of rational choice or rational belief that normative and descriptive scientists have used in erecting models for representing Creature. Therefore, what is at stake in examining such constraints are the very bounds and limits of the applicability of such models to the project of understanding the behavior Creature produces.

The axioms of rational choice theory were seen in Chapter 2 to provide a set of constraints—on the ways in which Ask can interpret Creature's behavior and behavioral patterns—that amounted to a "model" that Ask could test through repeated interactions with (and interventions upon) Creature. Moreover, these constraints were seen to arise naturally from a minimal set of aims and goals that a self-interested Creature might possess—such as precluding someone from designing and implementing a money or utility pump that could be used to extract a positive profit from Creature. As such, they furnish Ask with a way of *justifying to Creature* the set of standards to which it holds Creature's behaviors. Is it possible to articulate a model of rational belief (BEL) that functions in the same regulative fashion as DEC?

2.1. *Architecture and Justification of BEL*

BEL is based on a commitment to representing epistemic states of an individual in terms of personal degrees of belief about the truth of different propositions (the "state space") and on a set of axioms that constrain the structure and behavior of this belief function. Ask is interested in these axioms in a way that parallels his interest in the axioms of DEC: He wants to use them to interpret Creature's betting behavior in ways that make it intelligible. As with Ask's interest in the axiomatic structure of DEC, he also wants to be able to *justify* to Creature the use of the BEL axioms to interpret Creature's behavior, thereby turning BEL into a regulative model of betting behavior.

Here, then, is the representation maneuver: A *personal degree of belief* is a probability measure created by assigning a unique real number $P(S_i)$ to every one of a set of propositions S_i that Creature holds to be relevant in a context. Because propositions can be quite complicated (they are often concatenations or functions of other propositions), many of the axioms of BEL are designed to guide the assignment of probabilities to combinations and permutations of propositions.

Contrary to what many decision theory texts argue or implicitly assume, BEL assigns probabilities to *propositions* and not to *events*—for the simple reason that there are many different ways to "propositionalize" a given event. In fact, there is an *infinite* number of ways to do so, as Ask will discover, to his own dismay, in due course. What to Ask may seem to be the event "Creature lights a cigarette" may, from Creature's perspective, be the series of events "reaching for a cigarette, pulling it out, playing with the cigarette, taking a sip of coffee, placing the cigarette between lips, ..." More troublingly, what to Ask may seem to be the event corresponding to "Creature has a pain" may, to his neurophysiologist friend, seem to correspond to the correlated sequence of events "Creature's brain regions A, B, and C are highly active"— even though the correlation between such neural activity and Creature's pain reports is not perfect or even very strong. Ask is then highly concerned to be precise and discerning about the "state space" on which Creature's beliefs are defined, and he introduces the distinction between an event (a set of "raw feels") and its propositionalization (the sentence understood to refer to or describe the event) as a way of heightening his own awareness that "Creature's state space" is to be posited but not assumed. Hence, Ask will ask Creature about the propositions to which degrees of belief are to be assigned *before* assessing whether or not Creature's resulting degrees of belief satisfy the axioms of BEL; Ask will also attempt to render Creature's responses meaningful by attempting to coordinate Creature's oral noises to external events that both Ask and Creature can perceive. In the context of BEL, such "asking" need not require an exchange of speech acts between Ask and Creature (i.e., a conversation), for Ask can simply (and silently) offer Creature well-defined bets on the truth value of various propositions and infer its degrees of belief in them through the application of BET*. Nevertheless, in order for Ask to make inferences about Creature's degrees of belief from the bets it accepts, he needs to impose some structure on Creature's degrees of belief—an "algebra" for Creature's measurable epistemic states—as follows.

B1: Boundedness from below and above (range). For any proposition S, $0 \leq P(S) \leq 1$: The probability of a proposition S will neither exceed 1 nor be lower than 0. *Why?* Because otherwise anyone, including Ask himself, could offer Creature a bet (or a series of bets) that (a) Creature is bound to accept if $P(S)$ is its true degree of belief in the truth value of S and (b) will lead

Creature to lose money (or whatever it stakes) *for certain*. In particular: If $P(S) = B/(U_t + B)$ and $P(S) < 0$, then Creature will be willing to accept a positive bet B on a lottery that pays $-U_t$ (so that the fraction $P(S) = B/(U_t + B)$ is negative by virtue of the denominator being negative, which happens only for U_t large and negative) if S is true and pays 0 otherwise; this would lead to a certain loss of at least B and at most U_t. On the other hand, if $P(S) > 1$, then Creature should be willing to lay a stake B on a lottery that pays $U_t < B$ if S is true and pays 0 otherwise—for a certain loss of at least $B - U_t$ and at most B. Call such (sure-thing money-losing) bets *Dutch books*.

Like the money-pump and utility-pump arguments for justifying the acyclicity axiom of DEC, the Dutch books argument for the axioms of BEL makes the obeisance of Creature to these axioms a matter of its self-consistent pursuit of self-interest. The arguments enable Ask to (a) *educate* and *argue with* Creature about the validity of BEL's rules and (b) *train* Creature in these axioms by engineering lotteries that punish it for transgressing BEL, extracting profits from Creature in a way that is independent of the truth value of S.

B2: Bets on tautologies and contradictions (logical structure). If S is a tautology (a proposition that is true regardless of the state of the world), then $P(S) = 1$. If S is a contradiction, then $P(S) = 0$. Why *should* Creature heed these conditions? Consider the tautology first. The case in which Creature assigns $P(S) > 1$ to a tautology is identical to the case discussed for Axiom B2 in which Creature assigns $P(S) > 1$ to any proposition S. If $P(S) < 1$, then Creature should be willing to place a positive bet B on a lottery that pays an arbitrarily small U_t *no matter what* (because S is true in any state of the world), yielding a certain positive loss of B minus an arbitrarily small U_t. This condition also means that Creature will certainly lose money if it accepts two simultaneous bets on the pair of propositions $(L, \sim L)$ because the disjunction $L \vee \sim L$ (read: "L or not-L") is a tautology and thus, by accepting such bets, Creature implies that its personal degrees of belief do not sum to 1. This means that, by betting B_L on the truth of L and $B_{\sim L}$ on the truth of $\sim L$ (to win U_L or $U_{\sim L}$, respectively), Creature is taking a bet on a tautology that entails its own degree of belief in the tautology does not equal 1.

As an example [Lo, 2004], consider the proposition L = *the NASDAQ composite index will rise by at least 1% by 4 p.m. tomorrow* and assume that Creature's personal degrees of belief are represented by $P(L) = 0.5$ and

$P(\sim L) = 0.75$. Then Creature will be willing to stake \$1 in order to win \$1 if L is true (bet 1) and willing to stake \$3 in order to win \$1 if L is false—that is, if $\sim L$ is true (bet 2). If Ask bets \$50 against L and \$25 against $\sim L$, then here is what happens to Creature: If L is true, then Ask loses \$50 on bet 1 and wins \$75 on bet 2 for a profit of \$25; if L is false, then Ask loses \$25 on bet 1 and wins \$50 on bet 2 for a profit of \$25. Thus, *no matter what happens* (i.e., regardless of whether L is true or false), Ask makes a profit of \$25 by betting against Creature. This means that if Creature's degrees of belief in L and $\sim L$ are, in fact, $P(L) = 0.5$ and $P(\sim L) = 0.75$, then Creature stands to lose \$25 *for sure* if it accepts bets that are compatible with these degrees of belief.

Now consider a contradiction that is a conjunction of both S and its negation: $C = S \ \& \ \sim S$. The case of $P(C) < 0$ is identical to that discussed in Condition B1 for $P(S) < 0$, where S is any proposition. If $P(S) > 0$, then Creature should be willing to lay B on a lottery that pays an arbitrarily small U_t no matter what—since a contradiction will always have a negative, or "false," truth value—and therefore to withstand a positive loss of $l = B$ minus an arbitrarily small U_t.

B3: Sub-additivity. The sub-additivity condition requires that the degrees of belief of Creature in a set of logically independent propositions that together "span" or propositionalize all possibilities inherent in a given situation will not be greater than 1. *Why?*—Creature may ask Ask. In the limit, where the propositions in question are collectively exhaustive, their disjunction (i.e., $L_1 \vee L_2 \vee \cdots$) will be equivalent to a tautology (which is true no matter what state the world takes); the argument then runs along the same lines as those in that for Condition B2. On the other hand, if the propositions in question are not collectively exhaustive, then Creature's degree of belief about the *complement* of the disjunction $L_1 \vee L_2 \vee \cdots$ (relative to a tautology S) must be assigned a personal degree of belief that is greater than 0.

B4: Disjunctive additivity. The disjunctive axiom requires that if Creature believes in the truth of proposition L with probability $P(L)$, believes in M with probability $P(M)$, and believes that L and M are mutually exclusive in the sense that they cannot both be true, then Creature will assign to $K = L \vee M$ a degree of belief that is equal to $P(K) = P(L) + P(M)$. *Why?* Because otherwise Ask can get Creature to bet separately on L and on M and *then* to bet on K, with the following effect. If Creature accepts a bet on L that is

TABLE 3.1. Payoff Matrix for Bets That Creature Would Accept If Its Personal Degrees of Belief Did Not Obey the *Disjunctive Additivity Condition*

L is	M is	Outcome of bet on L ($)	Outcome of bet on M ($)	Sum of bets ($)	Outcome of bet on K ($)	Outcome of sum of all bets ($)
True	False	7	−3	4	−5	−1
False	True	−3	7	4	−5	−1
False	False	−3	−3	−6	5	−1

consistent with a personal degree of belief $P(L)$ in L, a bet on M consistent with a degree of belief $P(M)$ in M, and a bet on K consistent with a degree of belief $P(K)$ in K that does not equal $P(M) + P(L)$, then Ask can bet on K at one set of odds and against K at another set of odds, thereby registering a sure profit from Creature on the resulting combination. For instance [Skyrms, 1986]: Suppose that L = *the stock of company X will* fall *by 10% by 4 p.m. tomorrow*, that M = *the stock of company X will* rise *by 10% by 4 p.m. tomorrow*, and that Creature holds that $P(L) + P(M) = 0.60$ and $P(K) = 0.50$. In this case, Creature will deem it fair to stake $6 on a pair of lotteries that together pay $4 if L is true and M is true and also to stake $5 on a lottery that pays $5 if K is true. If Ask turns into a bookie who takes Creature's bets, then what happens to Creature is summarized in Table 3.1.

B5: Conjunctive product rule. The conjunctive axiom requires that, if Creature holds L and M to be logically independent propositions and believes in their truth with respective degrees of belief $P(L)$ and $P(M)$, then Creature's personal degrees of belief in the conjunction $K = L \ \& \ M$ will equal $P(K) = P(L) \times P(M)$. *Why?* Well, suppose not. Then, by a procedure similar to that outlined in discussion of condition B4, Ask can get Creature to lay bets on both L and M (with respective implicit personal degrees of belief $P(L)$ and $P(M)$) and then, separately, to lay a bet on K (with implicit personal degree of belief $P(K)$) such that Ask makes a profit from Creature in any case. For instance, suppose Creature agrees: (a) to bet $1 on a lottery that pays $1 if L = *this toss of this coin will come up Heads* is true (implying that $P(L) = 0.50$); (b) to bet $1 on a lottery that pays $1 if M = *the next toss of this coin will come up Heads* (implying that $P(M) = 0.50$); (c) to bet $1 on a lottery that pays $1 if K = *this toss* and *the next toss of this coin will come up Heads* (implying $P(K) = 0.25$); and (d) to bet $1 on a lottery that pays $1 if $\sim K$ = *neither this toss nor*

TABLE 3.2. Payoff Matrix for Bets That Creature Would Be Willing to Accept
If Its Degrees of Belief Did Not Obey the *Conjunctive Product Rule*

L is	M is	Outcome of bet on L ($)	Outcome of bet on M ($)	Sum of bets ($)	Outcome of bet on K ($)	Outcome of sum of all bets ($)
True	False	1	−1	0	−2	−2
False	True	−1	1	0	−2	−2
True	True	1	1	2	2	4
False	False	−1	−1	−2	−2	−4

the next one will turn up Heads. Then Table 3.2 shows what happens to Creature in each possible case.

Although Creature does not lose money in all possible cases, the expected
value of the conjunction of lotteries on which Creature will bet in accordance with its personal degrees of belief will be negative (i.e., [(−2) + (−2) +
4 + (−4)]/4 = −1), which means that its degrees of belief—coupled with
Creature's choices in lotteries designed by Ask to take advantage of Creature's
counternormative belief structure—produce a class of situations in which,
on average, Creature will certainly lose money. By way of contrast, consider
the set of bets that Creature would be prepared to make if it estimates (i) that
successive tosses of the fair coin are independent and (ii) that the degrees of
belief associated with ensembles of independent events are the products of
the degrees of belief that Creature associates with each of the events making
up the ensemble, as summarized in Table 3.3 (i.e., Creature believes that if
$P(L) = 1/2$ and $P(M) = 1/2$ then $P(L \& M) = 1/4$, in which case the expected
value of Creature's bets becomes $0).

B6: Conditionalization. The conditionalization condition requires Creature to maintain consistency in the way it updates its degree of belief in a
proposition (*L*) in response to new information (represented by proposition
M) that it receives. *Coherent* conditionalization requires Creature's posterior
degree of belief in *L* (after Creature has discovered that *M* is true) to equal
its prior degree of belief in *L* conditional on *M* being true. Thus, if Creature
is coherent, its answer to "How probable would you consider *L*'s being true
if *M* were true?"—and thus its prior bet on the truth value of *L*—would be
identical to its answer (and degree of belief implied by its associated betting
behavior) to the question: "Now that you know *M* is true, how probable do

TABLE 3.3. Payoff Matrix for Bets That Creature Would Be Willing to Accept
If Its Degrees of Belief Followed the *Conjunctive Product Rule*

L is	M is	Outcome of bet on L ($)	Outcome of bet on M ($)	Sum of bets ($)	Outcome of bet on K ($)	Outcome of sum of all bets ($)
True	False	1	−1	0	−1	−1
False	True	−1	1	0	−1	−1
True	True	1	1	2	3	5
False	False	−1	−1	−2	−1	−3

you consider *L*'s being true?" *Why?* Because otherwise Ask could offer Creature separate bets—on or against *L* before Creature knows whether or not *M* is true and against or on *L* after Creature finds out that *M* is true—and thereby extract a positive profit from Creature provided that *L* is true (or break even if *L* is not true). *How?* By using the following scheme for exploiting a bettor's willingness to wager on the truth of the same proposition under different sets of odds ("*L* is true conditional on *M* being true") [Armendt, 1980]. First, if Ask is aware that Creature's degree of belief in *L*/*M* *before* it knows whether or not *M* is true, $p(L/M)$, is less than its degree of belief in *L*/*M* *after* it knows that *M* is true, $P(L/M)$, then Ask can proceed as follows. Sell Creature a lottery that pays $1 if *L* and *M* are both true and pays 0 otherwise as well as a lottery that pays $p(L/M)$ if *M* is not true and pays $0 otherwise—lotteries that Creature is guaranteed to buy for $p(L/M)$. Then, he can buy from Creature a lottery that pays $1 if *L* and *M* are both true and pays $0 otherwise as well as a lottery that pays $P(L/M)$ if *M* is not true and pays $0 otherwise—which Creature is guaranteed to want to sell to Ask for $P(L/M)$ provided it acts according to its beliefs. This leaves Ask with a profit of $P(L/M) - p(L/M)$ that is independent of *L*'s truth value. Second, if $p(L/M)$ is greater than $P(L/M)$ then the "buy" and "sell" operations are reversed: Ask will buy from Creature a lottery that pays $1 if *L* and *M* are both true and pays $0 otherwise as well as a lottery that pays $p(L/M)$ if *M* is not true and pays $0 otherwise—which Creature is guaranteed to want to sell to Ask for $p(L/M)$—and then sell to Creature a lottery that pays $1 if *L* and *M* are both true and pays $0 otherwise as well as a lottery that pays $P(L/M)$ if *M* is not true and pays $0 otherwise—which Creature is guaranteed to want to buy from Ask for $P(L/M)$. This leaves Ask with a profit of $p(L/M) - P(L/M)$ that is independent of *L*'s truth value.

Ask's ability to construct the conditionalization-driven Dutch book depends on his knowing whether or not Creature's degree of belief in L/M will rise or fall in response to Creature's finding out whether or not M is true. However, once armed with this information, Ask can extract positive payoffs from Creature (provided that M is true) regardless of whether or not L turns out to be true. For instance, Creature may believe the statement "L (= firm revenues will increase) if M (= the CEO is fired)" more strongly *after* the CEO is fired (i.e., once M turns out to be true) than it does *before* the CEO is fired (i.e., $P(L/M) > p(L/M)$). One reason for this discrepancy may be a failure of imagination that prevents Creature from distinguishing its degree of belief in M = *the CEO will be fired* from its belief in L/M = *firm revenues will increase if the CEO is fired*. Another reason is that, *before* finding out whether or not the CEO is about to be fired, Creature confuses its uncertainty about whether or not she will be fired with its uncertainty about whether or not revenues will go up *given that* she is fired.

On the other hand, Creature may exhibit a systematic bias toward simplifying complex sequences of causally connected events, a bias that drives it to believe that, *before* the CEO is fired, there is a causal connection between her firing and an increase in the firm's revenues (i.e., $p(L/M) = 1$); whereas, *after* the CEO is fired, Creature realizes that the causal nexus leading to higher revenues is more complicated and so many other conditions must be satisfied before revenues can increase. Hence Creature changes its degree of belief to $P(L/M) < 1$. The conditionalization-driven Dutch books argument allows Ask to *distinguish* between aspects of Creature's mental behavior, to *model* Creature's mental behavior in assigning conditional probabilities, and to *discipline* Creature by exploiting systematic biases that Creature exhibits in order to extract positive payoffs from Creature no matter what the situation is, provided that Creature's propositionalization of the situation remains unchanged.

Together, the rules that make up BEL provide a set of constraints on the kinds of personal degrees of belief that Creature has, *provided* that Creature is willing to make bets in ways that are consistent with these degrees of belief. It is possible to construct Dutch books that extract positive payoffs (either "for sure" or "on average") from Creature if its personal degrees of belief do not satisfy the rules of BEL. It is then reasonable to ask: What logical force does this possibility have for Creature?—in other words: Why should it matter to Creature that it knows there may be a bookie "out there" who might construct Dutch books against it? Is there any *other* reason that Creature has for disciplining its personal degrees of belief according to the structure of BEL?

With regard to the first question, the fact that Creature knows of the existence of a strategically minded bookie cannot reasonably determine the ways in which Creature structures its own private degrees of belief, for it can always choose *not* to lay the bets that are coherent with these degrees of belief. Thus Creature could maintain that there is nothing wrong with having personal degrees of belief that sum up to a number exceeding 1 or with holding that the probabilities of the conjunction of independent events exceed the probabilities of the individual events in question—*unless* (a) one is interested in maximizing personal gain, (b) one is always willing to lay bets that are consistent with one's degrees of belief, or (c) one suspects or knows that there is a bookie who will exploit counter-BEL bets or groups of bets. Creature may choose to "opt out" of the betting game and thereby protect its personal beliefs from exploitation by bookies intending to exploit its epistemic shortcomings.

The answer to the second question is that there are *no* other reasons for Creature to observe BEL that are as good as the ones based on the possibility of Dutch books. There are, of course, other persuasive maneuvers that Ask can use to induce Creature to acquiesce to the conditions on the "correct" usage of personal degrees of belief. Ask can, for instance, embarrass Creature into accepting the probability calculus by publicly demonstrating their coherence to Creature (via Venn diagrams or set-theoretic constructions of probability spaces), rhetorically invite Creature to refute Ask's demonstrations, and then use Creature's difficulty at doing so to convince Creature of their validity. Such maneuvers, however, are not conceptually unassailable: Fuzzy logic, for instance, models epistemic states by propositional beliefs whose associated measures do not necessarily obey the laws of the probability calculus. Additionally, Ask will also find that such maneuvers are not sufficiently incisive to produce the right commitment within Creature: Even if "persuaded" of the rightness of some conditions placed upon its degrees of belief by a logically connected demonstration, Creature may not be sufficiently motivated to produce betting behavior that is consistent with them. Ask's use of Dutch books

TABLE 3.4. Reconstructing the Dependence of Creature's Patterns of Choice on the
Riskiness of Structured Lotteries as a Function of the Size and Probability
of the Risky Payoff

Variations in probability of risky payoff		Variations in size of risky payoff	
Lottery 1	Lottery 2	Lottery 1	Lottery 2
$100 for sure	$1,000 if S is true, $p(e) = 0.10$; $0 otherwise	$100 for sure	$1,000 if S is true, $p(e) = 0.10$; $0 otherwise
$100 for sure	$800 if S is true, $p(e) = 0.125$; $0 otherwise	$10 for sure	$100 if S is true; $p(S) = 0.10$; $0 otherwise
$100 for sure	$500 if S is true, $p(S) = 0.20$; $0 otherwise	$1 for sure	$10 if S is true, $p(S) = 0.10$; $0 otherwise
. . .	. . .	. . .	. . .

and of Dutch books arguments to explain his choice of a model of epistemic
rationality for interpreting Creature's actions is motivated by precisely this
concern with making concepts and models speak as closely as possible to
Creature's behavior.

Even if there exists no definitive *logical* injunction that bids Creature to
lay bets according to its internal degrees of belief, Creature's unwillingness to
lay bets is of *practical* significance to Ask: Creature is not willing to "walk the
talk" that it produces. Exculpatory reasons such as mere risk aversion on the
part of Creature can be ruled out independently by reconstructing Creature's
risk aversion profile, which can be accomplished by (a) asking Creature to
choose between lotteries that pay $\$U$ no matter what state the world assumes
and lotteries that pay $\$U/p(S)$ if some proposition S with probability $p(S)$
turns out to be true and pay $0 otherwise (i.e., lotteries with expected values
of $\$U$); and then (b) record variations in choice patterns as a function of both
U and p. See Table 3.4.

If Creature chooses not to bet on the truth of its beliefs, or if constructing
such bets and credibly offering them to Creature is too costly, then can Ask
still hope to extract useful subjective information from Creature? Perhaps,
under some conditions—which Ask will turn to next.

3. SCORING RULES FOR PERSONAL DEGREES OF BELIEF

Ask may not always be in a position to offer Creature bets—or all of the
necessary bets—from which it can infer Creature's personal degrees of belief,

or to induce Creature to take these bets. If Ask is a principal and Creature is an agent in Ask's firm, getting Creature to place bets on all possible states of the world relevant to Creature's role in the business would be a long and costly project that may be difficult to justify in terms of a positive net present value. Moreover, as we have seen, Creature may coherently *refuse* to lay bets on propositions for which it *is* willing to state personal degrees of belief. In this case, whatever belief structure Ask imputes to Creature will not be testable by Ask through structured observations of Creature's betting behavior. What is Ask to do?

One solution is for Ask to question Creature directly about its degrees of belief regarding the truth value of a relevant set $\{S_k\}$ of propositions and then to record Creature's answers to those questions. To make sure that Creature's answers correspond to its *actual* degrees of belief, Ask can offer Creature an incentive contract that rewards Creature maximally for predictions that are based on only and all of the relevant information it possesses (i.e., the incentive contract will motivate Creature to make predictions based on the truth, the whole truth, and nothing but the truth). If Creature is asked about its degrees of belief regarding a set of collectively exhaustive propositions, then the incentive contract that Ask can offer Creature has the form shown in Table 3.5.

If Creature predicts that $S =$ *the CEO will resign* will be true by 5 p.m. tomorrow with probability $P(S) = 1/4$ and that $\sim S =$ *the CEO will not resign* will be true by 5 p.m. tomorrow with probability $P(S) = 3/4$, then the payoff to Creature (provided it accepts an incentive contract that has the form Table 3.5) will be $V(P(S)) = V(S)$. The question is: What is the value of the contract that maximizes Creature's expected value for revealing its true

TABLE 3.5. Payoff Structure of a Contract That Rewards Creature Contingently upon the Ex Post Truth Value of Its Ex Ante Probabilistic Predictions

Creature's prediction	Truth value of S_k	Payoff to Creature
$P(S_1) = P_1$	True	$V(P_1)$
$P(S_2) = P_2$	True	$V(P_2)$
$P(S_3) = P_3$	True	$V(P_3)$
$P(S_4) = P_4$	True	$V(P_4)$
$P(S_5) = P_5$	True	$V(P_5)$
$P(S_k) = P_k$	True	$V(P_k)$
...	...	...

degrees of belief?—in other words, that maximizes $\sum_{k=1}^{N} P_k V(P_k)$ subject to the constraint that $\{P_k = P(S_k)\}$ are degrees of belief that span all relevant possibilities (i.e., $\sum_{k=1}^{N} P_k = 1$). Bernardo [1979] solves the (more difficult) continuous-probability distribution problem,

$$\max_{\{p_k\}} \int P_s(S) U(P_s(S)) dS \quad \text{s.t.} \quad \int P_S(S) dS = 1,$$

to show that the optimal truth-revelation contract pays Creature $A + B$ $\log(P(S))$, which reduces in the discrete case to $V(P_k) = A + B \log(P_k)$. Thus, if Creature predicts that $P_k = P(S_k)$ and if S_k turns out to be true, then Creature is paid $V(P_k) = A + B \log(P_k)$, where the "log" function is to any base (Ask will choose base 2 in order to facilitate the transition to information-theoretic jargon) and where A and B are arbitrary constants (we will take them to be positive).

The functional form of this contract gives some intuitive sense of how the contract "feels" to Creature: If A and B are both positive then the contract "starts Creature out" with a fixed endowment A, and it "fines" Creature (specifically, in the amount $B \log(P_k)$) if S_k turns out to be true *and* Creature predicts that $P(S_k) = P_k$ (because the probability P_k will typically be less than or equal to 1 and so its logarithm will be less than or equal to 0). Creature will perceive the contract as a "free" grant of an endowment $e = A$ followed by a fine $f = B \log(P_k)$ for every prediction P_k that it produces. Of course, such a scheme does not discipline Creature's epistemic behavior in the same way as the threat of a Dutch book does. Unless Ask explicitly constrains it, Creature can announce probability values greater than 1 as a way of increasing its payoff. Ask must therefore use some of the discretionary power that this constructed situation gives him to at least weakly shape the range of allowable behavior from Creature.

What happens if Creature reports to Ask a P_k^* that is different from its "real" degree of belief P_k? Creature can only do worse than it could have done had it reported its "best guess," P_k, because any distorted prediction P_k^* (if it satisfies the finite sub-additivity axiom) will by definition take Creature farther away from its expected payoff maximum. Creature could try to cheat by announcing probabilities that are close to 1 on the truth values of *all* possible propositions (and thus violate the sub-additivity condition), but then Ask could explicitly "call" Creature on this violation of the probability calculus because Ask is the contract's designer and "principal." Ask can also incentivize Creature to play along with this game by making A—the payoff for perfect predictions by Creature—high enough.

Of course, the number of "games" that Creature can play upon Ask *after* it has accepted a $\log(P)$ contract on its predictions is still significant. For instance, suppose Ask (the CEO) convinces Creature (a vice-president of sales) to accept a $\log(P)$ contract based on forward-looking quarterly revenue numbers. Then Creature can define the prediction's propositional space in a way that renders the making of correct high-probability predictions easy (e.g., S_1 = *we will generate at least $10 million in revenue* and S_2 = *we will generate less than $10 million in revenue*); here $10 million is an "easy" target, with $P(S_1) = 0.999$ and $P(S_2) = 0.001$, so that the prediction has a high expected value and is also highly reliable.

More generally, given the incentive contract $V(P_k) = A + B \log(P_k)$ and given that Creature has access to choosing the number of propositions S_k *and* the probabilities that it associates with those propositions, Creature will try to maximize

$$\sum_{k=1}^{N} P_k V(P_k) = \sum_{k=1}^{N} P_k [A + B \log(P_k)].$$

It can accomplish this by maximally reducing the "state space" of possibly true propositions (ideally to a tautology T that is true independently of the state of the world) such that $P(T) = 1$; this means that the fine, $\log(P(T))$, equals 0. In this situation, Creature may say to itself: "T will be true no matter what, so I can just pocket A on the basis of having predicted $P(T) = 1$ and $P(\sim T) = 0$." However, if Creature must first persuade Ask that T is not a tautology and hence that $\sim T$ corresponds to a possible state of the world, before accepting the contract, then the peril is diminished. The sobering news for Ask is that some degree of adherence of Creature to norms of coherence must be either already in place, or enforceable by Ask, in order for a productive exchange of commitments to get off the ground.

In such cases, asymmetries of capability or skill between Ask and Creature become as relevant as the asymmetries of *information* seen in the usual treatment of imperfect contracting. For instance, suppose Creature knows that the value of some variable X is $\sqrt{2}$; then, provided that it believes that Ask does not know how to compute $\sqrt{2}$, Creature can "accept" a $\log(P)$ contract from Ask on the (suitably propositionalized) "event space" consisting of $T = $ *the value of variable X is* $\sqrt{2}$ and $T' = $ *the value of variable X is 1.419 . . .* ; announce probabilities $P(T) = 0.99999$ and $P(T') = 0.00001$; and pocket $A + B \log(0.99999)$ on the basis of that prediction.

In response to such tactics, Ask has two options. One is to amplify the fine relative to the endowment in the incentive contract (i.e., to make B large relative to A) so that even very small predictive errors will be sharply penalized. This move is likely to make the contract unattractive to Creature unless it is a risk seeker—and the whole scheme depends on Creature's acceptance of the contract. The second option is for Ask to generate the set $\{S_k\}$ of possibly true sentences about which Creature will generate predictions. For instance, Ask can request, as a prerequisite to Creature receiving the $\log(P)$ contract, that it provide probability estimates for *each* of the intervals in which forward quarterly revenue may fall: \$5 million $< R <$ \$7 million; \$7 million $< R <$ \$9 million; \$9 million $< R <$ \$11 million; and \$11 million $< R <$ \$13 million. This option requires Ask to be or to become sufficiently aware of the specific knowledge domain or information partition of Creature in order to generate an appropriate space of propositions on which Creature is to bet. The knowledge required of Ask to generate this space is sometimes minimal (involving, e.g., revenue forecasts or states of the weather); however, "complex" knowledge domains will make Ask's problem of defining state spaces a far more difficult one. In these latter cases, Ask will benefit from a communicative technology that allows him to efficiently grasp and understand Creature's knowledge domain—a subject that will be broached in Chapter 6.

3.1. *Can Betting Odds Be Used to Fix the Meaning of Sentences?*

The maneuvers and machinations described so far all rely on the transparency of the meaning of a particular sentence S. They rest on the assumption that Ask can unambiguously assign meanings to Creature's sententially structured oral noises, thereby making them intelligible. This is, in fact, a tall assumption and far from unproblematic. It calls for a theory of interpretation of sentences, which Ask must apply in order to understand what Creature is saying—or to understand how Creature understands what Ask is saying when it is Ask who generates the sentences on whose truth value Creature bets.

"Meaning" stands perched atop a three-pronged definitional structure consisting of "meaning as reference" (to what does a word or a sentence refer?), "meaning as consequence" (what are the consequences of uttering a word or a sentence in a context?), and "meaning as common usage" (what are the rules to which a meaningful utterance must conform?). Creature may utter sentences because doing so is in its best interest given the circumstances (meaning as consequence), because it wants to "refer" to certain states of affairs in an unambiguous way (meaning as reference), or because it is following certain rules in putting words and phonemes together that are coordinated to both context and consequence yet are guided by knowledge of a core set of principles that it believes others follow as well (meaning as common usage).

Ask thus has several possible "theories of meaning" to choose from that range from the simple-minded to the mindfully simple, and he would like to take into account all these possible meanings of "meaning." He can choose to assume that "words refer to objects" in the same way that a pointer sign "refers" to that to which it points. On this view, the word "rabbit" refers to a rabbit (an object). An ostensibility problem (a problem about how the meanings of words are learned by pointing at the objects to which the words refer) arises when Ask tries to coordinate his own mental picture of what "rabbit" refers to with Creature's. Pointing at a rabbit while uttering the word "rabbit" seems like a natural solution, but (as Quine [1951] points out) it is never clear whether one is pointing to the whole animal, to an undetached rabbit part, or to a space-time slice of a rabbit; still more troublingly, there is no fail-safe or algorithmic procedure for disambiguating the object of the act of pointing.

Failing in his attempt to take individual nouns as carriers of meaning, Ask could follow Tarski [1935] and take instead entire sentences to be bearers of meaning. The meaning of a sentence, on this view, is the set of conditions under which the sentence comes out true. For instance, $S = snow\ is\ white$ is true just in case snow is white, and it is false otherwise. This seems like a felicitous move because it apparently eliminates ostensibility problems from the picture. But it is something of a sleight of hand in that it creates a "double-decker" picture of language in general: the sentence "$T = 'S = snow\ is\ white'$ is true" is true in the upper-level language only if the claim "snow is white" is unobjectionably assertible (by Ask to Creature and vice versa) in the lower-level language. This shifts the question of *truth* of a sentence in the upper-level language to the question of *assertibility* of that sentence in the lower-level language. Ask is left "holding the bag" and asking himself: What behavior of Creature's corresponds to the unobjectionable assertibility of a sentence?

One solution [Davidson, 2005] is to retain the basic moves of making meaning a property of the truth value of sentences, rather than of the reference of predicates and variables, and to devise Ramsey-like procedures for extracting meaning from betting behavior on the truth value of sentences. As Davidson (p. 61) puts it:

> A speaker holds a sentence true as a result of two considerations: what he takes the sentence to mean and what he believes to be the case. The problem is that what is relatively directly observable by an interpreter is the product of two unobservable attitudes, belief and meaning. The problem is curiously like the problem of disentangling the roles of belief and [desire] in determining choices and preferences.

But rather than following Davidson in transforming Jeffrey's [1983] formulation of a calculus of desire and belief into a calculus of belief and meaning, Ask prefers to stay with Ramsey's simpler and more well-rehearsed procedure for extracting degrees of belief from bets on lotteries with controlled payoffs. Ask begins by offering Creature a bet on the truth value of S (e.g., "it will rain tomorrow") and extracting Creature's estimate of $P(S)$ from the stake that Creature places on a lottery that pays $\$U$ if S is true. Suppose that tomorrow comes but that Ask and Creature disagree on whether or not S is true: It drizzles, to be sure, but only in some places and intermittently. Ask internalizes this problem as one about "the meaning of S."

Unwilling to press the bet's enforcement at any cost, Ask proposes to re-contract for another, more precisely worded bet on tomorrow's precipitation level and proposes to resolve the problem of meaning by specifying tighter truth conditions on S. For instance, S will be considered true only if, in the 24-hour period 00:00–23:59 on the date in question, there is at least 1.5 mm of water accumulation over an area defined by particular GPS coordinates. Creature agrees and bets, and Ask extracts Creature's $P(S)$ using the normal routine. Once again, tomorrow comes; and there is an accumulation of 1.6 mm of water within the specified space-time hypervolume. Yet Creature still refuses to acknowledge that it rained, arguing that there was ambiguity in the precise meaning of "tomorrow."

Ask is surprised (if not worse), but he sticks with the scheme for identifying meaning with the truth conditions of sentences specified at recursively higher levels of precision. He decomposes the sentence "in the 24-hour period 00:00–23:59 on the date in question, there is at least 1.5 mm of water accumulation over an area defined by particular GPS coordinates" into subsentences that Creature will acknowledge to be true just in the case that the meaning Ask assigns to these subsentences is identical to the meaning that Creature assigns to them. For example: S' = *the number of hours that elapse from the moment a clock X at location Y indicates 00:00 to the moment when the same clock indicates 23:59 is equal to 24*; S'' = *if today is the Nth day of the year, then tomorrow will be the (N + 1)th day of the same year, except if . . .* ; and so forth.

The decomposition of S into subsentences or clauses for the purpose of analyzing its meaning does not make use of "definitional" clauses (e.g., clauses that *define* a date, an hour, a clock), which would merely transfer the problem of meaning from the definiens to the definiendum. Instead, the decomposition maps required definitional clauses into predictions. Thus S' is *not* "a 24-hour period that begins at 00:00 tonight and ends at 23:59 tomorrow night" but rather a *prediction* about some occurrence that is prima facie accessible to both Creature and Ask and that Ask believes Creature will propositionalize in an identical fashion to that in which Ask does ("the clock now reads 23:59"). Now, if Creature's degrees of belief obey the BEL conditions, then it is possible for Ask to audit the meaning that Creature assigns to S by considering the relationship between $P(S)$ (reconstructed from Creature's betting odds) and $P(S')$, $P(S'')$, and so forth. For example, if $S = S'$ & S'' and if S' and S'' are logically independent, then it should be the case that $P(S) = P(S')P(S'')$. *So what?* Well, "so nothing" if the interaction remains at the level of oral noises. However, if Ask can get Creature to lay separate bets on S', S'', and S, then the motivational logic of avoiding a certain loss gives bite to the logical force of the decomposition of S into S' and S''. *Bets turn logic into action* by mirroring logical structure into payoff and motivational landscapes.

There is, of course, no *guarantee* that this procedure will converge to an unambiguous shared meaning of S. Creature may, for all Ask knows, follow a different kind of logic altogether—obeying rules that differ from the rules of first-order logic. And if this were the case, then Ask would be hard-pressed to make inferences about Creature's logicality on the basis of interpreting Creature's bets via a schema that is founded on Ask's own logical rules. For this reason, *some* shared structure must be presupposed. But then, no guarantees were promised in any case. What Ask is after is a schema for iteratively eliminating possible sources of ambiguity in the meaning of sentences that is, in most cases, *recursively refinable*. This is what the Ramsey procedure provides.

4. A PRINCIPAL–AGENT MODEL OF AFFECT AND COGNITION

Ask will now take the scoring rules used above to induce Creature to disclose its degrees of belief in maximally truthful fashion and turn them "inwardly" to model the dependence of Creature's own beliefs on its visceral or emotional states. The modeling move made when Ask went from DEC to INT is that of maintaining the assumption that behavior is pulled by incentives while relaxing the assumption of "conscious will" of the initiation of the motivated behavior: Creature was assumed to react to micro-incentives yet to be only imperfectly aware of the basis of its own behavior. In the case of modeling the contents of Creature's (putative) "mind," "beliefs" are now again considered as outcomes of incentive-pulled (or at least incentive-sensitive) mental behavior—with the aim of producing a model of "belief changes" in Creature that can be tracked as a function of logically irrelevant but causally relevant changes in Creature's internal conditions, such as changes in Creature's blood sugar levels and levels of anxiety, fear, rage, panic, elation, or sexual arousal.

The model assumes that Creature's belief selection behavior is influenced by a $\log(P)$-type contract between two internal agencies: *Affect*, denoting the "feeling" part of Creature; and *Cognition*, the "thinking" part. Suppose Affect wants Cognition to make maximally accurate predictions and, as a result, Affect gives Cognition a(n optimal) $\log(P)$ contract on a set $\{S_k\}$ of propositions that Affect and Cognition implicitly "agree" to be relevant to Creature's survival or success. Because Affect and Cognition are co-located in the same person, there is no sustainable asymmetry of information that can be exploited by Cognition to Affect's disadvantage, or vice versa, and therefore Ask is not concerned to model "informational games" that Affect and Cognition can play with one another as they negotiate their agreement. Cases of "self-deception" on the part of Creature as a whole—for example, Creature may believe S in spite of also knowing R and knowing that R logically implies ~S—will be explained by Ask using his "internal contracting" model of Creature's epistemic state dynamics and without the need to invoke additional motives and mechanisms for manipulating and distorting information. The intrapersonal contract by which Ask models Creature's mental activity, then, is one under which Affect offers to pay Cognition $\log(P(S_k))$-type payoffs in the case that proposition S turns out to be true after Cognition has predicted that the probability of S is $P(S_k)$. The expected value of this contract for Cognition is $\sum_{k=1}^{N} P(S_k)[A + B \log_2(P(S_k))]$. The maximization problem for Cognition, then, is

$$\max_{\{P(S_k)\}} \left\{ \sum_{k=1}^{N} A P(S_k) + \sum_{k=1}^{N} B P(S_k) \log_2(P(S_k)) \right\}.$$

The first term of the sum will be equal to A (a constant) because $\sum_{k=1}^{N} P(S_k) = 1$; the second term is the *negative* of the Shannon entropy associated with the probability distribution function associated with S_k, multiplied by a constant (B):

$$\sum_{k=1}^{N} B P(S_k) \log(P(S_k)) = -B \sum_{k=1}^{N} P(S_k) \log_2\left(\frac{1}{P(S_k)}\right) = -B H(P(S_k)) = -BH.$$

The Shannon entropy uniquely measures the uncertainty associated with a probability distribution function (see the appendix to this chapter); therefore, in maximizing the expected value of its contractual arrangement with Affect, Cognition is choosing its $P(S_k)_{k=1,...,N}$ so as to mitigate the uncertainty associated with the ensemble $\{P(S_k)\}_{k=1,...,N}$.

An obvious question for Ask is: What is the *currency* that Creature's Affect uses to pay Cognition for its predictive successes and failures? There can be no question of "money changing hands" between Affect and Cognition. The Affect–Cognition contract works at the level of physiological utility. The model suggests that *predictive failures* on the part of Cognition are "punished" by Affect with strongly aversive or dysphoric states brought about, for instance, by the selective throttling of useful metabolic substances. States of "panic," for instance, may be associated with increased glucose consumption in parts of Creature's brain associated with dysphoric affective responses (producing a relative sugar deprivation of other parts of the brain normally used up by the agency we refer to as Cognition).

4.1. The Affect Dependence of Creature's Epistemic States: Measurements and Manipulations

Armed with this model of Creature's mental behavior, Ask is in a position to examine the visceral and affective dependence of Creature's epistemic states. To do so, he will first note that the model calls for Cognition to maximize the quantity $A - BH$, where A and B are positive constants and H is the Shannon entropy associated with a relevant belief set. This is possible only if H is *minimized*, and the value of the maximand depends on the values of the constants (A, B) that shape the value of Creature's "epistemic utility function." Ask interprets A as an *uncertainty budget*, the total resource constraint that governs how Creature will respond to uncertainty, and interprets B as an *uncertainty multiplier*, a term that determines the marginal rate of uncertainty-driven mental resource depletion on the part of Creature. Thus, A determines how much uncertainty Creature can afford to face in a given state or situation, whereas B determines the rate at which its "affective budget" is depleted as a function of the uncertainty Creature has allowed itself to be aware of.

Ask plausibly posits that physiological conditions, such as systematic sleep deprivation, will likely decrease A whereas "sugar hits," or euphoric states associated with the intake of excitatory neurochemicals, will likely increase A. In contrast, physiological states such as anxiety, fear, and panic will likely increase B, which will be lowered in states of calm, sedation, and collected reflection. Ask will distinguish between the effects of A and B on Creature's mental behavior by positing that the effect of B *may take time*—they may be delayed effects—because they supervene, depend upon, or "ride upon" the dynamics of an underlying physiological process; whereas Creature's "uncertainty budget," represented by the constant A, is always-already there for Creature. Therefore, Ask wants to model the temporal behavior of the coefficients A and B by the time-dependent functions $A(t) = Au(t)$ and $B(t) = B(1 - e^{t-T})$, where $u(t)$ is a step function that takes on the value 0 for $t \leq 0$ and

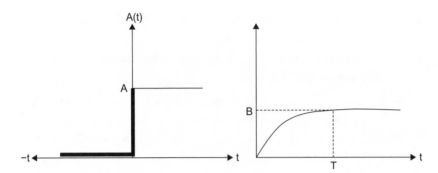

FIGURE 3.1. Temporal dependence of $A(t)$ and $B(t)$. *Note:* $B(t)$ has a functional form
that models the fact that it takes time before the (physical) processes
underlying Creature's affective response to uncertainty show their effects
on its mental behavior.

the value 1 for $t > 0$ and where T is some (short) time constant that can be
experimentally determined (see Figure 3.1).

Ask's goal is not to *measure* precise values of A, B, or T but rather to make
textured *predictions* about the direction and magnitude of changes in Creature's beliefs resulting from changes in states of affairs (information Creature
receives) and from its current and evolving physiological states. As an example, consider the problem of predicting how Creature will respond to its sudden awareness of a contradictory set of beliefs—that is, a situation in which it
simultaneously has good reason to hold S and good reason to hold $\sim S$. When
faced with the prospect of believing a logical contradiction, Creature has at
least four options available, as follows.

1. A *denial* strategy: Creature can *pretend* that it does not know $\sim S$
   (or that which it knows and knows to imply $\sim S$, or S itself), in
   which case the contradiction "vanishes"—albeit for reasons that
   have nothing to do with the truth values of S or $\sim S$. There is simply
   "no room" in Creature's mind to *behold* the contradiction.

2. A *reconciliatory* strategy: By tests of S and $\sim S$ and by arguments for S
   and for $\sim S$, Creature attempts to resolve the contradiction—possibly
   by seeking evidence for both S and $\sim S$ and then applying the principle
   of maximal reason or the principle of sufficient reason to choose
   between them.

3. A *fiat* strategy: Creature takes recourse in the logic of BEL and sets its degree of belief in the contradiction S & $\sim S$ to 0. It does so in an "automatic" fashion, goes no further, and does not attempt to resolve the contradiction.

4. A *dissolution* strategy: Creature accepts both S *and* $\sim S$, which it can do if it denies the logical axiom of the excluded middle, whereby "either S is true or $\sim S$ is true, but S & $\sim S$ cannot be true, nor can *both* S and $\sim S$ be false." Such denial consists either of rejecting the axiom itself (without recourse to an alternative) or of adopting a different kind of logic altogether (e.g., N-valued truth-functional logic).

The question for Ask is: What strategy will Creature use to guide its mental behavior vis-à-vis S & $\sim S$ as a function of physiological and psychological conditions or states that Ask can represent and observe or measure?

To answer this question, Ask deploys his model of "epistemic utility" together with a simple insight on the nature of logical contradictions, first discussed by Popper [1963]. The insight is that a cognitive commitment to both S and $\sim S$ logically entails a cognitive commitment to *any* proposition (say, R) whatsoever. For example, from believing S ("today is Tuesday"), one may infer that either S or R, where R is any proposition (e.g., "the president of the United States murdered his wife's pet"). Then, from $\sim S$ ("today is not Tuesday") and $S \vee R$, one infers R. Thus, from the conjunction *today is Tuesday* & *today is not Tuesday* one may infer a proposition that is semantically and materially unrelated to either of the propositions making up the contradictory conjunction. The implication of this insight is that Creature's epistemic state in beholding the contradiction is one of beholding a large and potentially infinite number of propositions and is therefore one of *maximal* uncertainty, as measured by the entropy of Creature's epistemic state space. It is a state of "anything goes."

Ask now has a simple model of the epistemic kinematics surrounding a contradiction, a model of the functional form of Creature's epistemic utility, and an interpretation of the parameters of the model (A, B) as measures of the uncertainty *budget*, A, and uncertainty *multiplier*, B, that characterize the *condition* (resource endowment) and *state* (rate of resource depletion) of Creature. He can now make a number of predictions about Creature's epistemic behavior, which can be classified into three regimes.

Regime 1 (high A, low B): Reconciliation and Deferral of Closure. The first regime is one in which Creature has a high uncertainty budget (high A) and a low uncertainty multiplier (low B). Here Creature's propensity to ascertain or acknowledge a contradiction is high, and the rate at which beholding the contradiction depletes Creature's resources for dealing with uncertainty (i.e., B) is low. In this regime, Ask expects Creature to acknowledge a contradiction among its beliefs and to be capable of delaying the resolution of the contradiction sufficiently to seek a reasonable reconciliation.

There are several different ways in which one might seek to reconcile the two sides of a contradictory statement, and some are costlier than others in terms of uncertainty. A costly approach, for instance, is one in which Creature fundamentally rethinks its beliefs in terms of an alternative logic (say, three- or four-valued logic) that dissolves the contradiction at the cost of setting up a number of other potential contradictions—for example, between its beliefs about different logical systems—which will also "call out" for reconciliation. A (physiologically and psychologically) "cheaper" approach is one in which Creature *accepts* the "excluded middle" axiom of first-order logic and seeks to differentially validate the two sides of the contradiction S & $\sim S$ in a way that allows it to shift its degree of belief either to S or to $\sim S$. In order to determine the relative influence of A and B on the mental behavior of Creature, Ask can perform one of the following two experiments.

THOUGHT EXPERIMENT 3.1
Decrease A by purposefully depleting Creature's resources (e.g., restfulness, blood sugar levels). This should produce a shift in its mental behavior concerning a contradiction *toward* denying that the contradiction exists. Creature may ignore $\sim S$ if it cannot deny knowing or believing S (or some proposition R that implies S), or it may ignore S if it cannot deny knowing or believing $\sim S$ (or some proposition U that implies $\sim S$).

THOUGHT EXPERIMENT 3.2
Increase B by purposefully inducing a state of high anxiety in Creature (e.g., by giving it worrisome news that is materially unrelated to the truth value of S or of $\sim S$). This should produce a change in Creature's

mental behavior concerning a contradiction *away from* reconciliation strategies, such as a principled reexamination of the fundamental logical axioms, that beget more uncertainty and *toward* "cheaper" reconciliation strategies, such as setting the degree of belief in the contradiction to 0 by appealing to the laws of the probability calculus and leaving matters at that. In contrast, *decreasing B*—say, by setting Creature's mind at ease regarding a difficult topic that is nevertheless materially unrelated to the truth value of S or merely by taking Creature out for a walk or a run— should produce states of mind in which Creature is willing to engage in physiologically or psychologically "costlier" reconciliation processes.

Regime 2 (low A, high or low B): Denial of Contradiction. A resource-depleted Creature will be likely to deny that the contradiction even exists (by the mechanisms outlined in Thought Experiment 3.1). Moreover, in a resource-depleted state, Creature will be likely to do so in a way that does not set up additional potential contradictions (for instance, by leading the conversation to another topic and ignoring Ask's attempts to refocus the conversation on the contradiction-riddled subject in question). Once again, Ask can perform experiments aimed at testing Creature's responses to contradictions in terms of its affective uncertainty processing model of Creature.

THOUGHT EXPERIMENT 3.3
Increase A by letting Creature rest or by soothing its hypoglycemic slump. This should produce a "sudden" awareness by Creature of the contradiction in question that cannot be explained by material changes in the information that Creature has about S.

THOUGHT EXPERIMENT 3.4
Decrease (resp., *increase*) *B* by engaging Creature in activities that typically soothe high levels of anxiety (resp., by tormenting Creature with worrisome new information, unexplainable "random" behavior, or reference to a problematic subject that is unrelated to the truth value of S). This should produce no effect (given the low-A regime) on Creature's mental behavior vis-à-vis the contradiction, since Creature does not have the resources needed to ascertain that a contradiction exists.

Regime 3 (high A, high B): Truncation of Contradiction. The last regime is one in which Creature has the resources to ascertain the contradiction but its resources deplete rapidly as a function of levels of uncertainty. In this case, it might be expected that Creature will recognize the contradiction but seek low-cost solutions to the problem of resolving it. Of course, Ask can discover what kind of regime Creature is in only by performing additional experiments aimed at uncovering the dependence of Creature's mental behavior on its psychological and physiological conditions, as follows.

THOUGHT EXPERIMENT 3.5

Decrease A by depriving Creature of sleep. This should produce a shift in Creature's mental behavior *away* from contradiction-resolving attempts and *toward* denial of the contradiction.

THOUGHT EXPERIMENT 3.6

Decrease (resp., *increase*) *B* by soothing (tormenting) Creature into a low-anxiety (high-anxiety) state. This should produce a shift toward "more complex" ("simpler") reconciliation strategies for the contradiction.

Armed with this array of possible regimes and potential interventions—and with the familiar Dutch books that can be built to take advantage of Creature's failure to police its degrees of belief by the rules of BEL—Ask can actively manipulate Creature's epistemic states by effecting changes in Creature's psychological or physiological conditions that are unobtrusive because they are seemingly unrelated to the beliefs that Creature is offered bets on.

THOUGHT EXPERIMENT 3.7

Ask can:
1. present Creature with evidence for *S* and with evidence for ~*S*;
2. offer Creature a bet on *S*;
3. increase Creature's *B* coefficient by having Creature focus on a problematic, difficult, or embarrassing aspect of its life;
4. decrease Creature's *A* coefficient by drawing out the conversation past Creature's mealtime;

5. calculate the direction in which Creature's degree of belief in S and ~S change as a result of the reconciliation strategies that Creature is likely to adopt (per Thought Experiments 3.1–3.5);

6. offer Creature a bet on ~S at odds that arbitrage the expected difference but that Creature is bound to take, given its new state of mind; and

7. pocket the sure profit.

More generally, Ask can combine the neuro-affective model of Creature's uncertainty response with the basic principles of Dutch book engineering in order to manipulate Creature into sure losses *or* to teach Creature (either by direct manipulation and subsequent debriefing or by logical demonstration) the basic dependencies among (a) Creature's belief formation, (b) its visceral or affective states and characteristics, and (c) the betting behavior produced thereby.

4.2. *Reasonableness of Epistemic Utility Functions*

When informed by Ask about the model he uses to interpret its behaviors, Creature could reasonably respond as follows: "I can understand why one *might* think and behave in ways that are consistent with choosing degrees of belief that minimize the entropy of their mixture, but why *should* I want this? Moreover, are there no instances in which I might want to hold personal degrees of belief that *maximize* the entropy of their mixture?" Both are reasonable requests. Ask, after all, has used the principal–agent model of the interaction between Affect and Cognition only to make predictions about changes in Creature's personal degrees of belief regarding propositions about the world; he has not made predictions about their values or distribution of values. On the basis of this model, Ask can hope to measure the degrees to which Creature's emotional and visceral states and predispositions drive it to change the spread of its personal degrees of belief, but the model offers no guidance about what that spread should be or aim to be in the first place. In order to find such guidance, Ask is well advised to construct some prototypical problems that Creature may try to solve—or to envision goals that it might have—when it constructs a distribution of personal degrees of belief on the basis of the information it possesses.

The first such problem relates to a betting situation in which Creature is trying to choose its betting odds so as to maximize its winnings after a sequence of bets. Suppose Creature is betting on the outcome of a NASCAR race among N drivers. If driver n wins, Creature makes v_n dollars for a bet of \$1 on that driver. Creature arrives at the race with U dollars and bets $b_n U$ of the money it has on each n of the N drivers in the race. At the end of the race, Creature will have multiplied its money by a factor $b_n v_n$ if driver n wins. Suppose that Creature believes that the sentence "Driver n will win" is true with probability p_n. After K races in which it bets on the nth driver, Creature's wealth will be $U_K = \prod_{k=1}^{K} b_n v_n$. The doubling rate of Creature's wealth [Cover and Thomas, 1991] will be

$$D(\{b_n\}, \{p_n\}) = E(\log(b_n v_n)) = \sum_{n=1}^{N} p_n \log(b_n v_n).$$

The optimal doubling rate is the one that maximizes D over the choice of proportions of its endowment that Creature bets on each of the N drivers (b_n); it is achieved by

$$D^*(\{b_n\}, \{p_n\}) = \sum_{n=1}^{N} p_n \log v_n - \sum_{n=1}^{N} p_n \log(p_n),$$

which is satisfied by the proportional gambling scheme $b_n = p_n$. Creature will have recognized the second term in the expression for D^* as the entropy of the probability distribution function that represents its degrees of belief over the sentences that describe the outcomes of a race, so it will recognize that lower-entropy races will have higher doubling rates than higher-entropy races. Hence Ask argues that, in such a case, Creature might (and perhaps should) seek to minimize the entropy of the probability distribution function that measures its personal degrees of belief.

Might Creature also want to *increase* the entropy of its epistemic states in some cases? Suppose, Ask posits, that Creature is seeking to construct its distribution of prior degrees of belief about the drivers in the race according to the principle that these priors best reflect a state of "perfect ignorance." In this case—and given that Creature accepts Ask's demonstration that the entropy of the probability distribution function measuring Creature's personal degrees of belief is a good measure not only of uncertainty but also of ignorance—Creature will seek the maximum entropy prior distribution and not the minimum entropy one. Information (private or otherwise) that Creature has about the race (in the form of the expected values of average winnings per driver, the mode of the distribution of winnings, the unitariness of the sum of the betting odds, etc.) can be incorporated in the resulting maximization problem as a set of constraints on the optimization problem [Jaynes, 2003]. In this case, Creature will choose $\{p_n\}$ at "time 0" so as to maximize $H(\{p_n\})$ subject to constraints supplied by the problem statement itself.

Ask notes that Creature attempts to solve different problems in these two cases. In the first case, it attempts to design an optimum betting policy given information that it already possesses. In the second case, it attempts to design a maximally sensitive estimator of the optimum betting odds for the race— one that will be most sensitive to information about every driver's chances of winning. These problems may correspond to different predicaments in Creature's life, one in which Creature actually bets on races on the basis of information it already possesses and the other in which it observes races and samples the information they provide in order to calibrate its betting odds before actually engaging in betting. Thus, entropy measures provide Ask with useful ways of capturing the objective functions of different kinds of problem statements that Creature faces, corresponding to either exploitative or exploratory goals; and this makes the ascription, by Ask to Creature, of the right problem statement or objective a critical step in his deployment of the entropy extremization "apparatus."

APPENDIX. UNIQUENESS OF ENTROPY
AS AN UNCERTAINTY MEASURE

This proof is based on Shannon and Weaver [1949]. Claude Shannon was interested in finding a function $H(\{p_i; i = 1, \ldots, M\})$, defined over the probabilities associated with an event space (space of possibly true propositions describing events in Ask's formulation; Shannon's more restrictive "event space" will be used here for brevity) with M possible events, that would measure the uncertainty of that space. He placed the following three conditions on such a function.

1. $H(\cdot)$ must be a continuous function of its argument, p_i.

2. For an equiprobable event space with M events, $H(\cdot)$ must be a monotonically increasing function of M.

3. If an event space is represented as a concatenation of event spaces conditional upon each other, then $H(\cdot)$ must be representable as a weighted sum of the entropies of the resultant event spaces.

For example, an event space described by the probabilities $p_1 = 1/2$, $p_2 = 1/4$, and $p_3 = 1/4$ can be represented by two event spaces: the first with probabilities $p_1 = 1/2$ and $p_2 = 1/2$ and the second (conditional upon occurrence of the first event) also with probabilities $p_1 = 1/2$ and $p_2 = 1/2$. By Condition 3, the entropy of the first event space, $H(1/2, 1/4, 1/4)$, must be representable as the sum $H(1/2, 1/2) + H(1/2, 1/2)/2$.

It is of interest to show first that the entropy of an M-event space is given by $H_M = -\sum_{i=1}^{M} p_i \log_2(p_i)$. Shannon proceeds by considering the entropy of an equiprobable event space,

$$H\left(\frac{1}{M}, \frac{1}{M}, \ldots, \frac{1}{M}\right) = A(M),$$

and then uses Condition 3 to decompose the entropy of an equiprobable event space with S^m possibilities into m equiprobable event spaces each with s possibilities; thus, $A(s^m) = mA(s)$. Choosing t and n distinct from s and m, Shannon also obtains $A(t^n) = nA(t)$. Choosing m and n appropriately then yields the inequality $S^m \leq t^n \leq S^{m+1}$. Now taking logarithms and dividing through the inequality by $n \log_2(s)$, one has

$$\frac{m}{n} \leq \frac{\log_2(t)}{\log_2(s)} \leq \frac{m}{n} + \frac{1}{n}.$$

If n is chosen arbitrarily large, the inequality becomes

$$\left| \frac{m}{n} - \frac{\log_2(t)}{\log_2(s)} \right| < \varepsilon$$

for ε arbitrarily small. By Condition 2, which requires that $A(n)$ be monotonically increasing, one has $A(s^m) \leq A(t^n) \leq A(s^{m+1})$, which by Condition 3 can be written as $mA(S^m) \leq nA(t) \leq (m+1)A(s)$. After we divide through by $nA(s)$, the result is

$$\frac{m}{n} \leq \frac{A(t)}{A(s)} \leq \frac{m}{n} + \frac{1}{n}$$

or, equivalently,

$$\left| \frac{m}{n} - \frac{A(t)}{A(s)} \right| < \varepsilon.$$

By adding the two resulting inequalities (after reversing the sign of the term in the absolute-value brackets), Shannon obtains

$$\left| \frac{A(t)}{A(s)} - \frac{\log_2(t)}{\log_2(s)} \right| \leq 2 \Rightarrow A(t) = -K \log_2(t);$$

here $K > 0$ by Condition 2.

To derive the entropy of an arbitrary event space, Shannon partitions an event space with $\sum_{i=1}^{n} n_i$ $(n_i \in I)$ possibilities into the concatenation of an event space with n possibilities having probabilities $p_i = n_i / \sum_{i=1}^{n} n_i$ $(n_i \in I)$ and an event space with n_i equally probable possibilities. He then uses Condition 3 again to calculate the entropy of the event space with n possibilities as follows:

$$K \log_2 \left(\sum_{i=1}^{n} n_i \right) = H(p_1, \ldots, p_n) + K \sum_{i=1}^{n} p_i \log_2(n_i).$$

Multiplying $K \log_2 \left(\sum_{i=1}^{n} n_i \right)$ through by $\sum_{i=1}^{n} p_i = 1$ will have no effect on the value of the former. Therefore, we have

$$H(p_i, \ldots, p_n) = K \left[\sum_{i=1}^{n} p_i \log_2 \left(\sum_{i=1}^{n} n_i \right) - \sum_{i=1}^{n} p_i \log_2 (n_i) \right].$$

Since $p_i = n_i / \sum_{i=1}^{n} n_i$, it follows that

$$H(p_1, \ldots, p_n) = -K \sum p_i \log p_i.$$

CHAPTER 4

CALCULATING, REASONING, AND "DOING THINGS WITH THE MIND"

Wherein Ask seeks to understand Creature's mental behavior by building models of Creature's thinking, reasoning, and high-level perception processes. He models Creature's mental behavior as representable by a finite set of computational states whose execution is pulled by marginal incentives for thinking and stopping to think. Ask uses his models to build an economics of Creature's mental behavior on the basis of a canonical representation of the problems that Creature applies itself to solving, which allows Ask to sharpen his predictions about when and whether Creature will think through a problem, how deeply it will think the problem through, and how it will go about selecting the kinds of problems it will think about and the kinds of solution procedures it will seek to apply. Ask uses the model to characterize Creature's mental behavior on a scale of computational intelligence that ranges from imbecility to meta-computational sophistication, whereby Creature optimizes the allocation of its own mental energy to solving different problems using various solution procedures. Ask extends his model to include situations in which Creature's mental behavior is intelligent but unconscious and not based on an explicit representation of either the problem it faces or the solution procedure it follows, and he arrives at measures of the "computational complexity of Creature's being" that productively blur the boundaries between mental behavior and physical behavior.

AS SOON AS ASK understands that mental objects or symbols can be manipulated by Creature and that the consequences of this manipulation matter to Creature's mental states, he will see the need to consider ways of modeling Creature's mental behavior. Ask wonders: *Does Creature think?* And, if so: *How can the import of such thinking to Creature's mental states and to its behavior be modeled?* The problem of knowledge of *other minds*—so intractably hard to analytical philosophers ever since one of them [Russell, 1910] posed it sharply—is one that Ask must resolve as a matter of course in his interactions with Creature.

Ask should, for instance, be able to distinguish between cases in which Creature knows it should do *X* but fails to do so, which are cases of imperfect self-control and self-command (and treated in Chapter 2), and cases of cognitive failures and other mental mishaps wherein Creature may know that *Y* is true and know that the truth of *Y* entails it should do *X* yet fail to do *X* simply because Creature does not know the logical consequences of what it already knows. Ask will also want to distinguish between cases in which Creature's actions can be explained as a choice on the basis of its current options and cases in which Creature *chooses not to choose* but rather to "think about it some more," to reflect on its current option set with the aim of mitigating the uncertainty—or uncovering and resolving otherwise hidden logical inconsistencies—associated with the option set in question. Put this way, the related problems of logical omniscience, logical diligence, and logical sloth acquire a special significance for Ask, who can reasonably query: *When does Creature stop in order to think, and when does Creature stop thinking? When should it stop to think or stop thinking?*

1. LOGICAL OMNISCIENCE, DILIGENCE, AND SLOTH

Consider the following instances of mental acts and mental behaviors that Ask could be called upon to model, predict, or control.

The case of the missing algorithm: Creature is asked to value a lottery that pays $1,000 if the value of some variable x (to five decimal places) is equal to 1.41421 and pays $0 if the value of x is equal to the square root of 2 (correct to five decimal places). Unbeknownst to Creature, it turns out that— to five decimal places—the value of the square root of 2 is 1.41421. Thus, the choice problem is either *ill-posed* (if Ask himself does not know that the square root of 2 to five decimal places is 1.41421) or a *trick* question (if Ask does know this). Suppose Creature chooses to buy the lottery for $10; how is Ask to interpret this choice? As a failure by Creature to engage in the calculations necessary to find out that the two possible outcomes are in fact one and the same? As a deliberate attempt by Creature to "play stupid" in order to somehow make a $990 profit by afterward threatening to sue Ask for defrauding it? Some model of the *kinematics* of Creature's mental states are needed to make progress on this question. In particular: What kind of mental behavior is Creature willing and able to engage in? Relatedly, to what standards of mental behavior should Ask hold Creature if it does in fact engage in this behavior?

The case of the expensive algorithm: Ask first educates Creature on Newton's algorithm for iteratively computing the square root of 2 (starting from an initial guess of 1, say) and then asks Creature to assign a value to a lottery that pays $100 if the value of x to five decimal places is 1.41421 and pays $0 if x equals the square root of 2 to five decimal places. Suppose that Creature assigns a value of $10 to this lottery. What does Ask conclude? That Creature *temporarily forgot* how to compute the square root of 2 at the precise moment in which this was most relevant? Or that it was *not efficient*, on a cost–benefit basis, for Creature to engage in the iterative application of Newton's algorithm to compute the square root of 2 to five decimal places, because Creature values the (estimated) time required for the calculation more highly than the expected benefit of knowing the output of that calculation? This example highlights the need for a model of *the economics* of Creature's mental behavior that will answer such questions as: Under what conditions will it pay for Creature to perform computations prescribed by an algorithm it knows in a situation to which this knowledge is relevant?

A case of imbecility: Creature is told that "all companies in the telecommunications industry 'space' are valued at $N = 3.5$ times annualized quarterly revenue." Creature is then told that C is a firm that operates in this space and is asked to assign a probability (i.e., to bet in accordance with the relevant betting odds) to the statement $S = C$'s value will reflect a 3.5 multiple of its annualized quarterly revenue. Suppose Creature bets in a way that reflects a (risk-aversion-adjusted) personal probability of 0.5, which makes it appear that

Creature has not made use of the "self-evident" rule that if A is true and if A entails B, then the probability of B is 1—a rule that Ask has independently ascertained that Creature knows and believes to be valid. Is Ask justified in assuming that Creature is an *imbecile* in the strict sense that it is unwilling or unable to engage in a low-cost calculation that yields positive-value results? This example might be interpreted to justify an axiom of thought that enjoins Creature to always calculate the logical implications of all the propositions that it knows. But does it justify such an axiom?

A different case of imbecility: Ask teaches Creature (on Thursday 23 November 2080 at 5 p.m.) the algorithm for computing the number π— that is, one quarter of the ratio of the area of a square of side d (i.e., d^2) to that of a circle of diameter d. Ask then observes the following behavior: As of Thursday 30 November 2080 at 5 p.m., a (by now) malnourished, jobless, homeless Creature is still computing the decimal expansion of π according to the algorithm it has learned. When Ask inquires why, Creature replies that it is following the injunction of always calculating the logical consequences of whatever it knows to be the case so that, if it knows that some proposition A is true, it will also come to know all of the logical consequents of A. Is Ask then justified in inferring that requiring *logical omniscience* of Creature also leads to (a different form of) imbecility? If so, then what is the Archimedean point at which Creature thinks "just enough" about something?

Rumination redux: Ask poses to Creature the problem of deciding between two different weight-loss strategies—one based on meditation and the other on dieting and intense physical exercise—and asks Creature (i) to "reason out loud" as it makes its decision by writing down everything that goes through its mind while deliberating and deciding, (ii) to make the decision, and (iii) to act in ways that are consistent with this decision. Creature records all of the personal costs and benefits associated with both courses of action, computes probability estimates on the different assumptions that have entered its calculations, discounts the assumptions by its probability measures defined on the assumptions, recalculates the present value of its costs and benefits in a way that incorporates its personal degrees of belief, assigns probabilities to future states of the world on which the various costs and benefits depend, and then stops. *Why?* "Because," says Creature, "it is now time to make a decision between deciding on the basis of current information and *thinking some more* about the decision." When Creature opts for the latter option (to think some more), it finds that some of its assumptions have changed, that some of its cognitive commitments to the validity of its assumptions have changed, and that some of its degrees of belief about the expected values of future costs and benefits have changed. At this point Creature again stops, and the same episode repeats itself. To Ask's puzzled question, Creature replies that it now faces the same choice: to decide or to think some more. In fact, the process repeats itself for a large number of times (see Figure 4.1), with the overall result that Creature appears to Ask to be ruminating in a decreasingly productive fashion. Ask, reasonably, queries: What, if any, should be the *stopping rules* (for calculative reasoning) to which Ask should try to hold Creature or Creature should hold itself?

Reflection redux: Some might be tempted to legislate *all* ruminative reasoning away, but consider again the problem of the first "imbecile" example. Creature stops to think before assigning a subunitary probability to a tautology (i.e., to B given that it knows both A and the implication "if A then B"), *realizes*—as a result of stopping to think further—that it is indeed betting on a tautology, and revises its probability estimate (to 1). Hence, Ask reasons,

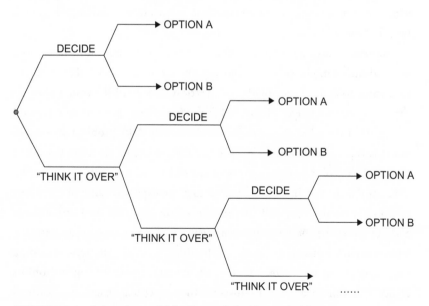

FIGURE 4.1. A recursive model for Creature's decision to decide.

there are cases in which apparently ruminative reasoning is useful, which sets up the obvious follow-up question: Can these cases be captured in a model of Creature's mental behavior that does not, at the same time, turn Creature into an imbecile of either type?

The mental kinematics of betting on a coin toss: Suppose Creature is asked to bet on the next toss of a coin that Creature itself can toss and is given a finite amount of time in which to obtain information that will be useful to its bet. Creature has (at least) the following two options. It can toss the coin as often as possible within the prescribed time—thus treating the coin as a "black box" that is modeled by the random sequence of heads and tails that its tosses yield. Alternatively, Creature can (a) build a *causal* model of an idealized coin toss based on applying its knowledge of Newton's laws, of the gravitational acceleration constant ($g = 9.8$ m/s^2), and of the initial conditions of the coin toss (angular velocity, vertical velocity, height from the ground, etc.) to derive the *range* in the values of the initial conditions that will allow it to predict the outcome of the toss with a certain desired precision; then (b) *practice* tossing the coin until it achieves the required level of control over these variables, thereby iteratively *increasing* the probability that it can exactly predict the outcome of the next toss by increasing the precision with which it can measure and control the independent variables of its causal model of the coin toss.

Suppose that Creature in fact knows classical mechanics sufficiently well to build such a model correctly, and suppose Creature believes that it can, in fact, come to control the angular and vertical velocity of the coin and to estimate the vertical height of its hand at the time of the toss through a period of practice that is less than the period allowed by Ask's problem statement. What is Ask to conclude if Creature, nevertheless, goes with the black-box model of the coin? Is there a component of the "mental costs" of building a model that has nothing to do with either the expected value of the information the model generates or the sum of the marginal and opportunity costs of using the model to generate new information? Endowed with the answer to such a question, Ask should be able to make predictions, regarding the "cognitive style" of Creature, that allow him to make inferences from its choice behavior to entities as "distant" (in conceptual space) as Creature's marginal propensity to engage in causal versus black-box modeling of a particular situation (e.g., to engage in "technical" versus "fundamentals" analysis of a firm's value).

2. COMP: MODELING CREATURE'S MENTAL BEHAVIOR

In order to answer such questions, Ask uses a model that undergirds (often inadvertently and implicitly) the "cognitive revolution" in psychology—namely, a model of Creature's mental states as the computational states of a machine [Turing, 1950]. (See, for instance, Gigerenzer and Goldstein [1996] for a discussion of the concept's impact on the field of cognitive psychology; note that the concept of thinking as "symbol manipulation" is implicit in most of Herbert Simon's theorizing about how minds work.) The computer whose operation serves as a model of the workings of Creature's mind can be as close as one desires to real or ideal computers. Real computers are characterized by finite (and relatively small) read-only and random access memories, finite and configuration-dependent computational resources, and finite rates of information transfer among memories and between memories and computational resources. Idealized computers, such as a Universal Turing Machine (UTM), are characterized by infinite effective memory sizes and negligible interface restrictions; if necessary, they can also be used to emulate the operation of any real computer. Ask has the freedom to define the "operating language" of his computational model of Creature's mental processes and to configure the elementary operations on the resulting computer to be one of two types. Operations may consist of the execution of single, typically assembly-language instructions that command real microprocessors. Alternatively, the computer's operations may consist of the execution of higher-level instructions, such as elementary forms of deductive inference like *modus ponens* and *modus tollens*, that usually depend or supervene on the successful completion of many assembly-language-level instructions for their proper execution. Ask also has the freedom to make assumptions about the kinds of memory features with which the computational model of Creature's mental processes is endowed: Does Creature's mind use more or less memory while working out the solution of a problem? What kinds of memory does it use: the kind that it can access "at will" in a deterministic way, or the kind that can only be accessed probabilistically (depending on "mood," external surroundings, social milieu, or some other state of mind)? Finally, Ask can also choose among various models of the input–output interface that represent the way in which Creature passes information back and forth internally (e.g., by transferring information from its long-term memory into its working memory) or externally (e.g., by "saying," visibly "emoting," or "perceiving").

The canonical computational model places such choices at the discretion of Ask, the model's designer and user. However, what is *not* placed at Ask's design discretion is a "hard core" of basic building blocks for COMP—a canonical model of Creature's mental processes whose purpose is to help Ask make sense of behaviors (including oral noises and visible expressions) that are produced by Creature and may be plausibly assumed to rest on some underlying "mental activity."

1. ALG: The computational processes that model Creature's mental behaviors are *algorithmic* in the sense that each elementary unit of mental behavior is modeled as the execution of an elementary instruction for processing a unit of information such that (a) the output of the execution of each instruction is the input to the execution of the following instruction and (b) the input to the first instruction is a finite unit of information. In this approach, Creature's instantaneous "state of mind" is modeled as a state of an unfolding computational process that is linked to both its precursor and its postcursor by a set of local rules, which may be deterministic or probabilistic in nature.

If Creature's mental states are to be modeled by the computational states of a device, then it is important that Ask rule out nonalgorithmic states in his modeling approach. This does not mean, of course, that nonalgorithmic states of mind do not exist; rather, they do not count in the model that Ask will use to interpret Creature's mental behavior. Thus, Ask uses a model of thought as symbol manipulation without the metaphysical baggage normally associated with that model—namely, the stipulation that mental states *are* nothing but computational states—but rather with the instrumental assumption that nonalgorithmic mental states fall outside the range of applicability of the model insofar as they cannot be reduced to computational states. Ask does not posit that Creature's mental behavior is *nothing but* symbol manipulation operations; rather, Ask posits that such operations are all that the model can refer to. Thus the modeling assumption is a strong one but is not a *metaphysical* one. It does not seek to answer the question *What is the true nature of mental behavior?* but instead the more modest question *What is a model that allows Ask to usefully represent and intervene in Creature's mental behavior by capturing relevant observable and controllable variables?*

2. *FINCONV:* The computational processes used to model Creature's mental behavior must *converge* to an answer or a decision in a *finite* number of operations. Idealized computational devices can run either forever or at infinite speeds—and thus execute an infinite number of operations in a finite amount of time—but Creature's mind is not so endowed. Of course, FINCONV does not require that Creature know ex ante whether or not the problem it is trying to solve is solvable in a finite amount of time by its own mind. Indeed, if the problem with which Creature's mind busies itself is not solvable in a finite number of operations, then FINCONV allows that Creature may *truncate* the processes by which it is trying to solve that problem at a point that is arbitrary or to be determined by further considerations—which may require the deployment of additional constraints, rules, or axioms of the basic model. FINCONV seems to say that Creature will not solve problems it cannot solve. This apparent circularity is not troublesome to Ask, for he interprets it as suggesting that if Creature solves a problem then there exists a computational model that incorporates FINCONV and can be used to represent the process by which Creature solved that problem. Ask understands that this is not an existence proof for COMP or for any of its conditions but instead is a modeling hypothesis, a guidepost for Ask's own modeling efforts.

3. *FINMEM:* The information required by the computational processes that model Creature's mental behaviors—including the "input" data or information partition as well as the set of instructions making up the algorithm that constitutes Creature's mental strategy vis-à-vis solving a particular problem—must be finite. This *finite memory* requirement is not only one that makes the model physically plausible: If we think of memory as somehow physically embodied or realized, then "infinite memory" would entail that Creature had an "infinite brain size." The finiteness requirement is also a restriction on the kinds of computational processes that Ask can deploy to model Creature's mental behavior. With access to an infinite memory, for instance, Creature could simply store all logically possible sentences encoding all physically possible states of nature and develop a class of computationally simple algorithms (lookup tables) for figuring out (a) which one of

the logically possible states of the world the actual and physical world has assumed and (b) what is the optimal action to be taken in such a case. This would make the analysis of the computational complexity of Creature's mental behavior irrelevant, since all computational processes that model mental processes would be at most as complex as that of a table lookup algorithm, and the most interesting part of COMP would be the map of Creature's infinite memory. With finite memory, however, several interesting problems appear for Ask. For example: How does Creature make mental choices between algorithms that use more memory and algorithms that require a greater number of operations until they converge to an answer or to a decision? How does Creature make decisions between algorithms that have different levels of computational complexity, as measured by the number of operations they require to get to a solution, which can take the form of a decision or some other answer?

4. OPT: It is precisely Creature's ability to make such choices that OPT addresses: OPT states that Creature's mental behavior is the result of its choices made in ways that extremize some objective function and that are, in that sense, *optimal*. For example, they may minimize the psychic or physical energy required by Creature to engage in a particular mental behavior subject to attaining an end state; or they could maximize—subject to constraints on time, memory, and computational capacity—the precision or accuracy with which Creature's mental processes calculate the value of a particular variable that Creature finds relevant. The elementary computational operations that are used to model elementary units of Creature's mental behavior have start-up, marginal, and opportunity *costs* as well as short- and long-term *benefits* associated with them. Thus, Ask models Creature's mental behavior as the embodiment of a process of optimization, just as he modeled Creature's mental states as the outcome of an optimization process.

This stipulation leads Ask to the following conundrum: "Meta-mental" behavior is itself mental behavior in that it, too, is modeled as computational and algorithmic. An infinite regress seems to arise from this maneuver: If the optimization process by which Creature chooses its mental behaviors is itself a mental behavior, and if this mental behavior must (*ex hypothesi*) be modeled by a computational process whose costs and benefits can *also* be measured and subjected to a further optimization that is also a computational process, . . . , then will not the resulting *global* model of mental behavior be infinite in a way that is ruled out by FINCONV? Ask's answer is: "Yes, it will; but that is precisely why I deployed FINCONV in the first place." In the words of optimization analysis: Even if the global problem of jointly optimizing thinking, thinking about thinking, thinking about thinking about thinking, and so forth may be uncomputable, it is nevertheless true that each subproblem—say, "optimizing what one thinks about and what kinds of algorithms one deploys in order to think about these problems"—is *not* uncomputable. Thus, given a set of resource constraints and a particular information set, Creature's mental behavior can be declared to be optimal or suboptimal given what it knows or beholds in memory even without being aware of it, and what it can do with what it knows or beholds.

Moreover, since Ask has significant discretion over the practical tailoring of his model to fit his purpose of modeling Creature, he can stipulate that Creature's mental behavior is based on *long-term* or *average-case* optimization processes—and thus distinguish them from Creature's other behavioral choices, which he will take to be based on *short-term* optimization processes. On this view, *how* Creature thinks may be modeled by a set of mental routines or habits that are optimal over a wide range of possible scenarios that Creature might encounter. On the other hand, *what* Creature thinks may be the outcome of interactions between *how* Creature thinks and *what is the case* at any particular moment in time. If criticized for the ad hoc nature of his assumption, Ask will retort (with some irritation) that it is indeed a choice, and no more ad hoc a choice than that made by cognitive psychologists who purport to investigate "the way people think" through forced-choice experiments that fix the time scales on which experimental subjects can think through or make sense of a situation. A choice of time scales on which a behavior is studied, Ask argues, is one of the first choices an experimentalist makes; and it is embarrassing that most experimentalists make this choice implicitly and in ignorance of the consequences. Ask's model acknowledges that the intelligent design of mental behavior may take longer than the intelligent design of physical behavior, but it remains open to new insights about the time scales on which the most relevant mental behavior (changing beliefs, changing the ways in which Creature changes its beliefs) takes place.

3. THE MENTAL ECONOMICS OF SIMPLE CALCULATIONS

OPT sets up the following principle that Ask can deploy to understand Creature's mental behavior.

> INT**. *Interpret each mental behavior as a step in a computational process whose execution is a choice that Creature makes on the basis of operation-level micro-incentives.*

In other words, Creature chooses whether or not to think at each step—and chooses whether or not to think in a particular way—on the basis of a local objective function it is trying to optimize. To articulate this utility function, we need a general characterization of a problem statement: an initial epistemic state from which Creature starts to think. For both deterministic and stochastic variants, problem statements assume the following general form.

> **PROBLEM (DET).** *Find the approximate value A_ε of the answer to the problem of finding (the exact answer) A satisfying conditions $\{C_k\}_{k=1,\ldots,M}$ such that $\|A - A_\varepsilon\| \leq \varepsilon$.*

> **PROBLEM (STOCH).** *Find the approximate value of the answer A_ε to the problem of finding (the exact answer) A satisfying conditions $\{C_k\}_{k=1,\ldots,M}$ such that $\Pr(\|A - A_\varepsilon\| \leq \varepsilon) \leq P_{\text{threshold}}$.*

In the *deterministic* version of a problem statement, Creature looks for a "good enough" answer, as measured by the distance ε between the approximate answer A_ε and the exact answer A. In the *probabilistic* or stochastic version of the problem statement, Creature looks for an approximate answer that is "likely" to be within an acceptable distance of the exact answer, where "likely" is measured by the threshold probability $P_{\text{threshold}}$. In either case, Creature's local mental behavior—a single "calculation" or "operation" aimed at getting it closer to the answer in question—can be understood as being regulated by a local objective function that informs Creature's choice to "stop thinking" or to "think further."

Two principal factors enter into the calculating this objective function: the computational costs and benefits. *Computational costs* include the following.

1. Creature's start-up costs C_S(PROB), the costs of articulating the problem statement and the solution algorithm and beholding them in working memory along with the information needed to solve the problem by applying the algorithm to the data.

2. Creature's marginal costs $c_M[n]$ of a computation (operation), indexed by n, using the solution algorithm it has chosen.

3. Creature's opportunity cost $c_O[n]$ of one additional computation (operation) using the chosen solution algorithm; this represents the cost of forgone opportunities for Creature to think about other matters, engage with other tasks, or try out a new algorithm on the same problem.

4. Creature's "along-the-way anxiety" cost $c_{atwa}[n]$, which is the cost of Creature's incremental "worry" about whether or not its solution algorithm will converge to an answer within the specified tolerance level within the allotted amount of time (past which the value of an answer begins to decrease or vanishes altogether).

The *computational benefits* of a local calculation may be summarized as follows.

1. Creature's marginal benefit $b_m[n]$ of one additional computation (operation), indexed by n, as prescribed by the solution algorithm. This benefit can be measured in terms of the number of *bits of information* by which Creature is closer to the acceptable answer A_ε, after performing the nth operation, multiplied by the *value* or *utility* of one additional bit of information about A_ε. If Creature does know how many more bits of information the next computation will bring, then it can *extrapolate* the function that relates information gain to iteration number (i.e., $b_m[1], \ldots, b_m[n-1]$) by using a more or less sophisticated "extrapolator" function that will be linear in the simplest case: $b_m[n] = n(\partial b[k]/\partial k)$, where $k = 1, \ldots,$ $n - 1$. For stochastic problem statements, the informational gain can be measured by the *decrease* in the entropy associated with the probability distribution function of A_ε multiplied by the utility of that decrease to Creature: $b_M = -\delta H(P_{A_\varepsilon}(A_\varepsilon)) \times U(\delta H(P_{A_\varepsilon}(A_\varepsilon)))$.

2. Creature's long-term benefits B_L of having carried out a computation or operation of a particular kind (i.e., its "learning by doing"

benefits), which are realized if Creature completes the computational process of solving the problem. That is, $B_L = 0$ for $n < N_{tot}$, where N_{tot} denotes the total number of operations needed to arrive at A_ε.

Equipped with this framework for interpreting micro-local mental behavior, Ask can derive Creature's objective function for a problem-directed thinking episode that takes up N_{tot} operations as follows:

$$U(P, \alpha, N_{tot}, A_\varepsilon) = -C_S + \sum_{n=1;n\in\alpha}^{N_{tot}} \{F(b_m[n]) + B_L\delta(n - N_{tot}) \\ - c_m[n] - c_O[n] - G(c_{atwa}[n])\}, \tag{1}$$

where α denotes the algorithm that Creature has used to attempt to solve problem P; $F(\cdot)$ and $G(\cdot)$ are monotonically increasing functions; and $\delta(\cdot)$ is the Kronecker delta function. The implicit discount rate for the process is set to 0 here, but for long calculations or reasoning processes this rate may become relevant and can be inserted into the model without loss of generality. If Ask assumes, to make matters simpler, that Creature's start-up and opportunity costs are 0, that Creature is not capable of computing (and so is not aware of) the long-term benefit of completing the calculation to its end, and that $F(\cdot) = G(\cdot) = 1$, then Ask will predict that, at the margin, Creature will engage in the nth computation (operation) if

$$b_m[n] - c_m[n] - c_{atwa}[n] \geq 0: \tag{2}$$

in other words, if its marginal net benefit of an additional computation is weakly positive. This "marginal local utility of thinking" analysis allows Ask—based on his own knowledge of the problem that Creature is trying to solve, the algorithm it is using to solve the problem, and estimates of Creature's marginal costs and benefits—to make predictions regarding Creature's *marginal propensity to think further* about a particular problem whenever Creature is actually thinking about the problem in question. By observing Creature as it "reasons out loud" through a well-defined problem, Ask may also attempt to infer Creature's marginal benefit of an additional operation.

Ask can also *calculate* the marginal benefit of an additional computation from the problem statement and knowledge of the algorithm that Creature is likely to use to solve the problem for a wide class of problems—as will be elaborated in what follows. If Ask assumes that the marginal cost to Creature of an additional mental operation is constant, then the critical term in inequality (2), the expression for the marginal utility of an additional calculation, is Creature's along-the-way anxiety cost of an additional computation, $c_{atwa}[n]$. Creature's along-the-way anxiety at operation n should rise if Creature feels it is "not making progress" toward a satisfactory answer (e.g., if the net benefit of the previous computation is 0 or negative), and it should fall if Creature believes that it *is* making satisfactory progress toward an acceptable answer. The problem for Ask, of course, is to figure out what counts or should count *for Creature* as "satisfactory progress toward an acceptable answer."

In order to do this, Ask must develop a model of the *rate* at which Creature's solution algorithm produces useful information—which gets Creature closer to an answer. Call this rate $r_I(\alpha, n)$ (measured in bits per operation n and specific to algorithm α) and suppose the rate is tracked by Creature as it computes A_g. Then, at the nth iteration of the solution algorithm α, Creature (provided it has made no errors in applying α to its problem statement) will have generated $\sum_{k=1}^{n} r_I(\alpha, k)$ useful bits of information. Provided that a total of I_A bits of information are needed to get Creature from the problem statement P to the good enough answer A_g, Creature's along-the-way anxiety should measure the difference between the total amount of information needed to get to the good enough answer and the useful information its calculations have already produced—that is, $c_{atwa} = L\left(I_A - \sum_{k=1}^{n} r_I(\alpha, k)\right)$, where $L(\cdot)$ is a nondecreasing, well-behaved (continuous and at-least-once-differentiable) function. Thus, if Creature knows that it has N_{tot} operations in which to generate I_A bits of information, then at iteration n it should also know (provided it knows at least the first-order logical consequences of what it knows) that it has $N_{tot} - n$ operations in which to generate $I_A - \sum_{k=1}^{n} r_I(\alpha, k)$ bits of information and *worries* in proportion to the information that it still has to produce in order to get to a good enough answer in a short enough time (measured by N_{tot} in this case). This analysis of c_{atwa} works well enough to give Ask an "anxiety meter" for testing whether Creature knows just how much information it needs to produce to move from a state of zero knowledge about A to a state of knowledge of A that is at least equal to A_g.

But what happens when Creature does *not* know the total amount of information it has to produce to get an answer, let alone the total number of steps that *should* take Creature from a state of zero knowledge to a state of satisfactory knowledge? After all, computational complexity theory, the theoretical analysis of computational processes, and operations research are all disciplines that have developed precisely in response to the desire of many Creatures for ready-to-hand *measures* of the number of operations that a satisfactory solution to a particular problem will take *before* attempting to solve a problem, but their application is not part of everyone's skill base. Hence Ask would not be justified to assume, in general, that Creature will have special insight into the computational complexity of its own thought processes, or that Creature will be able to optimize its thinking on the basis of anything other than the most local sorts of optimization.

Nevertheless, most untrained Creatures have some "primitive intuition" about how difficult solving a certain problem will be for them. Because they are untrained in the art of estimating the computational complexity of a problem before attempting to solve it, it must be—reasons Ask—that a Creature's hunch and intuition about the difficulty of the problem it faces has to do with the instantaneous epistemic state in which it finds itself when looking at the problem statement. It is of great interest to Ask to come up with estimates of the types of functions that could represent the dependence of Creature's along-the-way anxiety on its current epistemic state. The simplest (and perhaps most intuitive) such estimate is to make Creature's along-the-way anxiety cost of the kth computation track the *marginal changes in the benefit* of the $(k-1)$th and $(k-2)$th operation (i.e., $c_{\mathrm{atwa}}[k] = C(b[k-2] - b[k-1])$), so that if the $(k-1)$th operation produces *fewer* bits of information than does the $(k-2)$th operation then $c_{\mathrm{atwa}}[k]$ is positive and is a real cost, whereas if the $(k-1)$th operation produces *fewer* bits of information than does the $(k-2)$th operation then $c_{\mathrm{atwa}}[k]$ is negative and can be interpreted as a *confidence boost* due to local progress. The along-the-way anxiety cost of more sophisticated Creatures can be modeled as more sophisticated estimates of the marginal informational gain of each operation. Note that if Creature uses the same extrapolation methods to estimate the net informational gain of the kth computation and the along-the-way anxiety cost of that computation, then the only way that the marginal net benefit and marginal along-the-way anxiety cost of the kth computation would *not* cancel each other out is for the functional dependence of Creature's utility and along-the-way anxiety on its informational gain to differ from each other ($F(x) \neq G(x)$) or for Creature to weigh psychic costs and psychic benefits differently.

How does this analysis work in the case of an actual problem? Consider a situation in which Creature is engaged in computing the exact value of x (i.e., with $\varepsilon = 0$) such that x satisfies the equation $5x + 2 = 3x + 1$. At each step of its thinking through this problem, Creature is trying to minimize the spread of the probability distribution function of its answer, x_A. Assume Creature has understood the problem statement and knows the basic algorithm for solving the problem, which goes roughly like this: "Group all terms in x on one side of the equality sign, group all constant terms on the other side, divide the resulting constant term by the coefficient of x, and observe the addition and multiplication rules of arithmetic (and their inverses) as well as the rule that taking any term across the equality sign changes its sign (from negative to positive and vice versa)." Now consider a plausible version of Creature's step-by-step process of thinking its way to a solution.

Step 1: If Creature is asked to "eyeball" x based on the problem statement alone, without giving it any time to "crank through" an application of the algorithm, then it might reasonably estimate that x should be less than 0 (it can be quickly verified that no positive x will satisfy the equation) but greater than -10 (again, based on quick verification). Lacking further information, Creature will assign a uniform probability distribution function to the values of x in the interval $(0, -10)$.

Step 2: Following the algorithm it knows, Creature groups the terms of the equation that end in x on the left-hand side of the equality sign (and the constant terms on the right-hand side) and then carries out the additions and subtractions according to the rules of arithmetic to arrive at $-2x = 1$. Now, *without* performing the division by 2, Creature can eyeball the value of x and narrow its estimate to a value in the range $(-1, 0)$, thus narrowing its probabilistic estimate of the value of x to the uniform probability distribution function on $(-1, 0)$. So, if pressed at this point of its calculation, Creature can do better than it could do at the end of Step 1 but may still not be able to narrow its estimate of x down to a single value.

Step 3: Creature now carries out the division by 2 to obtain $x_A = -1/2$, thereby narrowing its probabilistic estimate for the value of x to a large (but still subunitary) probability—for example, $\Pr(x_A = -1/2) = 0.99999$. Ask can extract this information from Creature either by asking it directly or by offering Creature suitable bets on the value of x lying in various ranges.

Step 4: To get from this estimate to "certainty" (i.e., to $\Pr(x_A = -1/2) = 1$), Creature verifies its estimate by plugging $x_A = -1/2$ back into the equation in the problem statement (i.e., into $5x_A + 2 = 3x_A + 1$ and gets $5(-1/2) + 2 = -1/2 = 3(-1/2) + 1$, which indeed confirms the result of its calculation and allows it to finalize its probability estimate to $\Pr(x_A = -1/2) = 1$.

Creature's sequence of epistemic states vis-à-vis the value of x_A is summarized in Table 4.1. Ask can become far more precise when analyzing Creature's marginal net benefit (of using a particular algorithm to think further about a problem) by calculating in advance the marginal informational benefit of an additional computation at each step of applying the algorithm that Creature will apply to the problem statement. To do so, Ask needs to compute the benefit to Creature of each additional application of the algorithm to its problem statement, which he can accomplish by asking: "How many additional bits of information does the nth operation in the algorithm give Creature?" This, in

TABLE 4.1. Creature's Epistemic States as a Function of Progress
              in a Simple Calculation

Computational step and updated problem statement at end of step	Verbal description of step	Range in estimate of x_A	Probability estimate $P(x_A)$
1: *Find x_A satisfying* $3x + 1 = 5x + 2$ *such that* $P(x = x_A) = 1$	Behold problem statement and store in short-term memory; perform quick computation to find initial range for x_A	$-10 < x_A < 0$	$P(x_A)$ is uniform on $-10 < x_A < 0$, $P(x_A) = 0$ outside $-10 < x_A < 0$
2: *Find x_A satisfying* $-2x_A = 1$	Group like terms on same side of equality sign, minding rule for sign change of numbers across equality sign; carry out additions and subtractions	$-1 < x_A < 0$	$P(x_A)$ is uniform on $-1 < x_A < 0$, $P(x_A) = 0$ outside $-1 < x_A < 0$
3: $x_A = 1/(-2)$	Carry out the division of the constant term by the coefficient of x_A	$x_A = -1/2$	$P(x_A = -1/2) = 0.9999$, $P(-1 < x_A < 0; x_A \neq -1/2) = 0.0001$
4: *Check that* $3(-1/2) + 2 = -1/2$; $5(-1/2) + 1$	Verify that x_A satisfies the problem statement	$x_A = -1/2$	$P(x_A = -1/2) = 1$

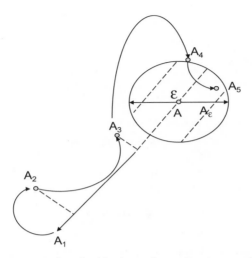

FIGURE 4.2. Dynamics of an algorithmic set of operations in a search space. *Key:* Here A denotes the exact answer and ε is the diameter of an acceptable error region around A; the A_k are successive approximations of A, outputs of successive iterations of the solution algorithm.

turn, will inform the more important question: "How much closer will the nth iteration of α get one to an acceptable estimate A_ε?" See Figure 4.2. To be sure, Ask will have to address this question with respect to each particular algorithm α that he believes Creature is using to solve a problem, so he will require knowledge of both the problem statement and the solution algorithm.

To exemplify the use of this pico-analysis of thinking, consider once again the case where Creature is attempting to find the value of the square root of 2 correct to five decimal places (i.e., 1.41421) using Newton's algorithm for estimating the root of an equation, setting $x^2 - 2 = 0 = f(x)$ in this case. Here $\varepsilon = 0.00001$, which means that Creature will be indifferent between the answer 1.414212 and 1.414214 or that a "good enough" approximation to the square root of 2 lies between 1.414205 and 1.414215 (i.e., $1.414205 \leq A_\varepsilon \leq 1.414215$). Newton's algorithm is based on first picking two numbers, A_0 and a_0, that bound A (the square root of 2) from above and below, respectively (i.e., $a_0 < \sqrt{2} < A_0$), and then sequentially narrowing the interval that contains A (until its magnitude falls below ε) via the following update equations.

Update for A_0:

$$A_{n+1} = A_n - \frac{f(A_n)}{f'(A_n)}. \tag{3}$$

Update for a_0:

$$a_{n+1} = \frac{a_n(f(A_n) - f(a_n))}{A_n - a_n} - \frac{f(a_n)(A_n - a_n)}{f(A_n) - f(a_n)}. \tag{4}$$

Assuming Creature starts with initial estimates ($A_0 = 2$; $a_0 = 1$) at step $n = 0$, its "progress" through the calculation from step n to step $n + 1$ can be calculated in terms of the number of (decimal) units of information ("digits," hence the base 10 for the log function) via $I_{n:n+1} = \log_{10}[(A_n - a_n)/(A_{n+1} - a_{n+1})]$, which yields the results (up to $n = 3$) shown in Table 4.2.

Given this calculation, Ask can, after each step, perform "surgical" inquiries into Creature's epistemic states vis-à-vis x_A—by asking it for verbal estimates of the value of x_A, by getting Creature to lay bets on the value of x_A after each operation, or by asking it for verbal estimates of the probability that x_A falls in any particular range R, under the safeguard of a $\log(\Pr(x_A \in R))$ contract that Ask gets Creature to accept beforehand. Thus armed, Ask can perform "intrusive" experiments into Creature's mental behavior by interrupting Creature at various steps in its thinking process and asking it to make estimates, bets, or predictions regarding the answer to the problem it is thinking its way through—possibly, again, safeguarded by incentive contracts aimed to extract maximally truthlike estimates of probabilities from Creature.

Because it has a reliable estimate of the marginal benefit of each additional calculation to Creature—and assuming that opportunity costs are nil and that marginal costs of additional calculations are constant—Ask can figure out if Creature's mental behavior is "rational" in the sense that Creature

TABLE 4.2. Information Gain from Iterating Recursive Algorithm for Calculating the Square Root of 2

Step $n =$	A_n	a_n	Information gain from previous step (digits)
0	2	0	—
1	1.5	1	0.60205
2	1.4	1.41666...	1.47771
3	1.41420	1.41422	3.06042

proceeds to the next computation only if and when the net benefit derived from this computation is positive. For instance, it is clear from Table 4.2 that (a) the third iteration yields handsome payoffs for Creature in terms of additional precision in its estimate of the square root of 2 and (b) the marginal benefit of an additional computation increases from $n = 1$ to $n = 3$. Given this information, Ask can find Creature's mental behavior "irrational" if Creature gives up on its computation at $n = 2$ (claiming that "this is too hard") even though the marginal benefits of the previous two computations were positive and increasing. Ask may attribute Creature's truncation of the computation to a spike in its along-the-way anxiety costs—which Ask will find to be irrational because Creature's decision to stop calculating is not based on a decrease in the marginal benefits of additional computations.

Of course, such an independent estimate of the calculation's local payoff landscape may not be available. Creature's calculative processes may not always be representable by an algorithm that is as well-behaved as that of Newton's algorithm for calculating the square root of 2 to n decimal places. In this case, Ask will want to revise his model of Creature's internal economics of thinking to take into account not only Creature's subjective perception of the costs and benefits of each additional operation but also Creature's choice of a solution algorithm, since a practical problem that Creature faces may have many different solution algorithms for any one problem that, moreover, satisfy different criteria for accuracy and convergence.

A promising candidate for a building block for such a model is the entropy measure introduced in the previous chapter as a measure of uncertainty. Ask can model Creature's internal thinking processes as a set of serial operations individually and jointly aimed at mitigating the uncertainty "cloud" around the answer that Creature is trying to calculate; see Figure 4.3. Suppose that Creature's degrees of belief about where the answer A might lie before performing any calculation (along a line for a 1-dimensional problem, in a hyperplane for an n-dimensional problem) can be represented by a (discrete, in this case, but possibly continuous) probability distribution function $P_n(A_n)$, where $\{A_n\}$ are Creature's guesses at the possible values of A. Then Creature's uncertainty in its "dead reckoning" state of mind—before it begins to crank through its calculations—can be measured by the entropy of $P_n(A_n)$; that is, $H_0(p_n(A_n)) = -\sum_n p_n \log_2(p_n)$. At each operation in a sequence of

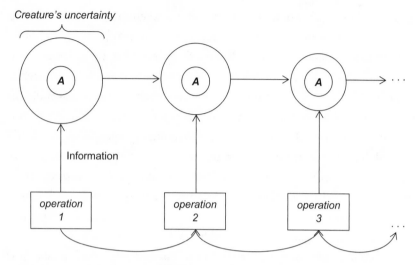

FIGURE 4.3. Calculation modeled as an information-producing process. *Note:* Each individual operation reduces the uncertainty (as measured by the entropy) associated with Creature's guess at an answer, whose exact value is denoted by *A*.

operations corresponding to a uniformly convergent algorithm, Creature's uncertainty (modeled by the entropy of the probability density function of its estimates of the answer) is reduced by the production of new and relevant information: Computation-driven information gain drives the benefit of each new operation to Creature. Thus, if the *k*th operation in the sequence produces β_k bits of information, then Creature's uncertainty at the *k*th step will have decreased from H_{k-1} to $H_{k-1} - \beta_k$. After *k* operations, the entropy measure of Creature's degrees of belief regarding the range of possible answers will be $H_k = H_0 - \sum_{i=1}^{k} \beta_i$, from which Ask can calculate—at any point along the way—the information that Creature estimates it needs to reach the answer *A* (i.e., $I_k = H_k$ if Creature is aiming for an exact answer, one about which Creature's uncertainty will be 0).

Using this simple model for the relationship among computation, information, and uncertainty, Ask can build a more elaborate model for Creature's marginal benefit of an additional calculation and its along-the-way anxiety cost of each additional operation. Hence Ask can make even tighter predictions about the relationship between (a) Creature's natural ability for performing calculations of a particular type (measured by the inverse of its marginal cost of an operation), (b) Creature's "state of mind" and proneness to the kind of anxiety that pre-empts or aborts its calculative activities, and (c) Creature's foresight and insight regarding the local marginal benefit of thinking. To do this, Ask needs something akin to the more elaborate model of Figure 4.4, where Creature's thinking process is modeled as a succession of states of a computational device that is represented by a Turing Machine. Each one of Creature's elementary thinking steps is represented by an operation of the Turing Machine (or algorithm) chosen to represent Creature's thinking process. Therefore, at each step along the path of its thinking, Ask will model Creature as making a *mental choice* between stopping—and using the approximation to the answer that is currently available—or continuing to think about the problem (and aiming to refine its approximation by reducing the uncertainty around its current estimate of the answer). This choice (Figure 4.4) is driven by Creature's subjective costs and benefits of performing an additional calculation. If each operation k changes Creature's uncertainty from H_{k-1} to H_k, then Creature might estimate the benefit of an additional calculation to be proportional to (or to be a monotonically

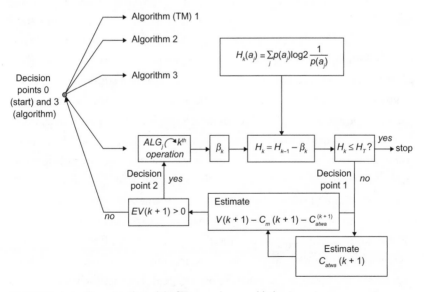

FIGURE 4.4. Functional model of Creature's mental behavior using an operation-by-operation uncertainty metric (entropy), an uncertainty-dependent net-benefit function, and an uncertainty-dependent set of stopping and switching rules.

increasing function of) the difference $H_{k-1} - H_k$; that is, $v_k - v_0(H_{k-1} - H_k)$. Moreover, Ask models Creature's along-the-way anxiety cost as being proportional to (or a monotonically increasing function of) H_{k-1}: $c_{atwa} = c_0 H_{k-1}$. The model entails that Creature reacts, without foresight, to its own instantaneous epistemic state and the "anxiety" that it triggers—which is Ask's zeroth-order approximation to the way in which the fear of thinking further works in human creatures. Assuming that the marginal cost of an additional operation (net of Creature's along-the-way anxiety cost) is a constant c_m, Ask can estimate the net benefit of the kth operation for Creature as $v_N(k) = v_0 (H_{k-1} - H_k) - c_m - c_0 H_{k-1}$. This measure of Creature's psychic utility of an additional calculation can be used to predict whether or not Creature will use a particular solution procedure or algorithm to "think further" about a problem.

Ask will require one more element in his model, and that is a set of *stopping rules* for Creature (the stopping rules are marked in Figure 4.4's block diagram of the model). A *positive* stopping rule tells Creature when to stop calculating—either because it has reached the exact answer it required or (more realistically) because it has arrived at an approximation that is close enough to the answer it required. Ask can model this proximity by the *tolerance* or the *spread* of values of the answer that Creature sees at any point during its thinking process or by a threshold *entropy* of Creature's subjective probability distribution H_T over the range of possible answers. The test *Is H_k either less than or equal to H_T?* gives Ask the required stopping rule for his model of Creature's thinking process: Creature will stop thinking (about a particular problem, using a particular algorithm) if $H_k \leq H_T$; otherwise, it will continue. Ask's model also contains a *negative* stopping rule, which takes effect when Creature's net benefit for an additional operation drops below 0—that is, when $v_0(H_{k-1} - H_k) - c_m - c_0 H_{k-1} < 0$. This rule tells Creature when to stop calculating because the path it has taken (the algorithm it has chosen) leads it progressively *farther from* the answer with each operation.

Ask knows better than to assume that, once stopped, Creature reverts to a vegetable-like state of mind (and "does nothing"). He remembers his own injunction that Creatures never "do nothing" and that their behaviors always have a positive content. Ask therefore conjectures that, once Creature realizes that its current algorithm no longer returns positive per-operation net benefits, it may widen its search to other algorithms that could provide a solution to its problem (see Figure 4.4). Thus Ask's model allows that Creature can make both intra-algorithm and inter-algorithm choices, which can be modeled as value-maximizing acts using the entropy-dependent net-benefit measure just described. By the logic of the model, Creature will choose the algorithm (the associated Turing Machine in Ask's model of Creature's thinking) that minimizes the prior entropy of its probabilistic estimate of the answer; that is, Creature will choose so as to minimize $H^0_{\mathrm{TM}_i}$, the entropy of its estimate of the answer using the ith Turing Machine (algorithm) at step 0. There is a sense in which Creature's algorithms function like lenses through which it perceives the answers to its problems.

Having developed this more precise model of Creature's mental states, Ask can now perform experiments, similar to those put forth in the previous chapter, that aim to probe Creature's anxiety-proneness and resourcefulness.

THOUGHT EXPERIMENT 4.1

Ask tests for Creature's *marginal cost of calculating* by subjecting it to a computationally difficult task ("calculate the Nash equilibria of a competitive game using iterated elimination of dominated strategies") in a nonstressful setting (no punishment for inexact or incorrect answer or for delays above a certain threshold). Ask can then repeat the test under stressful conditions (time constraint, large error and delay penalties) and record the number of operations that Creature performs under the new conditions. Now, Ask can compare the two results. The difference can be accounted for by the along-the-way anxiety cost, which kicks in as a result of the error and delay penalties that Ask imposes on Creature by the structure of the problem statement.

Ask can also turn this experiment into a device for measuring the susceptibility of Creature's calculative reasoning process to visceral or emotional factors that (a) decrease Creature's capacity for thinking in a clear, connected fashion and (b) introduce additional costs, in the form of suboptimal mental behaviors, into Creature's thinking process.

Ask can also check for Creature's resourcefulness in finding alternative or additional ways of solving the problem (algorithms), as follows.

THOUGHT EXPERIMENT 4.2

Ask repeats Thought Experiment 4.1 after equipping Creature with several different algorithms for computing Nash equilibria and records Creature's solutions and solution times when Creature uses each one of these algorithms. Ask can then infer, using the model in Figure 4.4, Creature's algorithm-specific marginal cost of calculating for each algorithm. Then, after ensuring that Creature understands all the algorithms it can use and establishing stressful conditions (large penalties for both error and delay), Ask can use reasoning-out-loud protocols to test for Creature's stopping rules *within* an algorithm ("when does Creature stop calculating because it cannot 'see its way' to an answer any longer?") and switching rules *between* algorithms ("when does Creature switch algorithms?") for the same problem.

Ask can use such experiments in combination with the models BET and BEL to probe even more deeply into Creature's thought processes and local epistemic states as it is calculating. Guided by the imagery of Figure 4.3 for the way in which calculation can reduce subjective uncertainty and thus computation-driven uncertainty, Ask can elicit from Creature a sequence of bets that the answer to its problem lies in a particular range $A_L \leq A \leq A_H$ and then measure the increase in the betting odds that Creature is willing to take on the answer's lying in that range as a function of the number of operations (or the amount of time) that Creature has already expended. The increase in the betting odds that Creature is willing to take should track the decrease in Creature's uncertainty about where the answer lies.

The moral of this modeling strategy is simple: Creature sees its way to an answer to a problem through the prism of the algorithm it applies to that problem. Each operation corresponds to a sharpening of the focus with which Creature sees the answer and aims to narrow the uncertainty Creature currently perceives as a cloud that surrounds its estimate of the answer. The modeling approach allows Ask to probe into Creature's thought processes by getting it to make choices or lay bets—or by observing its verbal behavior, as in the case of reasoning-out-loud protocols—and to make plausible and informed inferences from Creature's physical behavior to its mental behavior.

4. CANONICAL ALGORITHMS AS THOUGHT ENGINES

Ask needs one more element in his computational model of Creature's mental behavior, and that is a set of basic mental routines or ways of describing
Creature's "cognitive productions" (see Newell and Simon [1972]; Newell
[1990]); he needs a set of basic *algorithms* (sets of logically linked operations)
that can be used to model Creature's mental behavior. A *model* of Creature's
mental behavior serves as a prototype and can be used to produce a *map* of
any of a large number of such behaviors. Hence Ask would like to have a
way of characterizing, in a canonical fashion, Creature's *mental production
function(s)*—the set of algorithms that typically pattern and shape Creature's
thinking. He will be concerned, then, by such questions as *How much representational power does the concept of an algorithm give me?* and *How large a
library of canonical algorithms must I build in order to be a competent modeler of
Creature's mental behavior?*

Suppose Creature is attempting to solve the problem of picking out the
largest number from the list (213, 7, 4, 8, 9, 1120, 3678, 3198, 4111, 2101).
Ask might model what Creature's mind does in order to accomplish its task
by an algorithm, MAX, which bids Creature to (a) focus on the first two
numbers on the list, (b) compare them in magnitude, (c) place the smaller
number first and the larger number last, (d) move on to the next pair on the
list and perform the same operations, and (e) repeat (a)–(d) until the end
of the list is reached. Of course, Creature may use its mind in ways that are
different from those prescribed by MAX. It may first just pick the 4-digit
numbers and compare them to one another, and it may compare the first
digit of the 4-digit numbers it has identified to more quickly select the largest number. This would be a simplification of MAX for this particular case,
one based on Creature's incorporation of problem-specific information in its
design of a search algorithm; however, the simplification will not work as well
in other situations (e.g., when there are many 4-digit numbers to choose from
or when some 4-digit numbers have decimal points). What MAX gives Ask
is an intuitive, mechanical, first-level representation of Creature's mental behaviors, one that Creature can employ for a "brute force" solution. Ask thinks
of MAX as a *best worst-case* algorithm: best because it is reliable and "performs" in all plausible sorting scenarios of this kind; worst because it is more
complex than many possible shortcuts that Creature might take to picking

the largest number. Its "algorithmicity" is the essential part that Ask is after, since it allows Ask to understand Creature's mental behaviors as being simultaneously rule-bound and incentive-sensitive and also to model Creature's "innovations" in problem solving via shortcuts and improvements vis-à-vis a canonical, best worst-case scenario.

Thus conceived, algorithms are integral to most of the models that Ask uses to make sense of Creature's behaviors. Even models (such as DEC) of the ways in which Creature produces purposive, intelligent behavior require that Creature perform a set of identifiable, linked, rule-bound operations that allow it to figure out what it prefers from a list of possible options—that is, at least partially sort a list of options in descending (or ascending) order of value in answer to the question *What do I want to do in situation X?* Descriptive and normative approaches to explaining Creature's choice processes are usually silent about the computation required of Creature before it can make a "rational" choice; therefore, appeals to "bounded rationality" or "biased decision making" to explain deviations of Creature's behavior from normatively mandated patterns of behavior are not tethered to a specific analysis of exactly what is bounded, how it is bounded, and why it is bounded because the "algorithms of rationality" have not been specified. Introducing specific algorithms into his models of Creature's behavior allows Ask to venture hypotheses about cases and conditions in which Creature does not want to perform the calculations necessary for the instantiation of a rational choice because it is not in Creature's all-things-considered best interest to do so—perhaps because the computational costs of a comprehensive optimization process are too large with respect to the expected value of the benefits. In everyday language, Creature might say "it is not worth thinking about," a seemingly uninformative turn of phrase that Ask finds deeply interesting. The circumscription of such scenarios allows Ask to posit a zone of *cognitive indifference* for Creature, a zone wherein Creature does not have sufficient local incentives to engage in the rule-bound reasoning required to instantiate a rational "decision process."

Since an algorithm can be understood as a progression of linked epistemic states and since ascribing an algorithm to a Creature requires some knowledge of these states, it follows that knowledge of what Creature is likely to know and to do with what it knows—and when and under what circumstances—is important for producing viable models of Creature's mental behavior.

In particular, what matters to the production of such a model is *who knows what when*, as follows:

1. *Ask's knowledge* of the algorithm that models Creature's mental behavior and of its complexity allows Ask to figure out the total computational cost of producing the mental behavior that is modeled by the algorithm;

2. *Creature's knowledge* of the algorithm that models its own mental behavior and of its total computational costs allows Creature to make cognitive choices that are sensitive to *global* costs and benefits in producing certain thought patterns;

3. *Ask's knowledge of Creature's knowledge* of the algorithm that models Creature's mental behavior allows Ask to reasonably *ascribe* to Creature a (meta-cognitive) process by which Creature rationally plans its overall mental activity;

4. *Ask's knowledge* of the marginal benefit (to Creature) of an additional calculation—within the context of an algorithm that it has deployed to solve a particular problem—allows Ask to calculate Creature's *local* mental behavior (*when to stop thinking?*) as a function of the local or along-the-way cost–benefit ratio of an additional calculation, provided that this mental behavior is driven by local cost–benefit calculations performed by Creature;

5. *Creature's knowledge* of the marginal benefit (to itself) of an additional calculation—within the context of an algorithm that it has deployed to solve a particular problem—allows Creature to locally adapt its mental behavior (*when to stop thinking?*) as a function of the local or along-the-way cost–benefit ratio of an additional calculation;

6. *Ask's knowledge of Creature's knowledge* of the marginal benefit (to itself) of an additional calculation—within the context of an algorithm that it has deployed to solve a particular problem—allows Ask to validly ascribe to Creature locally adaptive mental behavior (*when to stop thinking?*) as a function of the local or along-the-way cost–benefit ratio of an additional calculation.

Of course, not all of this knowledge is necessary, and Ask can make much progress by making reasonable assumptions along the way. The algorithmic picture of Creature's mental states and processes is a useful schema in part because it is adaptive to situations in which Ask has more or less information about Creature's mind.

How does this work in practice? If Creature is trying to compute the value of the square root of 2 to three decimal places (i.e., 1.414) using Newton's algorithm, then Creature can be understood (from the binary representation of 1.414) as attempting to generate approximately 5.13 bits of information. Each iteration of the algorithm requires 18 operations, and the first three iterations produce (respectively) 0.60, 1.47, and 3.06 bits of information. Given this "computational landscape" of Creature's thinking, Ask can proceed to model Creature's mental behavior as follows. If Creature knows the information production rate of its algorithm (Table 4.3) and can estimate its cost per operation before it begins computing, then it can figure out whether or not it is worthwhile to engage in each additional operation. If Ask has this information as well, then he can also calculate whether or not it is worth Creature's while to compute the required quantity. If Ask knows that Creature knows the computational landscapes of its own thought process, then he can interpret Creature's mental behavior as being responsive to the cost–benefit calculus of thinking one step further. It may seem that Creature cannot know how many bits of information the successful completion of an operation will bring it, but this appearance is misleading. The number of bits of new information resulting from a calculation does not necessarily determine Creature's epistemic state after the operation, and there are situations (to be described in what follows) in which Creature can have a good estimate of the amount of information that the execution of an operation will bring it before actually carrying out the operation.

On the other hand, if Ask does *not* know the full computational landscape of Creature's thought process but can at least locally estimate the number

TABLE 4.3. Creature's Computational Landscape for Calculating the Numerical Value of the Square Root of 2 to Three Decimal Places

Step $n =$	A_n	a_n	Information gain from previous step (digits)	Number of operations/iterations required to produce estimate
0	2	0	—	—
1	1.5	1	0.60205	18
2	1.4	1.41666...	1.47771	18
3	1.41420	1.41422	3.06042	18

of bits produced per operation, the number of operations per iteration, and Creature's personal (psychic or even physiological) cost per operation, then he can still make conjectures about Creature's local tendency to engage in one more calculation. If Creature does not know its own full computational landscape but can estimate its local costs and benefits for an additional operation or iteration (i.e., if Creature knows or can estimate the bits generated per iteration and the number of operations per iteration at Step 1 in Table 4.3 just before it attempts the first iteration), then it can make locally cost–benefit-sensitive adaptations in its thinking patterns. Finally, if Ask knows that Creature knows the local computational cost and informational benefit of each operation or iteration, then he can ascribe to Creature boundedly but intendedly rational adaptations to its cost–benefit calculations.

Algorithms are useful things for Ask to know about because (a) they are basic building blocks for interpreting mental behavior and (b) they can be used to generate the micro-local costs and benefits of thinking—the computational landscape of Creature's mental behavior. Ask considers the collection of algorithms assembled for interpretive purposes as an open set of mental production functions that operate on lower-value information partitions (the problem statement and the input data) to produce higher-value information partitions (approximations) to a particular end (the answer or solution). This end need not always be a prediction. It may be that Creature attempts to generate mental objects that are "self-therapeutic"—as with myths and narratives as well as scientific models that are used not for predictive purposes but instead solely for explanatory purposes (even in the absence of a core belief that explanation is nothing but "prediction in reverse"). In such cases, Ask can still use his knowledge of Creature's mental production function (and of the goals toward which Creature deploys them) in order to generate conjectures about the workings of Creature's mind—in particular, about how far Creature will go on thinking given that its mental behavior can be represented by the deployment of a particular algorithm to generate information to a particular end.

Algorithms can be understood as rule-bound sequences of linked operations. Operations can be understood as mappings from one epistemic state of Creature to another. An operation comes in many different flavors, and it need not be restricted to the kind of operation that a computer accepts as input. Ask can posit as operations: numerical addition, subtraction, multiplication, and division; logical negation, conjunction, disjunction, and so forth; meta-logical quotation and dis-quotation; and 1-, 2-, and 3-dimensional correlation, convolution, and deconvolution. Ask will use operations as the basic units of analysis of an algorithm, and he will describe the working of an algorithm in terms of such operations.

Operations are primitives in Ask's models of Creature's mental behavior, but they are neither given nor infallible. Ask can add new operations to his modeling tool kit. For instance, *modus ponens* (making it the case that *B* is true if *A* is true and if the statement "if *A* then *B*" is true) can be introduced as a basic elementary operation, even though it is composed of several, simpler operations (i.e., read "if *A* then *B*"; look up its truth value; look up the truth value of *A*; then assign a truth value to *B*). Unlike a programmer, who can only employ a closed set of operational primitives when specifying a program as an input to a computer, Ask *qua* modeler of Creature's mental behavior is free to posit the basic vocabulary of mental operations in terms of which he describes the algorithms used to model Creature's thought patterns. A key difference between Ask and an Artificial Intelligence expert lies precisely in the additional level of hermeneutic freedom that Ask has in specifying the basic operations in terms of which Creature's mental behavior is analyzed. Thus Ask trades not in artificial intelligence but rather in *intelligent artificiality*: the use of algorithmic methods to abstract patterns of thought from living Creatures in ways that make them more intelligible to other Creatures—and to Ask.

5. TIME COMPLEXITY AND AN ALGORITHMIC "LIBRARY OF FORMS"

In building models of Creature's mental behavior, Ask can derive useful guidance from a basic maneuver of computation theorists that assigns complexity measures to various algorithms or, equivalently, assigns measures of difficulty to various algorithmically solvable problems [Cormen, Leiserson, and Rivest, 1993; Papadimitriou, 1994; Hromkovic, 2003]. The *time complexity* of a solution algorithm is measured in terms of the number of operations required for the algorithm to converge to an answer (see Figure 4.2) by the convergence criterion defined in the problem statement.

Suppose Ask combines DEC and BEL to represent Creature's choice
as the outcome of a decision, which he models as the output of a process
whereby the corresponding outcomes are represented by the utilities or payoffs they entail and the probabilities of their occurrence. The "expected utility" (subjective or objective) of a given option (a set of outcomes) is calculated
by vector multiplication of the probabilities and utilities corresponding to it,
and the option with the highest expected utility is chosen. This account of
choice lays bare a minimal algorithmic structure of the decision problem: If
there are N options each of which is probabilistically linked to a set of M outcomes, then the number of operations in a step-by-step account of Creature's
decision process (and the number of operations required) can be determined
in two steps.

Step 1. (Repeat N times.) Calculate the expected utility of each option by
multiplying the probabilities and utilities of the associated outcomes:
N options $\times$ (M multiplications plus $M - 1$ additions) = $N(2M - 1)$.

Step 2. Pick the option with the largest expected utility from the list of
N options: $N - 1$ "compare" operations.

How "difficult" the problem of deciding is for Creature (assuming it
already knows the probabilities and payoffs of each outcome and is seeking
to pick the maximal option) can be understood by Ask as: How many operations will this algorithm "cost" Creature as a function of the number of
variables (the number of different outcomes and options)? The total time complexity of the CHOICE algorithm sketched above is $T(N, M) = N(2M - 1) +
N - 1 = 2MN - 1$ operations. This time complexity (so called because op-
erations take time and because more operations take more time if they are
performed serially) grows linearly in both M (the number of outcomes per
option) and N (the number of options): $dT/dM = 2N$ (which is constant for
given N) and $dT/dN = 2M$ (which is constant for given M).

It is possible for Creature to perform the calculation in fewer than
$T(N, M)$ operations—for example, by eyeballing the option with the largest expected utility from the list of options after Step 1 of the algorithm was
carried out (in which case the $N - 1$ "compare" operations would reduce to a
single operation) or by "guessing" at the highest expected utility option after
eyeballing the payoffs associated with the various outcomes (in this case, the

complexity of the algorithm's Step 1 would be reduced from $N(2M - 1)$ to MN and the time complexity of Step 2 would be reduced to 0). In each case, Creature's mind takes a shortcut to the solution; this reduces the number of operations from that entailed by the step-by-step method, though at the cost of increasing the possibility of a mistake—of "eyeballing the wrong solution." As before in the case of the algorithm MAX, $T(N, M)$ must be considered a best worst-case bound on the time complexity of CHOICE: "best" because it is maximally reliable; "worst" because it is more costly, since it is fully explicit and does not take advantage of shortcuts.

5.1. *Types of Problems and Associated Solution Procedures*

Ask can reduce the question *What kind of mental behavior will Creature engage in when faced with this problem?* to the more precise questions of *What kind of algorithm will Creature use to solve this problem?* and *How will Creature trade off time complexity against accuracy or reliability?* Ask can use the taxonomy of known time-complexity measures as a guide to the classification of Creature's mental behaviors. He can accordingly represent "easy" mental production functions by algorithms that require a number of operations (to arrive at an answer of acceptable tolerance) that is at most a *polynomial* function of the number of free or independent variables in the problem that Creature is trying to solve. Such problems are commonly referred to as *P-hard* problems [Garey and Johnson, 1979; Cormen, Leiserson, and Rivest, 1993]. If the number of operations required (to compute an acceptable answer or solution) varies linearly with N, the number of free variables of the problem, then the algorithm is deemed computationally "inexpensive" or at least "tractable" and the associated problem relatively "easy." In contrast, hard problems are those solvable only by algorithms requiring a number of operations that is a greater-than-any-polynomial (e.g., an exponential or super-exponential) function of the number of free problem variables. The key distinction in this taxonomy concerns how the time complexity of solving a problem—and hence Creature's cumulative computational cost—*scales* with the number of problem variables.

A useful heuristic for telling the simple from the complex is to think of a solution algorithm as a *search procedure* [Pólya, 1957; Newell and Simon, 1972] among possible solutions to a problem. In this view, a problem statement—once it is understood—defines a space in which Creature's mind searches for the solution to its problem; and an algorithm is a *strategy* for searching that space. This metaphor allows Ask to ask: Are there typical structures of a search space that correspond to simple and complicated algorithms (and correspond to easy and difficult problems) that guide Creature's mental behavior?

Suppose Creature is trying to figure out which one of *n* possible familiar objects (on a list or in its working memory) a particular object it has suddenly perceived really is. This problem seems counterintuitive only because most human Creatures perform it unconsciously or subconsciously; however, it is one of the most basic problems that Creatures solve on a second-by-second basis. Creature must search its inner list to figure out which one of the objects on the list the unknown object most closely resembles. Each object on this list is identified via a group of (say, *m*) properties such as "redness" and "hardness" (see Figure 4.5) and a quantitative measure of the degree to which the object possesses the property in question—or the degree to which the object possesses *more* of the properties in question than does some reference object. In modeling the process by which Creature ascertains the relative

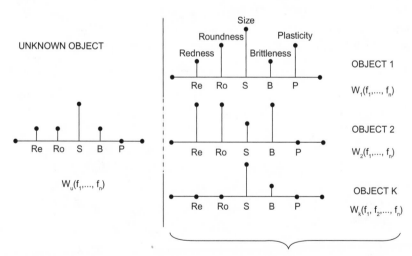

LIST OF SALIENT OBJECTS STORED IN WORKING MEMORY

FIGURE 4.5. Representation of a typical "list search" problem. *Note:* Creature is trying to figure out which—among a series of possible objects $\{W_1, \ldots, W_k\}$, each distinguished from the other on the basis of $n = 5$ properties or features—an unknown object W_u is most likely to be.

similarity between a new object and the objects on the list within its short-term memory, Ask can use a correlation algorithm whereby Creature measures the correlation between the numerical degrees to which the new object possesses each property and the degrees to which every object on the list possesses these properties. If Ask takes a basic operation as an addition or a multiplication, then Creature will require a total of $m^2 - 1$ operations per correlation (between the new object and any one object on the list) multiplied by n, the number of objects: $T(n, m) = n(m^2 - 1)$.

Creature can do better—in terms of the numbers of operations it requires—by keeping its working memory organized in the form of a tree (see Figure 4.6) and by "quantizing" the properties it assigns to each of the objects in its memory. For example, *red–not-red* is a decision node in the tree, as is *hard–not-hard*. Under this organization, the number of operations required

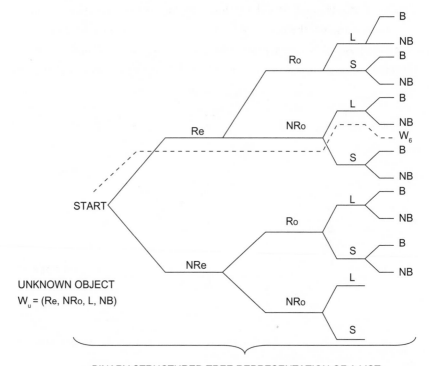

BINARY STRUCTURED TREE REPRESENTATION OF A LIST

FIGURE 4.6. Representation of a "tree search" process modeling Creature's solution to a typical classification problem.

to search the tree (to establish whether any one object in Creature's memory corresponds to the new object) can be reduced even further—to $T(n, m) = n \log_2(m)$, which is more efficient than $n(m^2 - 1)$ because $\log_2(m)$ grows far more slowly with m than does m^2.

The class of P-class algorithms provides Ask with a significant library of building blocks for representing mental behaviors such as "frugal" patterns of inference. Descriptivists have used "heuristics" as a catchall class for nonsystematic patterns of thinking aimed at forming quick judgments from incomplete information [Gigerenzer et al., 1999]. Heuristics in this sense of the word can be understood as algorithms that perform "well enough, on average" and have a manageable computational complexity. Ask interprets "manageable" as "being of at most quadratic complexity." Surveys of human judgment formation and inference that consider the underlying algorithmic structure of heuristics used to make inferences [Martignon and Laskey, 1999] turn up a set of procedures that can indeed be modeled as P-hard algorithms. Table 4.1 showed the most frequently analyzed heuristics put forth to date to explain the judgment of humans in M-variable, N-cue problems of inference from incomplete information along with their time complexity. The prototypical test question for Creature here is of the type *Which (of Munich, Mannheim, Manchester) is the more populous European Union city?*—having ascertained first that Creature does not independently know the correct answer.

Recognition is an example of a "super-simple" heuristic. If it uses this heuristic, Creature will pick the first city that it recognizes (say, Manchester) and pick a random city from the list if it does not recognize any (its stopping rule here). This strategy entails that Creature will, in the worst case, have to read the entire list (here, three cities; in general, N cities). The heuristic will be "ecologically successful" (i.e., successful over the range of inference scenarios Creature is likely to face) if the most (subjectively) recognizable city from a random list is also the one with the largest number of inhabitants. Thus, if confronted by Ask for being "simple minded" in its choice of an algorithm, Creature can advance the hypothesis that a city it is more likely to (subjectively) recognize is (objectively) more likely to be more populous. In turn, Ask can test this hypothesis independently and duly modify or maintain his model and judgment of Creature.

Creature may also use multiple criteria to make its judgment. For instance, it may recall (from its online searches for air travel routes) that Munich comes up as a connecting airport more frequently than do the other cities (criterion 1). Creature may also know that Manchester has a prominent soccer club with well-known players who often vie for the European Championship and the World Cup (criterion 2). Finally, Creature may remember that Munich is a well-established center of industry and culture (criterion 3), being home to several large firms and to a well-known—though infrequently recorded—philharmonic orchestra. Creature may then tally up the various aspects under which each city "wins" (2 for Munich, 1 for Manchester, 0 for Mannheim) and venture "Munich" as the answer on this basis. In this case, the computational complexity of its heuristic will be proportional to the number of criteria (3 here, M in general), to the number of variables (3 and N, respectively), and to the operations required to tally the score for each of the variables among which Creature is trying to discriminate. Once again, Ask can take the three-criterion discrimination algorithm that Creature uses and subject it to empirical scrutiny to determine if it does perform well enough in problems of this type or in most of the problems that Creature faces. These are two different cases, which provide Ask with an additional distinction: Creature's algorithm may indeed be well suited to Creature's usual judgment problems but not to the problem at hand. Ask may then conclude that Creature's shortcoming is not one of choosing too simple an algorithm but rather of failing to adapt the algorithm to a problem with different structure; and this failure may occur either because Creature does not realize that the problem has a different structure or because, even though it does realize this, Creature knows of no alternative heuristic that it can deploy.

Ask's attempt to "model Creature's everyday mental behavior" (as opposed to mental behavior it produces to solve a problem that is given and structured by Ask) usually entails that Ask attempt (a) to figure out (e.g., on the basis of hearing Creature reason out loud or carefully interviewing Creature) the heuristic or set of heuristics that Creature uses to arrive at its judgment, (b) to produce an algorithmic model of the resulting heuristic or bundle of heuristics, (c) to measure the complexity of the resulting algorithmic model of Creature's pattern of thinking or bundle of patterns with the aim of being able (d) to track Creature's progress through a particular problem (e.g., how much does getting to an answer *cost* Creature relative to the value of the right answer), and (e) to train his model on Creature's mental behavior by predicting the "breaking points" of Creature's mind—the number of variables or operations at which Creature gives up thinking and "just guesses."

Ask is interested not in models of the way most people think (or, more accurately, the way most undergraduates think when participating in forced-choice experiments) but rather in honing a precise representation language for Creature's mental behavior that will allow him to audit Creature's mental state experimentally, dialogically, and—if possible and reliable—neurophysiologically by connecting Creature's brain to measurement apparatus (e.g., functional magnetic resonance imaging, positron emission tomography, electroencephalography scanners). Toward this end, Ask will want to be precise about the objectives that guide Creature's thinking and structure its mental behavior, and he finds the concept of a "problem" a useful mental object for doing just that. The definition of *problem*—a mismatch, as perceived by Creature, between current and desired conditions—that shaped work in artificial intelligence and cognitive science for some 40 years has been sharpened in several ways in the course of its development.

First, the notion of a "solution search space" [Simon, 1973] was introduced to deal with the set of (physically and/or logically) possible paths that connect initial to final conditions. Second, "well-structuredness" [Simon, 1973] was introduced to deal with the notion of invariance of the search space relative to the problem solver's efforts to search it. If a chess player searches the solution space of the problem of choosing the best next move by *actually* (rather than fictitiously) making the move, then by virtue of having moved she changes the search space of possible moves by altering the topology of the chess board. On the other hand, a *fictitious* move (and, in general, the fictitious exploration of the search space) does not change that space—except, of course, insofar as the fact that the chess player *could* have moved at any one time but *did not*, choosing instead to simulate the consequences of possible moves, itself changes the structure of the game by influencing the opponent's beliefs and *her* resulting search processes. Finally, an important distinction between *types* of problems was made in the literature on the theory of computation [Hromkovic, 2003] that allowed for the definition of classes of problems in terms of the problem statement's grammar.

A *decision problem* is a problem defined by a triplet (L, U, s), where L is a set of allowable solutions (a language), U is the set of all solution candidates, and s is an alphabet for the language L. An algorithm A (a Turing Machine) solves (L, U, s) if and only if, for every $x \in U$, we have $A(x) = 1$ if $x \in L$ and $A(x) = 0$ if $x \in U - L$. *Is there a checkmate in two moves?* is a decision problem, as is *Is the minimum-length path that connects Canada's 4,663 cities less than 700,000 kilometers?*

An *optimization problem*, in contrast, is determined by a set L of candidate solutions belonging to an alphabet s; a mapping $M : L \rightarrow O$, where O is the set of feasible solutions; and a function COST $(x \in O)$ that measures the cost of any solution in the feasible set. The problem is guided by the goal of either minimizing or maximizing COST. *Find the fastest way from Newbury Street and Massachusetts Avenue to Harvard Square* and *Find the minimum-length path that connects Canada's 4,663 cities* are both examples of optimization problems.

Well-defined, well-structured problems require a mapping of observable current conditions into (time-bounded and measurable or, at least, observable) desired conditions via an algorithmic search of the space of possible solutions, which is invariant with respect to the implementation or operation of the particular search algorithm used. Ask further decomposes such problems into decision or optimization problems in ways that allow him to narrow down even more the range of possible search algorithms that he can plausibly ascribe to Creature. Upon doing so, and additionally equipped with the distinction between different classes of problem complexity, Ask can proceed to prospect Creature's mental behaviors in a way that is guided by (a) the problems he ascribes to Creature, (b) the algorithms he ascribes to Creature, and (c) the economics of Creature's mental behavior. Ask accordingly wants to circumscribe Creature's problem-solving routines by representing them in algorithmic form and then grouping the resulting, canonical problem statements according to their worst-case time complexity.

Polynomial-Time-Hard Problems.   Polynomial-time-hard problems (Figure 4.7) form a promising subset of such canonical problems because their time complexity grows "relatively slowly" (subexponentially) with the number of variables in Creature's problem statement; but Ask will find use for several additional distinctions within the P class.

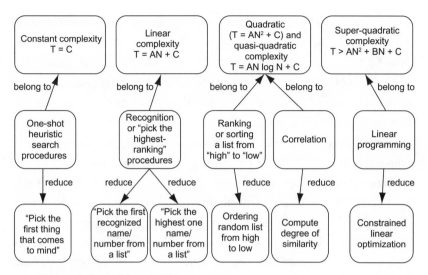

T = complexity of solution algorithm
N = number of variables in problem statement
A, B, C are arbitrary constants.

FIGURE 4.7. Complexity regimes, I: The P class.

Constant complexity problems have time complexities that are *invariant* with the size of the input. Although it would seem that no solution algorithm could be blind to the size of its input, "pick the first one on the list" from our example list of cities is a constant-complexity algorithm that happens to minimize search time ($T = 1$) in the case where Creature knows nothing about or relevant to the relative populousness of European cities and also *knows* that it has no such knowledge. Of course, if Creature *does not know that it does not know* this, then it may end up choosing a city at random or choosing the first city on the list—but only after first reading through the entire list of cities, in which case the heuristic is no longer of constant complexity.

Linear complexity problems have solution algorithms with the property that $T(N) = O(aN)$, where *a* is some positive constant. The recognition heuristic described previously is an instance. If asked, Creature can rationalize its use of this rule on the grounds that the largest city is also the one it is most likely to recognize. Using this heuristic to pick the best option from a list entails a worst-case time complexity of $T(N) = N$—that is, in the worst case, Creature must read the entire list before coming to a city that it recognizes.

Ask can also devise more sophisticated algorithms to represent Creature's ordering of random lists according to, say, *Which is the best element under criterion C?* Such algorithms range from the tree searches that Ask used before $(T(M, N) = N\log_2(M))$ to multicriteria choice models that require Creature to revisit the list several times and order according to each new criterion. Ask can represent analogical reasoning—as well as the automatic processing involved in pattern recognition in high-level vision [Marr, 1982]—via the problem of computing the *correlation* between two arrays. If the time complexity of correlating two vectors of lengths N and M is given by $T(\text{Corr}(X, Y)) = 2MN - 1$, the time complexity of the 2-dimensional correlation of an $N \times N$ array of samples ("pixels") with an $M \times M$ array of samples will be proportional to M^2N^2. In this case, Ask can deploy his algorithmic models not only to the study of Creature's mental behavior when faced with problems that are articulated in natural or formal languages but also in situations where Creature "orients itself" by solving visual pattern recognition problems. Ask can also observe the effect that getting Creature to think explicitly about a problem that it usually solves implicitly will have on Creature's ability to solve that problem more or less efficiently.

Ask can use linear programming (LP) problems to model the way in which Creature solves *n*-variable linear optimization problems under L constraints. If Ask believes, for instance, that Creature is trying to figure out its optimal allocation of time to one of N tasks in a given day—assuming that Creature knows the marginal value of allocating a minute to each task, the costs of each task and each transition between tasks, and the total number of working hours at its disposal—then Ask can use an LP problem to simulate the mental behavior, conscious or otherwise, in which Creature engages when it plans its day. Karmarkar [1984] shows that the complexity of such problems is super-quadratic in the number of optimization variables and linear in the length (in bits) of the total input; that is, $T(n, l) = O(n^{3.5}l)$. Ask can attempt to map bits and pieces of Creature's mental behavior as it attempts to solve the problem of planning its day to the relevant bits and pieces of a constrained optimization algorithm, and he can study Creature's mental behavior "piecewise" by using his collection of algorithmic operations as a guide to Creature's local optimization behavior.

NP-Hard and NP-Complete Problems. Whereas P-class problems are solvable by a deterministic algorithm in a number of operations $T(N)$ that is at most a polynomial function of the number of the problem variables (i.e., $T(N) \leq P^k(N)$), *nondeterministic* polynomial-time problems (or "NP problems") are solvable by a deterministic algorithm in a number of operations that is a super-polynomial function of the number of problem variables ($T(N) > P^k(N)$) and is typically an exponential or super-exponential function of that number ($T(N) \geq e^N$). Note that NP-class *optimization* problems are referred to as NP-hard, whereas NP-class *decision* problems are referred to as NP-complete. NP-class problems are solved by *non*deterministic algorithms in a number of operations that is a polynomial function of the number of problem variables, and the problem of verifying that a candidate solution to an NP-class problem is viable is itself P-hard—two facts that will come in handy when Ask attempts to model how Creature deals with "hard problems."

NP-complete problems (see Figure 4.8) are reducible by polynomial-time transformations to a problem already proven [Cook, 1971] to be NP-complete (whereas the associated optimization problem is provably NP-hard):

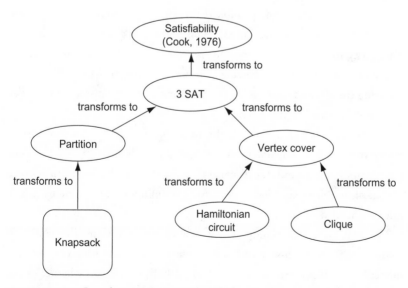

FIGURE 4.8. Complexity regimes, II: The NP class.

the k-satisfiability (kSAT) problem for $k > 3$. Subsequent proofs of the NP-hardness or completeness of an arbitrary problem take the reductive form of transformations of any problem onto a kSAT problem (or onto a problem that is polynomial-time reducible to a kSAT problem; see Fortnow [2009]).

The kSAT problem is a decision problem that asks for an assignment of truth values to a set of elementary propositions that satisfies a k-variable formula (or clause) expressed as a Boolean function of the elementary propositions. Suppose that Creature considers the problem of finding the set of truth assignments to the elementary propositions X_1, X_2, X_3, X_4 (where 0 denotes False and 1 denotes True) that satisfy the formula $F = (X_1 \vee \sim X_2 \vee X_4)$ & $(X_1 \vee \sim X_2 \vee \sim X_3) = 1$ (True), where "$\vee$," "&," and "$\sim$" are respectively the standard operators "or," "and," and "not" of Boolean logic. If Ask knows this, then he knows that Creature is trying to solve a "difficult" problem, one that maps to an NP-complete problem when stripped down to a canonical form. The problem is difficult in the intuitive sense because all possible truth assignments of X_1, X_2, X_3, X_4 (each of which can take on the value of 1 = True or 0 = False) must be checked against F in order to determine whether or not they satisfy it; and the intuition is validated by the proof [Cook, 1971] that solving the problem indeed requires an exhaustive search of the space of all possible truth assignments to X_1, X_2, X_3, X_4. For a deterministic search process of a kSAT solution, Ask can estimate the time complexity to be $T(k) \approx e^K$. He can use this time complexity as a measure of the difficulty of the associated *maximization problem*, MAXSAT (that of assigning truth values to X_1, X_2, X_3, X_4 that maximize the number of satisfied clauses of F), which is NP-hard.

Ask deploys kSAT as a versatile modeling device to represent various pieces of Creature's mental behavior. Cook [1971] uses kSAT to encode theorem-proving procedures in general. This suggests that Ask can use this canonical problem to model *deductive* reasoning more generally, which can be encoded as the problem of figuring out whether or not a formula (a "theorem") is logically compatible with a set of assumptions (the "axioms"). Cooper [1990] uses this canonical problem to model the problem of causal inference via probabilistic networks [Pearl, 1990], which asks whether or not a set of causal hypotheses—now playing the role of axioms in kSAT—provide a causal explanation for a set of data points or evidence statements. The "maneuver" that Cooper makes is to model conjunctions of causal hypotheses and single data points as Boolean formulas, whereby the problem of finding a set of hypotheses that provides a minimally acceptable "inference network" becomes that of finding a truth assignment to the variables of kSAT that satisfy the resulting formulas. Ask can analogously use kSAT to model Creature's *causal reasoning*—or reasoning aimed at inferring one or more *probable causes* from a set of possible causes, a set of observed effects, and a set of degrees of belief that link each possible cause to each observed effect. Thus, Ask uses kSAT to encode not only deterministic problems of deductive construction but also problems that incorporate incomplete information and uncertainty and admit multiple possible causal inferences.

Ask can also use kSAT problems (in particular, 3SAT) to model *abductive* reasoning processes within Creature—that is, reasoning whereby Creature seeks to make an "inference to the best explanation" [Peirce 1998]. An abduction problem takes as input a set D of data to be explained, a set H of hypotheses, and a mapping $e(\{h_i\} \rightarrow \{d_j\})$ from subsets of H to subsets of D. The problem that Ask takes Creature to be solving in this case asks for an *explanation* in the form of the *minimal* subset of H that completely explains D. Bylander and colleagues [1991] reduce the problem of determining whether or not an explanation exists (i.e., a subset of H exists that explains all of D) to 3SAT by first assigning a variable in the 3SAT problem and its negation to an incompatible set of hypotheses and then assigning each Boolean expression— a function of the variables corresponding to the hypotheses—to a datum to be explained. A complete explanation exists only if the Boolean expression that corresponds to a datum is satisfiable by the assignment of truth values to the set of explanatory hypotheses.

Canonical SET COVER problems come in two versions, both of which are of special interest to Ask: COVER and EXACT COVER (EC). The latter asks whether or not there exists a collection of pairwise disjoint subsets of a given finite set S whose union is equal to S. Aragones et al. [2003] show that EXACT COVER can be used to represent the problem that Creature faces when it seeks to learn by linearly regressing a set of predictors on a set of data and aiming to find the set $\{X_1, \ldots, X_K\}$ of predictors for a set $\{Y_j\}$ of observations that contains at most k elements, subject to a fixed bound on the acceptable squared prediction error. The time complexity of a brute-force solution to EC is intuitively given by the complexity of enumerating all possible subsets of S (i.e., $T(EC(S)) = 2^{|S|} - 1$), and the reduction of EC to kSAT [Karp, 1972] assures Ask that the problem is indeed NP.

Ask posits that Creature can learn not only by deduction, abduction, and multiple linear regression but also by induction. The problem of *induction*—of finding the minimal set of rules or generalizations that are consistent with a set of data—is transformable to the COVER problem, which asks whether or not there exists a set of n subsets of S whose union is equal to S [Aragones et al., 2003]. If the data are encoded as a matrix whose (i, j) entries represent the degree to which sample i has attribute j, then a *rule* is a statement of the form that no sample with property l will fail to exhibit property k. Creature will seek the minimal set of rules by seeking the smallest set of subsets of the data set that exactly correspond to the minimal set of rules. Relatedly, Ask can also model the situation in which Creature is trying to solve the problem of *parsimonious abduction*: figuring out the minimal set of hypotheses that together explain a data set. This problem maps to a version of the COVER problem [Bylander et al., 1991] that asks for the minimum set of subsets of a set whose union is the set itself (is "collectively exhaustive"). Ask will use the set in question to encode H_{min}, the set of explanatory hypotheses of at least minimal plausibility, in which case the problem of parsimonious abduction maps to the optimization version of the COVER problem. If Ask further specifies that allowable explanations sought by Creature must consist of "mutually exclusive" hypotheses, then the parsimonious abduction problem maps to the optimization version of the EXACT COVER problem.

At this point, Ask is in possession of a library of canonical problem statements—with associated complexity measures (Table 4.4)—for tracking and auditing various plausible patterns of thought that Creature can deploy to reason

TABLE 4.4. Ask's Encoding of Creature's Modes of Inferential Thinking into Canonical Forms of Measurable Time Complexity

Mode of thinking	Algorithmic model	Time complexity/class
Analogical	Correlation	Super-quadratic (P)
Deductive	Satisfiability	Exponential (NP)
Linear regression	Set cover	Exponential (NP)
Inductive	Set cover	Exponential (NP)
Abductive	3 sat, cover, exact cover	Exponential (NP)

analogically, causally, deductively, inductively, or abductively. Ask will use this library of forms as a set of putative "mental production functions" that model how Creature thinks its way from a problem to a solution, given a context; and he will use the associated time-complexity measures to make inferences about the cost structure of Creature's mental behavior. Ask can also reconstruct the full computational landscape that Creature's mind navigates by positing (a) a value function that measures the value Creature places on the (optimal) answer to the problem it is solving, (b) a function that assigns various levels of uncertainty (entropy) to Creature's estimate of an answer at any point during the problem-solving process, and (c) a function that assigns increments of Creature's subjective value function to various levels of computational depth to which Creature thinks and that will correspond to more or less precise estimates of the solution Creature seeks. Aware that Creature might use different modes of reasoning (deductive, inductive, associative, causal) in different contexts or might alternate among different modes of reasoning while thinking about a given problem, Ask can use the library of canonical modes of thinking to inquire into the conditions (payoff for a solution of a desired precision, cost of producing that solution in a given amount of time) under which Creature will, as a function of the local costs and benefits of its mental behavior, prefer one mode of reasoning to another or alternate between two different modes of reasoning.

Ask is interested not only in the general forms of reasoning that Creature can engage in (inductive, deductive, abductive, analogical, causal) but also in crafting canonical representations of run-of-the-mill problems that Creature faces in its everyday life. In these cases as well, Ask's basic strategy of reducing everyday problems to canonical problems will serve him nicely.

The *traveling salesman problem* (TSP) represents the problem faced by a salesman who must find the minimum-distance (or minimum-time) circuit that takes him to each of N cities, given that he knows the distance (time) separating any pair of cities. The problem is polynomial-time reducible to the *Hamiltonian circuit problem* [Karp, 1972], which in turn is polynomial-time reducible to the kSAT problem. The intuition behind the TSP's complexity measure is that the number of paths that must be searched is proportional to $N!$, which entails (by Stirling's formula) that

$$T(N) = (N/e)^N \sqrt{2\pi N} > P^k(N) \quad \text{for } N/e > 1,$$

and the reduction to a known NP-hard problem assures that this problem is at least as hard as the maximization version of kSAT. Ask can use the TSP to "encode," for instance, the problem that Creature is trying to solve when it behaves like a "shopper" (who knows roughly but not specifically what it wants and how much it wants to pay) as opposed to a "buyer" (who knows specifically what it wants and how much it is willing to pay for what it wants). As a shopper, Creature may be interested in minimizing the amount of time (or travel distance) between the stores that represent the search space for its shopping problem, in which case Creature may be said to be also engaged in solving the "meta-shopping" problem of searching among all possible routes that connect the stores in the search space of its shopping problem in order to determine the path that will take it to visit all of the stores in the minimum amount of time (or with the minimal traveling expense), given that it knows the geographic locations of the stores and, if necessary, the transit time and costs between any two stores.

Equipped with this knowledge, Ask can seek to infer—both from Creature's "browsing behavior" (represented by its shopping path on any given day) and from the amount of time that Creature spends optimizing its search strategy—Creature's mental production function for its path minimization problem. Ask can then use the resulting model, trained on Creature's shopping behavior by mapping nodes to shops and travel time or expense to the length of the edges connecting the shops, to make inferences about Creature's path optimization behavior. He can extend his model of Creature's path optimization behavior to other problems that are *computationally* isomorphic to the TSP problem and therefore of equal time complexity. If Creature appears to attempt no global optimization of its shopping path in its "shopping problem," then Ask may infer (a) that Creature does not sufficiently care about its search costs to engage in the meta-shopping problem, or (b) that Creature engages in a simplified search that is based on randomization or local search, or (c) that Creature does not, as a matter of course, engage in solving NP-hard problems. This last inference raises the possibility that Creature's mental behavior can be represented by a set of choices expressing cognitive preferences that are *lexicographic* in problem complexity class—which, further on, Ask will consider in some detail.

The *knapsack problem* (KSP) [Karp, 1972; Martello and Toth, 1990] typically models the problem faced by a hiker who wants to pack a knapsack of
known total volume V with a set of k utensils out of N possible options so
as to maximize the total utility of the set of utensils included, subject to all
utensils fitting in V, given that he knows the volume and the value of each
utensil. Under the constraints that no fraction of a utensil can be taken along
and each utensil can be included only once, KSP presents a search space that
comprises 2^N possible options (the number of subsets of N). This yields an
upper bound of $T(N) = 2^N$. The reduction of KSP to a problem (PARTI-
TION) known to be P-reducible to kSAT also confirms that KSP is at least as
hard as kSAT.

Ask can use KSP to represent many of Creature's optimization problems
that have integer constraints. For example, Creature's "daily planning problem" can be modeled as a linear programming problem if Creature's time is
continuously divisible. However, if Creature must choose among allocations
of a fixed amount of time (its day) to a subset of activities (analogous to the
knapsack utensils) with nondivisible durations ("a meeting with J takes one
hour," "traveling from Y to Z takes ten minutes," etc.), then the problem
becomes a KSP. Once again, Ask can "train" his computational eye on Creature's daily behavior to determine not only if Creature is a "planner" (*Is it at
least a weak optimizer of the value of its time? Does it make choices that reflect an
underlying time-value function that is consistent?*) but also if Creature is a "real
time" planner (*Does it seek the* optimal *reallocation of its time and resources to
the remaining activities given that a meeting it had scheduled was unexpectedly
cancelled?*). To the extent that Creature's self-control problem (of Chapter 2)
is not susceptible to "the application of fractions of self-control techniques"
being applied by Creature to its own states, this problem is also isomorphic
to the KSP—in which case Ask has found a potentially sound basis for being
able to say that "Creature is uncontrollable."

The VERTEX COVER (VC) problem is a decision problem related to
finding a subset v of at most K of the N vertices V of a graph $G(E, V)$, where
E denotes the set of connecting edges, such that v will include the vertices
that together touch all the edges E of G. The VC problem is proven to be
NP-complete by reduction to PARTITION [Karp, 1972], and a brute-force

algorithm will find the solution in $T(N, K) \approx 2^K N$. The associated NP-hard optimization problem is that of finding the minimum vertex cover of G (i.e., that of finding the minimal K).

Ask can use the VC problem to encode various of Creature's "social networking problems." For instance, it represents a plausible rendition of Creature's *networking strategy selection problem*—that of crafting a strategy for forming ties with other Creatures in situations where the position (or centrality) of a Creature in its network positively influences its status, informedness, fame, "power," respectability, and so forth. It is easy to encode social networking problems as graph problems of the VC type: Creatures are vertices, and the ties between them—of whatever kind (informational, pecuniary, affective)—are the edges of the graph that models the network of linked Creatures. The "most connected" Creatures will be precisely the ones that together *span* all of the network in the sense that there is no Creature in the network that is not somehow linked to at least one of them. If Creature is a competent "political animal," Ask reasons, then it will seek to form ties to the most-connected Creatures in the network and will actively seek ties with the Creatures that form the vertex cover of its immediate network.

Ask can reasonably deploy VC to model Creature's social network problem-solving behavior only if he has already ascertained that Creature *knows* all of the variables that enter the problem statement—in other words, if Ask has established that Creature knows its own network not only at the level of "who are my friends?" and "whom do I know?" but also at the comprehensive level of knowing its friends' friends' friends' . . . to a level that exhausts or nearly exhausts the fully connected network of which it is part. This is a stringent condition, and Ask must exercise diligence in trying to figure out what (if anything) Creature knows about its own network before positing that Creature is trying to solve some complex network optimization problem. However, Ask can derive important explanatory insight even if he realizes that Creature does *not* know its own network in spite of having good reason to know it—for instance, if Creature works in a relationship-intense industry or one in which "word of mouth" information transfer features prominently in the success of suppliers. In this case, Ask may venture that Creature does not know its own network because it does not *see* the reason why it should.

Yet even though Creature may realize the value of networking in general, it still may not see how to capture that value by solving VC-type problems for its own network. This may be (a) because it does not know how to set up and solve VC-type problems or (b) because, even though it knows how to set up and solve such problems, it does not engage in solving NP-hard problems—again because Creature harbors some lexicographic set of preferences over problem complexity classes that governs its choices among problems on the basis of their time complexity. Either inference will set Ask down additional paths of discovery, which by now he is equipped to pursue.

Ask can also use VC to encode problems related to understanding and manipulating the "epistemic networks" [Moldoveanu and Baum, 2008] that arise within groups of Creatures and that are relevant to the ability of these groups to coordinate or co-mobilize. An *epistemic* network is a network defined by a set I of Creatures, a set P of propositional beliefs, and a set of links among Creatures and beliefs that denote either the "knows" or "believes" operator. Creatures A, B, C and proposition $R \in P$ are linked by an epistemic path, for instance, if A believes B believes C believes P. The length of the edges connecting Creature A to Creature B to Creature C to belief P may be chosen to be the subjective degrees of belief of A in the truth of the proposition that B knows C knows P, of B in the fact that C knows P, and of C in the truth of P. The problem of figuring out the set of central beliefs in a network of epistemically linked Creatures turns into the problem of determining the set of propositions that together "span" the set of Creatures—the minimal vertex cover of the epistemic network of beliefs of that network. Such propositions may be important because they function as focal points in coordination and mobilization scenarios [Chwe, 1999; Moldoveanu and Baum, 2008]. Creature may reasonably want to learn the propositions that "most believe most believe to be true" or the propositions that "most believe most believe *they themselves* believe to be true," because knowledge of these beliefs will help it better coordinate and cooperate with other Creatures in the group. Once again, Ask will want to distinguish between the situation where Creature cannot solve a coordination problem requiring knowledge of higher-level beliefs (because it has not posed that problem to itself) and the situation where Creature cannot solve the coordination problem because it has not solved the associated (hard) problem.

The CLIQUE problem (CP) is a decision problem that asks whether or not a graph $G(V, E)$ of N vertices and L edges has a clique of size k (as defined by a fully connected subnetwork of G). The associated optimization problem asks for the minimal or maximal clique that graph G possesses [Garey and Johnson, 1979]. The intuitive time complexity of a brute-force approach to CP is $T(N, k) = N^k k^2$, and the reduction of CP to VC [Karp, 1972] attests to the fact that this complexity measure is not spurious or accidental. The CP has been used [Gilboa and Zemel, 1989] in its decision form to model the problems associated with finding a particular Nash equilibrium (NE) set of strategies that give a payoff of at least P in a competitive game, which include a NE in which a player makes a certain minimum payoff, a NE whose support contains a certain strategy, and a NE in which the aggregate payoff of the players exceeds a certain number. (The problem of finding *some* NE is one that can be represented by a linear programming problem.) More recent work [Chen and Deng, 2006; Daskalakis, Goldberg, and Papadimitriou, 2006] has shown that the problem of finding the NE of a game cannot, in general, be solved in polynomial time and that the problem is a subclass of TFNP (total function nondeterministic polynomial time)—the function-search equivalent (returning a function for an answer) of NP-complete decision problems (returning a 0 or 1 answer) and NP-hard optimization problems (returning a number or vector for an answer). Ask will find CP useful in his mental "examination" of Creature because he can use it to represent Creature's mental behavior as it attempts to make decisions with outcomes and payoffs that depend not only on Creature's actions and the way the world is but also on the choices that other Creatures make ("interdependent decisions"). If Creature indeed solves CLIQUE-type problems when it selects the strategy it is going to use in a competitive scenario, then Ask can get Creature to play games of various levels of complexity (indexed by the number of players and the number of strategies) and observe the evolution and optimality of Creature's strategies as a function of increases in the number of variables. If mental behavior is costly and if its costs to Creature grow quickly in the number of additional Creatures and their possible strategies, then Ask can estimate the marginal costs of Creature's strategic thinking via the payoff loss that Creature is willing to incur by taking shortcuts when playing a multi-Creature competitive game as the number of

Creatures grows. The time complexity measure of CLIQUE, then, gives Ask a blueprint for estimating the cost structure of Creature's mental activity in some strategic scenarios.

With these canonical problem statements (and their associated complexity measures) in hand, Ask has an expanded set of modeling choices to consider. He can model Creature's mental behavior as the outcome of a sequence of choices among different types of problems or, more specifically, as the outcome of a sequence of choices among problem complexity classes. Ask reasons that Creature, in its everyday life, faces *predicaments* and *situations*, not problems in the sense that Ask has defined them. And just as Creature can choose to *propositionalize* its experiences and perceptions in various ways (using sentences expressed either in natural language or in some more technical language), it can also choose to *represent* its predicaments using different problem statements modeled by problems of different complexity classes. Creature can, for instance, choose to approach an inference problem as a "recognition problem," as a linear regression problem given a tried-and-true set of regressors (as opposed to a minimal-variance–minimal-complexity set), as an abductive reasoning problem, or even as a theorem-proving procedure that starts from a set of facts or propositions Creature feels certain about and from which it can seek to deduce the truth or falsity of the proposition in question. Sensitized (by the descriptivist literature on cognitive heuristics) to the prevalence of computationally simple inference algorithms among Creatures at large, and mindful that Creature's psychic costs of solving NP-hard or NP-complete problems will grow rapidly in the number of variables of the problem, Ask may venture a *lexicographic* model of Creature's problem selection process as follows.

> LEXCOMP. *Creature prefers to represent its predicament in terms of P-hard problems rather than in terms of NP-hard or NP-complete problems.*

LEXCOMP is a lexicographic choice principle for interpreting mental behavior on the basis of observing Creature's predicament. It supplies Ask with an interpretive device for Creature's mental behavior, one that enjoins Creature from engaging in any NP-hard problem-solving task at all.

Against LEXCOMP, however, Ask will observe that run-of-the-mill Creatures in run-of-the-mill situations do sometimes engage in solving NP-hard

problems—particularly if there are only a few variables in the problem statement. Creatures of all kinds try to optimize their daily schedules in ways that
are heedful of the lumpiness of some activities that cannot be subdivided.
They can balance trays of hot liquid using sophisticated "force feedback"
algorithms that are subconsciously implemented. They engage in diagnostic reasoning (albeit in well-circumscribed domains) of the type that can be
closely modeled by the abductive reasoning reducible to COVER-type problems. Faced with this anecdotal and intuitive "body of evidence," Ask may
revise his model of Creature as follows.

> ADAPTIVE LEXCOMP. *Creature prefers to represent its predicament in terms
> of P-hard rather than NP-hard problems for problem variables that number
> more than n_C, which is a Creature-specific or Creature-invariant number.*

This new interpretation principle for Creature's mental behavior seems
more sensible to Ask because Creature's problem formulation process is rendered adaptive to the number of variables that Creature deems salient. It also
has some notable drawbacks. The first concerns Ask's choice to allow the
problem statement to vary while fixing the number of free variables in the
problem statement. Hence one possible objection is: "Why cannot Creature
choose to simplify its problem statement by choosing a problem in a lower
complexity class or by choosing a lower number of salient variables, which
would reduce the problem's complexity without changing its complexity
class?" Ask can turn this objection into a productive path of discovery by confronting Creature with forced-choice scenarios that allow Creature to choose
between pruning variables and changing the complexity class of its subjective
problem statement. Suppose that Ask requests Creature to control the temperature, air quality, and airflow rate (three variables) in a "clean room" with
very tight levels of precision by handling levers or buttons that control the
heat transfer, air filtering rate, and airflow rate using algorithms (sequences of
operations of the levers) that grow more or less quickly as a function of the
number of input and/or output variables. Then Ask can discriminate between
simplification strategies that have Creature reducing the difficulty of its problem by reducing the number of variables to which it attends and those that
do so by lowering the computational complexity of the control algorithms
Creature uses.

A second objection to ADAPTIVE LEXCOMP is rather more challenging for Ask to address. The objection focuses on the apparent propensity of some Creatures (engineers, operations researchers, game theorists) to attempt—and sometimes succeed in—solving NP-hard or NP-complete problems with large numbers of variables. One such example is the problem of finding the minimal path that connects Canada's 4,663 cities (4,663 variables), whose solution (shown in Figure 4.9) was generated using a "meta-algorithm" named after its inventors, Lin and Kernighan [1973]. The time complexity of the brute-force approach to the 4,663-city TSP problem is of the order of 10^{1300} operations, which easily overpowers any computational device available when his book was written. Ask therefore realizes that intractability need not entail unsolvability.

Ask becomes interested, as a result of such examples, in classes of meta-algorithms or Heuristics, where the uppercase H is used to distinguish them from the heuristics posited by those who limit their attention to intuitive rules of thumb that require no prior insight by Creature into the computational complexity of its problems. In contrast, Heuristics can inform Ask about Creature's mental behavior as it attempts to deal with problems that are

Problem:
"Find minimum-length tour connecting Canada's 4,663 cities"

Solution:

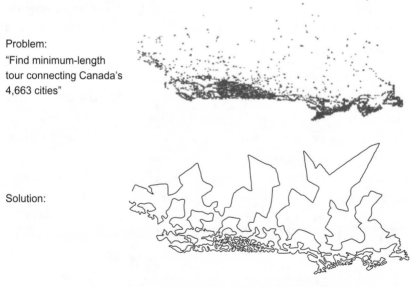

FIGURE 4.9. A TSP search space and solution using the Lin–Kernighan *neighbor exchange* local search.

technically intractable (NP-hard, NP-complete) *and* also have large numbers of variables. Analogously to his taxonomic approach to NP-class problems (where much explanatory work was done by a few prototypical problems), Ask seeks additionally from a small library of Heuristics that will help him make further modeling distinctions.

Ask will organize his library of Heuristics for modeling Creature's approach to intractable problems into two general approaches labeled Approximation Heuristics and Randomization Heuristics. *Approximation* Heuristics seek to arrive at an approximate solution to a problem whose exact solution is too costly to compute, and Creature can use them to "get to within x% of the answer." *Randomization* Heuristics, on the other hand, seek to arrive (with some acceptable probability) at the exact solution to a problem that would require Creature to perform too many operations to find 100% of the time. Accordingly, Creature can use them to "arrive at the answer y% of the time." (Mixed strategies, which Creature can use to "get to within x% of the answer y% of the time," are also feasible and sometimes effective.) Ask can use the assembled Heuristics (described briefly below) as templates for interpreting Creature's reasoning-out-loud renditions of its search strategy for solutions to intractable problems (or as maps to Creature's epistemic states along the way to searching a solution space) and thus further increase the precision with which he can predict and intervene in the mental behavior Creature produces when faced with "difficult problems."

Approximation Heuristics: Branch and Bound, Divide and Conquer, and Local Search. Branch-and-bound (BB) Heuristics are approximate solution techniques that rely on (a) partitioning the solution search space of a problem via a tree whose nodes represent binary decisions among different elements of a solution, (b) calculating bounds on the performance of a solution that will arise from various branches of the tree, and (c) removing from the search space those branches that are likely to result in a suboptimal solution. The key feature of a good tree structure for BB methods is that it is easily *prunable*: tight estimates of performance bounds for different branches can be calculated (lest an optimum be "missed" by the resulting search). A search tree for solutions to a four-variable MAXSAT problem with $F = (X_1 \lor \sim X_2 \lor X_4)$ & $(X_1 \lor \sim X_2 \lor \sim X_3) = 1$ appears in Figure 4.10.

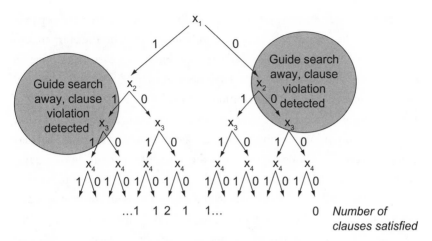

FIGURE 4.10. Branch-and-bound variable depth of search space $\{X_1, X_2, X_3, X_4\}$ for MAXSAT problem $(X_1 \vee \sim X_2 \vee X_4)$ & $(X_1 \vee \sim X_2 \sim X_3)$.

Creature can use the BB Heuristic to classify the various paths through the search tree and thus save time by searching only the most promising part of the search space.

For a TSP problem (with cities indexed by A, B, C, D, E), Creature can build a BB tree structure on the basis of whether or not a path contains a particular segment. The first node of the tree creates two "buckets" of possible routes: one containing routes that include AB and one containing routes that do not. For Canadian cities, for instance, Creature can create one set of paths that contains the Toronto–Ottawa segment and another set of paths that does not; accordingly, the first bifurcation of its BB search tree will be: "Does this path contain the Toronto–Ottawa segment?" Subsequent nodes of the tree— there will be a total of $N(N - 1)/2$ nodes for an N-city tree—will provide finer-grained partitioning of the space of possible paths. For Creature, the key to reducing the time complexity of the search is a tight characterization of the best-case performance that one can expect from any given subtree. Each bifurcation of the tree reduces the total number of required search operations by half, so Creature will seek to make estimates that trade off optimally between accuracy and speed.

Divide-and-conquer (DC) Heuristics are approximation techniques that involve (a) partitioning the problem search space into smaller search spaces that can be more efficiently searched and (b) piecing together the separate solutions to the smaller problems to form (approximate and therefore suboptimal) solution(s) to the intractable larger problem. DC Heuristics offer no guarantee that the concatenation of solutions to subproblems will in general be an optimal or even feasible solution to the bigger problem: The union of exact covers of subsets of a set will not, in general, be equivalent to the exact cover of the union of the subsets; and the shortest path connecting Canada's cities will certainly not be equivalent to the union of the set of shortest paths connecting cities north of the 50th parallel and the set of shortest paths connecting cities south of the 50th parallel. However, DC is an effective approximation method for some large problems (CLIQUE, for instance) and, like BB, it produces a "cognitive key signature" that Ask can recognize either in Creature's out-loud thinking or in the dynamics of its estimate of a solution along the way to solving the problem.

Relaxation to linear optimization (RL): Ask knows that the knapsack problem is difficult because of the "lumpiness" of the objects in the problem statement: No utensil can be subdivided for inclusion in the knapsack, and any utensil must either be taken or left behind—and thus cannot be taken/left with some probability (since utensils are not quantum-mechanical objects). Were utensils (product features, technical standard clauses, etc.) subdivisible or probabilistically includible in the knapsack, then the IP problem would "relax" to an LP maximization problem in N variables (under the single constraint of volume), a P-class problem. Hence Ask understands that an approximation procedure for KSP lies in the direction of relaxing the integer programming problem to an associated linear programming problem as follows:

1. *relaxing* the constraint that all numbers of utensils must be integers;
2. *solving* the associated LP problem;
3. *rounding* the resulting solution to the nearest set of integers;
4. *verifying* that the solution is feasible; and
5. *repeating* step 3 (with a different rounding criterion) and step 4 until a solution is found.

Ask may then suspect that Creature can "solve" KSP-type problems (e.g., optimally scheduling its day given how it values its time, how much time it has, and how much time certain activities need to take) not on the basis of literally solving an integer programming problem but rather on the basis of solving a linear programming problem and rounding off the result to the nearest allowable integers. Ask can test for this insight most sharply in cases in which the RL-based solution to the KSP differs markedly from its brute-force, exhaustive search solution—in which case Creature's solution when using the RL Heuristic will be significantly different from its solution when using exhaustive search to solve the KSP.

Local Search (LS) Heuristics: The procedure by which the 4,663-city TSP was solved [Lin and Kernighan, 1973] searches the $N!$-size search space of all possible paths by:

1. building an arbitrary, almost-complete tour of the cities—a *delta path*—that includes all of the cities exactly once except for the last one, which is a repeat (e.g., 1-3-2-5-6-3 for a six-city TSP); it is "almost complete" because the last link (return to 1) is missing and is replaced by a return to 3;

2. measuring the total distance of the delta path so generated;

3. selectively making switches between edges included in the delta path and edges that are available but not included;

4. comparing the total distance of the modified circuit with its last version;

5. retaining the more efficient path; and

6. reiterating steps 1–5.

Key to the (exponential) speedup achieved by LS (in the case of the TSP) is the manner of exchanging edges—which is usually two at a time (e.g., 1-3 and 3-2 replaced by 1-2 and 2-3) and thus entails a local search space of $N(N-3)/2$ for each application of the Heuristic. Local search allows that Creature may exclude "by inspection" many possible but absurd combinations of routes. In the 4,663-city TSP, Creature can thus immediately exclude such combinations as Toronto-Kelowna-Quebec (in central, western, and eastern Canada, respectively) without further evaluation. The speedup produced by local search is related to the replacement of the $N!$-size search space by a tightly coordinated sequence of moves along a trajectory of $O(N^2)$ search problems, and it is typical of both the architecture and the performance of well-designed LS strategies generally. Once he is aware of the architecture of LS, Ask can use it is as a "thought probe" to determine whether Creature is engaged in intelligent (as opposed to "blind") local search. The operative difference is that Creature must use significantly more memory if it employs a *k-exchange* LS Heuristic (i.e., it must remember the path lengths it has generated on past trials) than if it uses a blind local search process that responds to results of only the most recent trial. Therefore, Ask's probe for discerning among types of local search that Creature can use is *How much and specifically what do you remember about where you have traveled in the search space?*

Randomization Heuristics: Stochastic Hill Climbing, Simulated Annealing, and Genetic Algorithms. Ask recalls that NP denotes nondeterministic polynomial time (*not* nonpolynomial time) and refers to the solvability of intractable problems by nondeterministic algorithms in polynomial time. It is therefore not surprising that randomization can be used to significant advantage in the solution of computationally costly problems. Ask understands randomization Heuristics as *informed guessing* strategies. If he takes Creature to be using such an algorithm, then he can reasonably ascribe to it a search strategy aimed at maximizing the probability of arriving at an answer within a given number of steps (e.g., max $P(S = S^*)$ s.t. $T(N) < T^*$). The difficulty in searching the solution spaces of most hard problems is the vast number of local minima in which incremental procedures ("local hill climbing") can become trapped [Michalewicz and Fogel, 2004]. If Ask takes Creature to be using a randomization Heuristic for solving a computationally hard problem, then he will pay close attention to moves—such as sudden jumps in Creature's stream of thought—that help extricate Creature from local extremum traps. Ask can devise more sophisticated thought probes by understanding more about the micro-structure of randomization Heuristics.

Stochastic hill-climbing (SHC) Heuristics (see Hromkovic [2003]; Michalewicz and Fogel [2004]) attempt to free limited search processes from the constraints of local optima by probabilistically causing the searcher to "jump" to different regions of the search space. A Creature using SHC will exhibit the typically "jumpy" mental behavior ("ADHD-like" and "fugue of ideas" are terms that Ask may have encountered in the writings of some who understand little of the mechanics of randomized search) that Ask already understands to be the key signature of randomization more generally. Ask may specifically expect that a Creature using SHC to solve a problem will jump from one viable solution concept to another at a rate that is unrelated to the promise of the candidate solution currently under Creature's consideration.

Simulated annealing Heuristics, in contrast, are forms of SHC in which Creatures jump from one potential solution (or solution neighborhood) to another at rates that *are* related to the promise of the solution or neighborhood currently under consideration. Ask can interpret the rate of jumping as the "temperature" of Creature's mental behavior and can use it to distinguish between greater or lesser levels of adaptiveness of Creature's random search strategy to its local rate of success.

Genetic Heuristics (GH) and genetic algorithms combine the insight that randomization can induce probabilistic speedup of convergence to an optimal solution with a structured approach to the solution generation process inspired by the operations of mutation, selection, and retention that are the foundation of evolutionary explanations of biological structure and behavior. Ask expects that a GH-utilizing Creature will randomly generate primitive candidate solutions—for instance, delta paths in a Lin–Kernighan representation of TSP—and then perturb (mutate) and recombine (reproduce) them to produce new candidate solutions that it then prunes or filters (selects) based on the quality of the solution that they encode [Fogel, 1995]. The parameters of mutation rate, reproduction intensity, and selection pressure are under Creature's control.

Genetic algorithms provide Ask with another route to generate hypotheses for interpreting various "frenetic" states of mind that Creature might experience when trying to solve hard problems. Ask can distinguish, for example, between the "structured panic" of a randomization Heuristic based on a high-temperature genetic algorithm and "true panic"—the state of psychic disorganization that can arise from Creature *knowing* that it *must* solve a problem it also *knows it cannot solve* in the allotted time—by examining reasoning-out-loud transcripts of Creature's mental states and looking for the key signature patterns of genetic programming (variation, selection, retention) that are not likely to obtain in a state of "true panic." Additionally, Ask may be able to distinguish a Creature that searches using a genetic Heuristic

from one that searches using a SHC approach by focusing on the local coherence of Creature's thoughts and mental behavior patterns. If it uses some
form of stochastic hill climbing to guide its search, then Creature should be
able to give (to Ask) a relatively coherent account of "what it is seeking, where
it has been, and where it is going" in its search space. The answer may change
when Creature jumps to another hill, but it will be coherent. If it uses GH,
however, then Creature is not likely to give as coherent an answer because the
basic units of mutation and selection are likely to be short and randomly generated. Thus, Ask can use the intelligibility of Creature's self-reported states of
mind as a possible test for distinguishing between these different randomization Heuristics.

   A note on parallelization: What of parallelization? Ask can use the basic
insight of randomization methods ("start anywhere") to test the (ex ante implausible but potentially intriguing) hypothesis that Creature's mental behavior can be characterized by the parallel processing of subproblems ("start in
multiple places at once") even when Creature is actually aware of the unfolding of only one such process at any moment in time. Ask can test the
"parallelizability" of Creature's mental behavior by asking Creature for along-
the-way estimates of "where the answer might lie" in a search space (or by
offering it bets on this), *in addition to* questions about "what Creature's mind
is doing," and then looking for answer combinations that are inconsistent in
the sense that Creature could not know what it does about the answer's location if it is "only" doing what it believes itself to be doing.

   A Hierarchy of Models for Creature's Mental Behavior.   Ask now has at his
disposal a tool kit of models that will allow him to map Creature's mental
behavior at several levels of analysis and to represent several different degrees
of freedom of that behavior. He can model choices that Creature makes
among different kinds of problems by which it represents its predicaments
(in terms of problem complexity class), among different kinds of solutions it
can aim to produce (exact, approximate, probabilistic), and among different
algorithms and Heuristics for solving a particular problem to arrive at the
desired solution type. Ask can also model the choices that Creature makes
at the level of an operation or basic unit of calculation—once it has chosen
its problems and solution procedures. Ask now wants to rise above the exercise of building local models of Creature's problem-solving behavior and to

build not only a model of Creature's mental behavior but also a *hierarchy* of such models that represent different levels of computational sophistication that Ask could plausibly ascribe to Creature. He can do so by following the basic logic used for developing models of the local cost–benefit calculus of Creature's mental behavior. On the one hand, Ask has a library of canonical problem statements that he can use to represent Creature's mental behavior and to measure the (psychic) cost to Creature of arriving at a solution that is—by Creature's own criteria—good enough. On the other hand, Ask also has a way to measure the marginal benefit of an additional calculation or operation for a problem—namely, by the decrease in the entropy of Creature's estimate of the solution to its problem at any point in the process of trying to solve it. What Ask finally needs is a model that ascribes a value to arriving at a solution, regardless of whether the solution is exact or approximate and whether it was generated by a deterministic or stochastic solution search process. The time complexity of the algorithm Creature uses will give Ask an estimate of Creature's total cost of using that algorithm to generate a solution: $C(A) = c(m) T(S_A)$, where $c(m)$ is the marginal cost of an operation and $T(\cdot)$ is the time complexity of generating the solution S_A. However, the value $V(S_A)$ of the solution S_A generated by algorithm A will be different for different kinds of algorithms, as follows.

1. *Deterministic algorithms, exact solutions:* $V(S_A) = V(S)$ if the algorithm has converged to the exact solution and $V(S_A) = 0$ otherwise. Creature's along-the-way benefit is measured by the decrease in the entropy of its subjective probability estimates of the exact value of the solution, but the value of the solution is fully realized only if Creature actually computes it successfully.

2. *Deterministic algorithms, approximate solutions:* $V(S_A) = F_m(\|S - S_A\|)$, where $dF/d(\cdot) < 0$. The value of the solution generated by the algorithm at any step m is a decreasing function of (a) the distance between the solution produced by the algorithm (the approximation) on the mth iteration and (b) the exact solution to the problem.

3. *Randomized algorithms, exact solutions:* $V(S_A) = G(P_m(S = S_A))$. The value of S_A is proportional to the probability that the solution generated on the mth operation of the algorithm is the solution to the problem.

4. *Randomized algorithms, approximate solutions:* $V(S_A) = G(P_m(||S - S_A||$ $< \varepsilon))$, where $dG/d(\cdot) > 0$. The value of the solution produced by the algorithm at step m will be an increasing function of the probability that the solution produced at step m is within a small enough distance of the solution to the problem.

Ask can now reconstruct—for any given problem statement and algorithm or meta-algorithm that Creature chooses—the local net benefit of an additional calculation, which will determine whether or not it is "worth it" for Creature to keep thinking about a problem using a specific algorithm. The resulting marginal net benefit analysis can be used by Ask to create a hierarchy of models of Creature's mental behavior that characterize Creature as more or less sophisticated in terms of its level of insight, logical prowess, and awareness of its own problem-solving predicament. Proceeding in terms of increasing sophistication, Ask posits the following classes of computational potency for Creature.

Imbecility: Creature produces mental behavior that does not exhibit stable algorithmic patterns. It does not know even the first-order logical implications of what it knows. Creature can read a problem statement and repeat it back, but it can neither sketch an outline of a solution procedure nor reliably turn a narrative description of a predicament into a well-defined, well-structured problem—since this would entail performing basic logical calculations aimed at showing the equivalence of the problem statement to the salient parts of the narrative of its predicament.

Computational sloth: Creature uses only very simple heuristics (of constant or at most linear time complexity) to solve given well-structured problems, and it can structure narrative or fuzzy accounts of a predicament only in the form of problems that admit of constant-complexity or linear-complexity solution procedures or algorithms.

Computational adequacy: Creature tackles well-structured problems of different time-complexity classes, but it does not regulate its problem-solving behavior as a function of the marginal net benefit of an additional operation. Creature will tackle P-hard as well as NP-hard and NP-complete problems, but it will typically run out of time when tackling intractable problems with large numbers of variables.

Computational sophistication: Creature adapts its local thinking processes to the time it has at its disposal and as a function of the local costs and benefits of thinking further about a problem, but it does not adapt its problem formulation to these constraints. Creature will "move on to a different problem" once it realizes that the solution algorithm it has chosen for the problem it has formulated will not take it to the desired solution in the time it has to solve the problem, but it will not change its algorithmic search strategy or the problem's formulation.

Meta-computational sophistication: Creature will adapt its choice of algorithms (from exhaustive search to Heuristics for NP-hard problems and among different types of Heuristics for NP-class problems) to the local payoff structure of its thinking processes, but it will not modify the problem statements meant to capture its predicaments in ways that are responsive to the overall costs and benefits of its own mental behavior.

Wisdom: Creature will adapt its choice of algorithms to the local payoff structure of its thinking processes and will modify the problem statements meant to capture its predicaments in ways that are responsive to the overall costs and benefits of its own mental behavior. Under time and resource constraints, it will define well-structured P-class problems in lieu of NP-class problems according to the relative net benefit of solving the two different kinds of problems in a given predicament.

Meta-computational sophistication and wisdom both require that Creature make trade-offs among different types of problem statements and solution-generating processes on (at least) three different dimensions: the reliability of the solution-generating procedure, the accuracy of a solution that can be generated in a finite time, and the speed with which the algorithm converges to a solution of the required reliability and/or accuracy. (See Figure 4.11.) A wise or meta-computationally sophisticated Creature will choose algorithm A over algorithm B to solve problem *P* if and only if, in the most definitive case, algorithm A converges more quickly and more reliably to a more accurate solution than does algorithm B. If one algorithm does not Pareto dominate the other in terms of both of these aspects, then Creature will choose between the two algorithms on the basis of the relative value it places on reliability, accuracy, and speed in generating a solution. A wise Creature will additionally consider ways of reformulating the problem statement so that

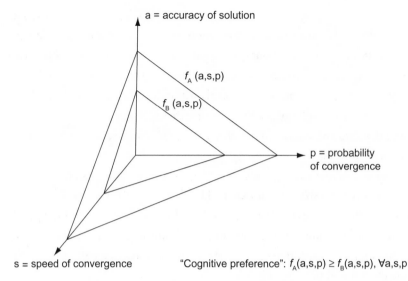

FIGURE 4.11. Three-dimensional measure of the value of a solution to a problem.
Note: The measure incorporates the reliability of the solution-
generating procedure as well as its expected precision and speed of
convergence.

it is a better match for Creature's algorithmic tool kit and level of computational prowess: the algorithms Creature knows how to implement along with
its estimate of (a) the total cost of computing a solution with these algorithms
and (b) the value of producing solutions of a particular reliability and accuracy within a given time constraint to the classes of problems that plausibly
capture its predicament.

5.2. *Thinking Instrumentally about Instrumental Thinking*

Ask realizes that meta-computational sophistication and wisdom are intuitively hard to come by in the sense of likely being both statistically rare and
computationally hard to instantiate, and he realizes that their putative rarity
may be linked to their computational difficulty. Ask would accordingly like
to know just how hard they are to come by. Toward this end, he formulates
(following his own templates) the problem of *meta-reasoning*—whereby Creature thinks in an instrumental fashion about the costs and benefits of its own
instrumental thinking. He can do so [Conitzer and Sandholm, 2003] by first
quantifying the performance of different algorithms on the problem(s) that

can plausibly be ascribed to Creature as a set $\{f_i\}$ of performance profiles of different algorithms i that are nondecreasing functions of the amount of time spent on solving a problem using a particular algorithm, a set $\{N_k\}$ of numbers of steps allocated to solving each problem, and a *minimum performance target* $V(S_k)$ as the minimal acceptable value of solutions to the k problems under considerations. Creature's meta-problem of thinking instrumentally about its own instrumental thinking then maps to the problem that asks whether or not there exists a set $\{N_k\}$ of operations expended on each of the k problems such that $\sum_k |N_k| \leq N$ while $\sum_k f_k(N_k) \geq V(S_k)$.

Ask sees that this problem is computationally isomorphic to the knapsack decision problem and is therefore NP-complete. Ask is thus led to the fact that he must make one more distinction: between Creature being sophisticated or wise (a) in the purely representational sense that it is aware of and always grappling with meta-reasoning problems of this type or (b) in the sense that it is actually solving such problems, often by Heuristic methods. Ask labels the former *platonic* sophistication and wisdom and the latter *pragmatic* (or *performative*) sophistication and wisdom. As a result of this distinction and the reasoning path that led him to it, Ask realizes that there is a strong sense in which performative meta-computational sophistication and wisdom require a certain degree of computational potency: To be "wise" in the performative sense, Creature must be "smart" in the computational sense.

6. INTERACTIVE COMPUTATIONAL SOPHISTICATION

Ask is, finally, interested in one more aspect of Creature's degree of computational sophistication, and that is its *interactive* sophistication: How sophisticated does Creature take other Creatures (with whom it is interacting) to be? The question of interactive reasoning in general has received significant attention in the epistemic game theory literature [Brandenburger, 1992], where inquiry has been oriented and structured by questions such as: "What is the minimal/maximal level of *interactive* thinking (i.e., of thinking about what each agent thinks, what each agent thinks other agents think, and so forth) that it is reasonable or sufficient to presume rational agents go through when they engage in thinking about decision problems with interdependent outcomes (i.e., games)?" More to the point: When Creature produces behavior of whatever kind, should Ask assume that Creature thinks about what Ask thinks, about what Ask thinks Creature thinks, about what Ask thinks Creature thinks Ask thinks, . . . ? Where should a reasonable regress stop, short of "common knowledge"?

If one of Creature's "strategies" is a logically linked set of choices that are responsive to what Creature thinks the situation will be and what Creature thinks other Creatures think the situation will be, then Ask will want to know: Can Creature make its mental choices *strategically*—that is, can it choose to think more or less deeply in ways that are responsive to its estimates of the level of computational potency of the other Creatures with whose actions Creature's payoffs are linked? Ask thus formulates Creature's problem of thinking strategically *about* thinking strategically as a two-step process of (i) choosing a canonical algorithm or family of algorithms that provide the "engine" for further thinking about a situation and (ii) choosing the level of logical depth to which the algorithm is carried out as a function of Creature's estimate of the logical or computational depth of some other Creature with whom it is interacting.

How might Ask operationalize this question about interactive computational sophistication? Ask can model a strategic interaction as a competitive game, define the solution as the competitive equilibrium point of the game, and then posit that Creature must choose the precision to which it wants to calculate this equilibrium—that is, its stopping rule. One-step computations will have Creature calculate its own best course of action; a two-step procedure will have it calculate its response to its estimate of its competitor's uninformed decision; a four-step computation will have Creature calculate its best response to its competitor's best response to its best response to its estimate of its competitor's "uninformed" decision; and an *exact* solution to the problem will have Creature calculate for as long as required to reach the Nash equilibrium strategy set.

In order to obtain estimates of Creature's responsiveness to the marginal costs and benefits of a calculation in an interactive setting, Ask restricts his attention, for the time being, to the class of uniformly convergent iterative algorithms, which generate sequences A_k of uniformly closer and closer approximations to an exact answer A. (This restriction is not critical; the basic method can be generalized to other classes of algorithms provided that Ask comes up with the right metric for the marginal cost and benefit of an additional computation.) Ask can calculate the value of the marginal informational gain of an operation (or an iteration of its algorithm) by considering the *loss* to Creature due to suboptimal levels of computation. Ask can set up an interaction between Creature and Kreature (another Creature, which can be Ask in the disguise of a software program to which Creature has access via a graphical user interface that fools it into thinking it is dealing with a real Creature) in a market where they are the only two competitors, who jointly face a linear and downward-sloping demand curve given by $q = a - p$; here a is some constant, q is the (total) quantity of units of good X sold on the market, and p is the equilibrium price of the good. Assuming c to be the marginal cost of the good, Ask can calculate the quantity that Creature and Kreature would have to produce of good X in order to maximize profits by differentiating the total profit of each competitor, $\text{Pr}_i = (a - q_i - q_j - c)q_i$ $(i, j = 1, 2)$, with respect to the quantity of good X produced to obtain two linear equations in two unknowns:

$$q_i^* = \frac{a - q_j^* - c}{2}; \quad i, j = 1, 2. \tag{5}$$

These two equations can be solved simultaneously to derive the Nash equilibrium output: $q_1^* = q_j^* = (a - c)/3$. This represents the (unique) quantity choice from which neither Creature nor Kreature can unilaterally deviate and be better-off.

Ask can now ask not only *What happens if the two competitors do not "find their way" to the Nash equilibrium on account of computational limitations or logical sloth?*—the traditional question posed in "bounded rationality" analyses of competitive games [Rubinstein, 1986]—but also *What is the (marginal) utility for Creature/Kreature to engage in (deeper) levels of computation?* Knowing this would give Ask an idea of the marginal utility of additional computations using a greater or lesser number of iterations of an algorithm in a particular class. To answer this question, Ask must formulate a plausible algorithmic model of the procedure by which Creature and Kreature reason their way(s) to a conclusion regarding output as an intuitive iterative procedure—a procedure under which the iterations carry real psychological "meaning" in that they capture a relevant component of a competitor's way of thinking about the problem. To arrive at such an algorithm [Saloner, 1994; following Milgrom and Roberts, 1990], suppose first that Creature decides to produce the (monopolistic) output of $(a - c)/2$. Kreature's profit-maximizing response to this choice is not $(a - c)/2$ but rather $(a - c)/4$. But if Kreature actually produces $(a - c)/4$ then Creature's profit-maximizing response will no longer be $(a - c)/4$ but rather $3(a - c)/8$. This line of reasoning maps out an infinite series of mutually adjustable "best responses" of Creature's moves to Kreature's moves and vice versa,

$$t_n = \frac{a - c - t_{n-1}}{2}, \quad n = 1, 2, 3, \ldots, \infty, \tag{6}$$

such that $\lim_{n \to \infty}(t_n) = (a - c)/3$. This allows Ask to measure not only the informational gain (in bits) of each iteration on the series but also the profit advantage to Creature to be derived from "thinking further" through the series—in other words, thinking about what Kreature thinks Creature thinks Kreature thinks Creature thinks. Table 4.5 shows a number of steps of the computational landscape associated with this game. Column 2 shows Creature's quantity choice, and column 4 gives Creature's best response (the profit-maximizing quantity selection) if Kreature plays the best response to Creature's actual move (which is shown in column 3). Every additional iteration buys Creature one extra bit of information (column 5), which represents the marginal benefit of an additional calculation. How much is a bit

TABLE 4.5.   Relative Benefits of Logical Depth of Creature's Calculations as a Function of the Game Structure and the Logical Depth of Kreature's Calculations

Iteration	If Creature chooses quantity . . .	Then Creature's profit-maximizing response is . . .	In which case Creature's profit-maximizing quantity choice should have been . . .	Information (in bits) gained per additional iteration	Information (in bits) needed to achieve best response level of output relative to actual output level
0	$(a - c)/2$	$(a - c)/4$	$3(a - c)/8$	1	2
2	$(a - c)/4$	$3(a - c)/8$	$5(a - c)/16$	1	2
3	$3(a - c)/8$	$5(a - c)/16$	$11(a - c)/32$	1	2
4	$5(a - c)/8$	$11(a - c)/32$	$21(a - c)/64$	1	2
5	$11(a - c)/32$	$21(a - c)/64$	$43(a - c)/128$	1	2
6	$21(a - c)/64$	$43(a - c)/128$	$85(a - c)/256$	1	2
7	$43(a - c)/128$	$85(a - c)/256$	$171(a - c)/512$	1	2

of information worth to Creature *in dollars*? Well, in this particular game Ask can directly calculate whether or not it will be *worthwhile* for Creature to engage in the additional computation by assuming a fixed cost c_I per iteration (and therefore per additional bit of information). Then an additional iteration of the best-response routine will be worthwhile for Creature if the computation's net benefit—that is, the difference between the net profit gain to thinking one step further and the cost of the additional iteration required to do so—is positive. (Of course, this reasoning assumes that Creature does not experience any along-the-way anxiety costs of thinking one step further.)

Using this approach, Ask can generate and examine the entire computational landscape of this game model, for a particular set of values of a and c, and so determine the *profitability* of each matched pair of outputs of Creature and Kreature corresponding to different levels of iterations performed by them. Part of this landscape is displayed in Figure 4.12. Profits of various computational strategy sets are plotted against the degree of computational depth to which Creature and Kreature iterate the sequence given by equation (6), which converges to the NE output levels $((a - c)/3, (a - c)/3)$ and the NE profit levels $((a - c)^2/9, (a - c)^2/9)$. After 20 iterations, convergence to within 0.01% of the Nash equilibrium level of output is achieved. (Depending on how much 0.01% of profits represents to Creature and how much it believes it represents to Kreature, Creature may truncate its iterations of the best-response routine at 20 repetitions. Ask will want to distinguish between the case in which Creature stops at k iterations because it has run out of time and the case in which it stops at k iterations because it has decided that it is no longer in its interest to continue; these cases correspond to different levels of computational prowess.)

How should knowledge of the game's computational landscape be treated by a Creature of interactive computational sophistication? If Creature knows that Kreature's mental behaviors are computationally bounded in some way that makes Kreature *unresponsive* to marginal incentives to reason or calculate more deeply, then it would be reasonable for Creature simply to choose the quantity that corresponds to the "best response" to the expected quantity selection of Kreature. For example, if Creature believes that Kreature will choose to produce $3(a - c)/8$ units, then it would be reasonable for Creature to produce the best-response quantity of $5(a - c)/16$ units rather than the

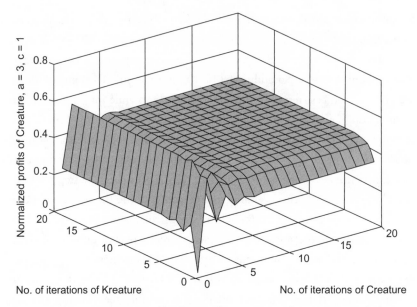

FIGURE 4.12. Computational landscape of interactive profit-maximizing calculations
in Cournot duopoly with two Creatures ($a = 3$, $c = 1$). *Note:* Horizontal
axes represent number of mental operations for Creature and Kreature;
vertical axis is the profit level of Creature (profit levels of Kreature are
symmetrical). The landscape converges to a Nash equilibrium output
of $(a - c)/3$.

$(a - c)/3$ units representing the NE quantity choice. It is, then, possible for a
computationally potent Creature to lose money if its play is based on a strategy that is logically "too deep" when playing against a computational sloth.
Thus, a Creature that is interactively computationally sophisticated will make
conjectures about its competitors' levels of logical potency and will tailor
accordingly the logical depth of the reasoning on which its actual strategy
is based.

7. STOPPING RULES: ON THE REFRAGABILITY
OF MENTAL ANCHORS

Where *does* thinking stop? Where *should* it stop? Where can Ask safely assume
that Creature's thinking will stop? What anchors Creature's thinking? These
are the questions that will matter deeply to any modeler of minds, for reasons
that can be made plain by considering a situation in which Creature is asked

to say *why* it believes that "the sun will rise tomorrow" (common language rendition of the claim that the patterns of planetary motion observed in the past will continue in the future), given that Ask has already ascertained that Creature *does* believe it. Inductively, Creature might say that its belief hinges on the fact that it has always seen the sun rise in the past and has never seen it not rise, leading Creature to believe that "the sun will rise" is either a true or a very probably true sentence. Ask could counter, however, with Hume's contention that so justifying this belief must rely on an *antecedent* belief in the uniformity of nature that is, itself, not justified. If Creature tries to escape the conundrum by arguing, meta-inductively, that inductive arguments are themselves inductively justified ("induction has worked in the past, therefore it will work in the future"), then Ask can reply that counter-inductive arguments are counter-inductively justified ("counter-induction has *not* worked in the past, therefore it *will* work in the future")—thus casting doubt on the validity of any circular argument of the type "induction is inductively justified" and "inference to the best explanation is justified by an inference to the best explanation as to why the best explanation is true."

In response, Creature could borrow a page from Popper [1959] and argue that its belief in the truth of the sentence "the sun will rise tomorrow" is based on the fact that the sentence follows deductively from the truth of a set of lawlike statements ("Newton's laws") that, though *unjustifiable*, have not yet been *falsified* in spite of repeated attempts made by humans intent on disconfirming them. Ask can, however, counter that the epistemic structure on which Creature's belief now rests must itself assume some inductive support for the statement that "laws that have not been disconfirmed in spite of repeated attempts to do so will continue to be valid in the future," in which case the earlier arguments against inductive inference are recapitulated.

Ask can also challenge Creature's belief in the validity of deductive reasoning itself, arguing that the validity of the rules by which syllogisms are produced is not deductively provable and thus not deductively *justified*—by the standards of justification imposed by deductive logic itself—as follows. In the manner of Gödel [1931], Ask assigns natural numbers to each well-formed proposition of first-order logic (made up of variables, constants, functions, and particles such as connectives and quantifiers) such that to every proposition there corresponds exactly one natural number. Although this is not the only possible arithmetization of first-order logic, Ask can assign the first ten natural numbers to connectives and constant signs, one prime number greater than 10 to each numerical variable, the square of a prime number greater than 10 to each variable denoting a sentence, and the cube of a prime number greater than 10 to each variable denoting a predicate. Thus, Ask can define $g(S)$ = *the Gödel number of proposition S* as the product of the Gödel numbers of the connectives, variables, predicates, and sentences that together constitute S—for example, $g(S) = 2^{g(a_1)} \times 3^{g(a_2)} \times \cdots \times p^{g(a_p)}$, where p is the pth prime number. Such formulas are (a) uniquely decodable, in the sense that each Gödel number encodes exactly one proposition, and (b) recursive, in the sense that the Gödel number of a higher-level proposition can be constructed from the Gödel numbers of the sentences that it comprises. Therefore, this Gödel numbering system maps a theory or language in first-order logic to arithmetic, a trick that Ask will find handy for producing the following argument about the impossibility of a deductive justification for deductive reasoning.

Ask first uses a result due to Turing (see Boolos and Jeffrey [1993]) to the effect that any recursive function is computable by a Turing Machine. Then, following Putnam [1985], Ask defines a procedure M that solves the decision problem of ascertaining whether or not a function is computable and defines a matrix $D(n, k)$ whose entries represent the kth number of the nth function that is proved by M to be computable, plus 1. Creature can "just see"—if it has followed the argument—that D *is* recursive and computable (Ask just showed how to compute each entry) and hence that it should be part of its own domain. However, Creature can see also that D cannot be proved by M to be computable, for otherwise $D(n, k) = D(n, k) + 1$. This maneuver *should* undercut Creature's belief that the ensemble of its deductive competences is reducible to the machine realization that makes formal proof possible. Adding 1 to a function (e.g., computing 2 from 1 by adding 1 to itself) is a trivial example of "computing a recursive function," but any reduction of Creature's competence on this score to a proof-theoretic procedure will either omit its capability or license a logical contradiction. Of course, Creature may continue to believe in, vouch for, and use deductive inferences notwithstanding Ask's demonstration that at least some part of Creature's deductive tool kit cannot be deductively proved to be valid. Such persistence is only a little less informative to Ask in his attempt to understand Creature than would be Creature's explicit disavowal—as a result of understanding Ask's arguments—of first-order logic as a technique for building syllogisms.

Ask can additionally challenge Creature to come up with a way of telling *what*, exactly, it is validating when it engages in inductive inference from a set of particular evidence statements to a general or universal law. He can put to Creature the paradox of time-dependent confirmation [Goodman, 1955], which runs as follows.

1. Define *grue* emeralds as emeralds that are green at or before time *t* in the future (e.g., 5 p.m. tomorrow) and blue thereafter; define *bleen* emeralds as emeralds that are blue at or before time *t* and green thereafter.

2. Therefore, if an emerald is observed to be blue at $T < t$, then it will confirm both the hypothesis "this emerald is blue" and the hypothesis "this emerald is bleen."

3. If an emerald is observed to be green at $T < t$, then it will confirm both the hypothesis "this emerald is green" and the hypothesis "this emerald is grue."

4. Therefore, confirmation is indeterminate: You (Creature) have no justifiable way of disambiguating a grue emerald from a green emerald and no way of disambiguating a blue emerald from a bleen one.

Creature may object that "grue" and "bleen" are pathological predicates because they link the name of a predicate to different points in time—and so run counter to the very principle that undergirds the use of objects in general, which is to refer to *time-invariant* entities and their properties—and therefore that nonpathological uses of language demand that Creature speak "blue-green" languages rather than "grue-bleen" languages. Ask can undercut this maneuver by showing that Creature's criterion for distinguishing between pathological and nonpathological languages does not deliver what it promises: From the perspective of someone who uses the language of grue and bleen, Ask argues, it is blue and green that impermissibly couple time into the definition of a predicate: "Green emeralds are emeralds that are grue on or before time *t* and bleen thereafter, and blue emeralds are emeralds that are bleen on or before time *t* and grue thereafter."

Ask can carry out an "anchors of thought" analysis not only on lawlike statements—that is, on statements (such as those about future states of affairs) that rest upon beliefs in lawlike or universal statements—but also on *particular* statements and their immediate interpretation. "Lo, there is a white swan," for instance, can lend support to the statement "all swans are white" and also to the statement "non-swans are non-white." This is the logical equivalent of setting up a situation in which a statement such as "there is a black car" can be said to lend (inductive) support to the statement "all swans are white": Cars are not swans and therefore their blackness confirms the proposition "non-swans are non-white," which is logically equivalent to the statement "all swans are white." Creature need not be "mindcuffed" by such examples, of course. It could counter that observing the color of a car cannot count as a statement that can lend inductive support to the color of swans and therefore should be excluded from the range of statements that are admissible as observations. This would reveal to Ask something about Creature's implicit philosophy of language: Creature is not willing to accept that the logical equivalence of two statements ("there is a white swan" and "there is a non-white (black) non-swan (car)") entails their material equivalence. Ask deduces that Creature first interprets "there is a black car" as "there is a car that is black" and then proceeds to eliminate the statement from consideration as a confirmation for "all swans are white" because the sentence speaks of cars and not of swans, directing Creature's attention to cars (the subject) and only then to their color. Ask will therefore conclude that Creature interprets propositions in first-order logic in ways that ascribe to them a temporal structure that they do not, in themselves, possess. Creature may itself be aware of this fact, and it can argue that *I went to the market and bought a machine gun* is different from *I bought a machine gun and went to the market* in ways that are obscured by a strictly logical use of the connective "and." Thus Ask can use inquiry trained on the ways in which Creature assigns weight and credence to various propositions in order to derive insight into Creature's personal epistemology.

Ask can also investigate the ways in which Creature's commitments to refer to certain entities by certain names ("the sun") respond to challenges aimed at destabilizing Creature. In particular, Ask can posit that what makes an object that which it is is a set of essential properties (large, hot, bright, visible on the horizon at 5 p.m., no longer visible at 11 p.m., etc.) that the object in question must possess. Ask can also posit that what makes a property essential ("hot") rather than nonessential ("five miles from the Atlantic shore") is the fact that it is a causal power of that object—in other words, the power of that object to *cause* certain effects to occur. If Creature agrees with this line of reasoning and is willing to pursue its logical implications, then it will agree: (i) that the "objecthood" of an object depends on the set of causal sequences (of the type "*A* causes *B*") that confer causal powers and therefore identity on that object; and therefore (ii) that whatever doubts Ask succeeded in raising in Creature's mind regarding the inference of causation from correlation (or regarding induction more generally) will also apply to its commitments and intuitions about "entitivity." Ask can take, then, a distinctly epistemological route to raising ontological concerns in Creature. He will be interested to observe Creature's response to such arguments and, in particular, to understand (a) whether Creature has any interest in resolving a challenge to its ontological commitments that arises from logical conundrums with induction (as opposed to simply ignoring the challenge and getting on with its day) and (b) how Creature will seek to address such challenges, given that it does so at all. Such observations should give Ask some guidance about the view that Creature takes of the epistemic bases of its own beliefs and judgments, which it could interpret in a purely instrumental way as locally useful guideposts to making predictions and everyday arguments or as foundational structures that must be perfected or repaired when challenged before Creature can use them as prediction engines.

The purpose of Ask's protracted questioning, then, is not the pursuit of the pleasure derived from destabilizing or untethering Creature's epistemic states; rather, its purpose is a structured reconnaissance of Creature's *anchors of thought* and of the importance and relevance of these anchors to Creature. The question is: On what premises, assumptions, or axioms is Creature willing to stop thinking further and "hang its hat," epistemically speaking? Creature can, at any point, withdraw from Ask's game by stating that it requires no further justification (e.g., for the validity of inductive inference) or that it feels no compulsion to pursue the dialogue—even though Creature may see the need, in an ideal world, for further justification of its position. Ask aims to reconstruct a basic map of Creature's anchors of thought and to state with some precision that, for instance, Creature *does not believe in inductive inference* on account of problems of inductive justification but *does believe in deductive inference* notwithstanding the problems of deductive justification that arise there. Ask may also be able to state that Creature *understands* the import of various paradoxes and epistemological dead ends to its beliefs but *does not feel compelled to change its beliefs on account of this understanding*, which will help Ask with the task of modeling Creature's mental and behavioral responsiveness to external reasons more generally.

Ask can specifically test for the possibility that Creature's epistemic states are simply unresponsive to the arguments that Ask produces against Creature's epistemic certifiers by first defining the relevance of a sentence T to a sentence S as [Jeffrey, 1983] $\text{Rel}(T \to S) = P(S/T) - P(S/\sim T)$—that is, as the difference between Creature's subjective degree of belief that S is true given that T is true and Creature's subjective degree of belief that S is true given that T is not true. Suppose now that T encodes a syllogism (such as Hume's argument) against the validity of inductive reasoning. Then Ask can ascertain Creature's responsiveness to that argument from the difference in the betting odds that Creature would be willing to accept on the truth of an inductively justified proposition before and after familiarizing Creature with the counterargument T.

8. THE COMPUTATIONAL COMPLEXITY
OF BEING-IN-THE-WORLD

Encouraged by the versatility of COMP, Ask may be tempted to extend its interpretive grasp to include *all* of Creature's behaviors—not just the mental behavior Creature produces for deliberating internally upon the optimal means for achieving its ends on the basis of some given representation of its ends (preferences, payoffs), and beliefs (probabilities) that link its actions and states of the world to payoffs that depend on them. In particular, Ask may be tempted by the following two extensions of COMP.

First, following a suggestion of Popper [1999] that "all life is problem solving," Ask can represent all of Creature's behavior—and not just its mental behavior—as being oriented toward solving problems, or resolving mismatches between Creature's current conditions (states) and its desired conditions (goals). An amoeba (Popper's example) "solves problems" when it feels its way around a pond foraging for food, but does so without (a) an internal representation of its search space, (b) a representation of its state space, and (c) a representation of the algorithms whereby it searches the space of possible solutions (its search space). In sorting its socks after washing them, for instance, Creature may performatively implement a more or less optimal sorting algorithm without knowledge of the algorithm and perhaps without even a conscious awareness of the mechanics of the sorting task itself. Just to make the point sharper, Creature may use sock sorting to "think about other matters," a task for which sorting socks serves as a useful sensorimotor "background."

Second, following a suggestion dating back to Heidegger [1927/1962] but phrased in more reductive terms by Brooks [1991], Ask is tempted to posit that *intelligence need not rely on representation.* Creature's behaviors may be seen as instantiations of the computational states of a machine that "solves problems" that are neither internally represented in "Creature's mind" nor consciously optimized for the efficient realization of the solution space search algorithm they nevertheless execute. In speaking to others, Creature can be seen as constantly but unconsciously ascribing meaning to their words, as seeking evidence that its interlocutors ascribe the same meaning to its own words that it does, and thus as constantly solving for the coordinative equilibrium of a sequence of language games—albeit without any precise representation of either the language game itself or of its space of strategies. In balancing a tray of cups filled with hot liquids, Creature can plausibly be modeled as solving a computationally nontrivial problem of optimal adaptive control without either a precise representation of the end state ("stable equilibrium") or of the space of possible strategies (combinations of forces applied in all possible directions to its wrist and finger joint abductors and adductors, as well as to the pronators and supinators of its forearm).

As a result of these two insights, Ask can posit the following more comprehensive ascriptive principle.

> KOMP. *Interpret Creature's behaviors as computational states of an*
> *algorithmic process that stops ("converges") when the process reaches an end*

state that can plausibly be ascribed to Creature as a goal or objective of its behavior.

KOMP supplants DEC and BEL and transforms Ask's attempt to interpret Creature's behaviors into an exercise aimed at (a) imputing plausible states and goals to Creature, (b) imputing to Creature plausible algorithms that map its states to a sequence of intermediate states to its end goals, and (c) mapping the correspondence of Creature's along-the-way behaviors to the set of intermediate states that link its states to its goals according to the algorithm ascribed to Creature. Creature, according to KOMP, is an unfolding computational process; this does not require (for KOMP's interpretive validity) that Creature *behold* either the algorithm that describes this process or the space of its own states and possible state–goal paths. Therefore, Ask can make use of the apparatus it has developed in the course of mapping Creature's mental behavior to make sense, in brief, of Creature's behavior—while retaining (if he sees fit) a principle such as RESP, which functions at the level of Creature expressing its agency in the choice of problems it attempts to solve and the solution algorithms it uses to search its solution space.

CHAPTER 5

LEARNING AND LEARNING
TO LEARN

Wherein Ask builds a model of learning that informs the way he learns about how Creature learns as well as the way Creature might learn about unknown states of the world, unknown ways of solving problems, and unknown behavioral blueprints and strategies. Ask posits a model of learning as problem-driven, model-based, and refutation-guided and then distinguishes learning from "inductive leaps" and from disembodied normative epistemology. Ask also reconciles the pragmatic and fallibilist model of learning that he uses to learn about Creature's learning with the calculus of beliefs that he uses to make sense of Creature's betting behavior.

ASK IS INTERESTED in modeling the ways Creature relates not only to objects and entities that form the object of its desires (DEC), to the effects of time on these desires (modifications of DEC that incorporate different discounting functions), to uncertainty (BET and BEL), and to the difficulty or relative tractability of the problems it faces (COMP); Ask is also interested in modeling the ways Creature relates to the *unknown*. How, specifically, does Creature *learn*?

This question is as pertinent to Ask's model of Creature as it is to Ask's model of *his own* interactions with Creature. Specifically, Ask attempts, through the deployment of representational models of Creature's physical and mental behavior and beliefs or epistemic states, to learn about Creature quickly, efficiently, reliably, and competently. These models shape his *interventions* upon Creature—the kinds of questions he poses to Creature and the kinds of treatments to which he subjects Creature through the design and implementation of experiments meant to elicit from Creature choices or behaviors that give Ask specific information that is *interpretable* through the prism of a model such as DEC, BEL, COMP, or KOMP. If what Ask does when he engages in his work can be called "learning," then what is the most general representation of this process that may be applied also to understanding what Creature itself does when it "learns"? What is the fundamental structure of a process called "learning," and how is it different from such processes as "choosing," "betting," "thinking," and "calculative reasoning"? If such a process can be distinctly referred to, then what are the minimal conditions that would have to be met in order for Ask to ascertain that Creature does indeed "learn"? Finally, when Ask and Creature are one and the same person—that is, when Ask turns his own models *upon himself*—then what conditions would have to be satisfied in order for Ask to be said to "learn" something thereby? Consider the following situations—all of which Ask might be interested in modeling.

Creature is trying to learn about the ways in which Kreature makes choices among options that have different levels of uncertainty: Creature articulates a model of choice under uncertainty—based, for instance, on a set of relationships between Kreature's beliefs and desires—and proceeds to collect data to test the model in question. Creature tests the model against the data by comparing the predictions of the model with the evidence statements that describe Kreature's actual behavior. At the end of this testing process, Creature will have either validated or invalidated the model it has built, depending on the data collected. If the model is invalidated by the data, then Creature attempts to build a different model, which it tests by the same process used to test the first model. If this model is validated, then Creature stores it in memory as a sort of generative engine for valid predictions of Kreature's behavior, which means that Creature can recall and deploy the model whenever appropriate in the future.

Creature is learning to speak a new language, such as a natural foreign language, a computer language (e.g., LISP or C++), or the axiomatized language system sometimes used by normative social scientists to generate models such as BEL and DEC. Creature learns the rules for building correct or intelligible sentences in the language; then it tests its skill in using the new language by attempting to communicate with skilled users of the language and observing their reactions. If it looks to Creature as if the skilled users of the language have understood the sentences that it has put together, then Creature will remember the rules it has used to construct the sentences in question as "correct." Alternatively, if its sentences are misinterpreted or not understood, Creature will remember the rules it has used to construct its sentences as potentially false or incorrect and will try either to adjust them, iteratively, so that they produce intelligible sentences or to exchange them for different ones altogether—which it will also proceed to test, adjust, and possibly discard in the same fashion.

Creature knows that the problem it is trying to solve is intractable (NP-hard or NP-complete) and learns, by trial and error, an efficient approximation scheme that yields an accurate enough solution in a short enough period of time. Creature may learn this scheme implicitly by trying out various approaches that are subconsciously guided by its understanding of the problem's peculiar structure. Alternatively, the scheme may be learned consciously via a route that has Creature discovering the computational structure of the problem, searching through Heuristics and algorithms that are candidates for solving the problem, and discovering an approximation scheme that works well enough given the problem statement.

Creature learns how to turn, seamlessly, at the end of the swimming pool for the purpose of being able to participate in swimming competitions. Creature breaks down the complex set of motions corresponding to an efficient turn into a sequence of smaller behavioral components, and it tries out different variants of each one of these components by putting different sequences of micro-behaviors together into a complete sequence that corresponds to the desired behavior. Creature then eliminates the sequences of micro-behaviors that do not lead to a successful turn and retains the sequences of behaviors that correspond to a successful turn. (This process may be quite lengthy: For a set of N micro-behaviors each taking on one of M possible states, there are M^N possible combinations to consider and hence there are M^N possible ways to "turn.") If several different sequences of micro-behaviors all lead to satisfactory turns, then Creature may remember all of these sequences as its "repertoire" of skills for turning at the end of a swimming pool. Otherwise, it will adjust, discard, modify, and so forth.

These situations are distinctive in that Creature, in each case, acquires an ability or capacity that it can reliably reproduce within the same situation and export to other situations. They are, accordingly, different from situations typically modeled by DEC, BEL, and COMP, wherein Creature is not necessarily seeking to create a capability for choosing and betting coherently or for solving certain types of problems. It is this *self-referentiality* of learning that makes it a specific and separate area of inquiry for Ask and helps him to distinguish between learning situations and non-learning situations. Ask will want to develop a model that makes this distinction and also distinguishes between cases where Creature has learned and cases where Creature has not learned in a given situation.

1. SOME BASIC MODELING CHOICES: DETERMINISTIC BEHAVIORISM, INDUCTIVISM, AND FALLIBILISM

Ask has a set of fundamental modeling choices to make before proceeding to craft a model for Creature's learning behavior. These choices are related to each other and to the basic question, which should be quite familiar by now and comes in different variants: *What is the basis for Creature's inference from past experience (behavioral, explanatory, or predictive success or failure) to future experience?* or *What is the basis for Creature's inference from observed facts (such as another person's past behavior) to unobserved facts (such as another person's future behavior)?* or *What is the basis for assuming that what has worked in the past (partial sequence of motions corresponding to a satisfactory turn at the end of a swimming pool) will also work in the future?* The answers that Ask chooses to give to such questions will inform the class and kinds of models of learning that Ask will contemplate and articulate.

There is no learning: One possibility is for Ask to assume that Creature *does not learn.* On this view, Creature produces behaviors on the basis of simple principles like the maximization of pleasure and the minimization of pain (both present and future), but these behaviors are determined by a set of internal physiological states and external conditions coupled to a set of "transition rules" that govern the passage from one state to another. Learning, in this case, is an *epiphenomenon* and thus the word "learning" is just a label attached to certain sudden and otherwise hard-to-explain changes in Creature's behavior by overzealous philosophers and social scientists—who are themselves "determined" by internal physiological states and external conditions to produce behavior that corresponds to "speaking about learning." However, the successes that Creature occasionally registers in learning how to swim or even to play or compose a fugue suggest some difficulties with this modeling approach: They show that Creature can effect intelligent, purposeful, intentional changes in its own behavior that are targeted to producing a novel kind of behavior. Accordingly, Ask would like to come up with a model of learning that can account for such "learning" phenomena.

Creature learns by a combination of induction and repetition: This is the traditional modeling approach to learning that continues to permeate several of the social sciences disciplines. In this model, learning is a purely *inductive* process. Creature learns rules associated with successful behavior by extrapolation of past successes to inferences about future successes. It does so in relative obliviousness to the difficulties that surround the justification of inductive inferences, and Creature may be quite unresponsive to Ask's reiteration of these difficulties. "Behavior B has worked for me N times in the past," Creature would reason if it learned according to this model, "and therefore it will work again in the future."

Suppose, however, that, behavior B has *not* produced the desired results every single time it was produced in the past; what does this entail for a model of Creature's learning processes? The inductivist modeler argues that the model should then be made *probabilistic* in nature, as follows: "If behavior B was produced M times in the past and produced the desired results $N < M$ times, and if M is a very large number, then the probability that it will produce the desired results in the future either equals N/M or will *converge* to N/M in the limit as N and M increase without bound." To Ask, this means that Creature should accept betting odds of N/M on the truth value of a proposition that predicts the behavior will produce the desired results in the future, conditional on it having worked N/M times in the past.

Suppose now that there are *several* behaviors that in the past have been successful (albeit to different degrees) in producing the effects that Creature desires. Then, the inductivist modeler posits, Creature should use some metric for comparing the success of the different behaviors and choose *the most successful* one—the one with the highest probability of producing the desired results given Creature's knowledge of past experience and current conditions. Bayes's theorem can then be deployed to allow Creature to update its estimate that a particular behavior will produce an intended effect in a way that incorporates the possibilities of other behaviors producing the same effect. In this case, the model can account for learning in situations in which (a) not every case of behavior has led to performative success or (b) several different behaviors have led to some performative success. This model thus allows for some "informed exploration" and for this reason is significantly better than a model in which no learning is possible: It allows for purposive changes in Creature's behavior in a way that is responsive to past experience, current conditions, and alternatives.

However, this probabilistic approach also has a flaw, one shared by all inductively buttressed models. Suppose Creature is trying to learn the laws governing the behavior of a complex system—such as itself—in a certain type of situation (e.g., one in which it is trying to calm its anxiety through a particular kind of breathing). Creature does not know, ex ante, whether any of the regularities (say, taking ten quick, deep breaths followed by a one-minute period of relaxed breathing) that it observes are physiological or psychophysical *laws* or mere coincidences, and it can hope to achieve better estimates of the probabilities that apparent coincidences *are* actual laws only by observing as many conjunctions of (supposed) cause and (supposed) effect as possible in the time allowed. In prototypical learning scenarios, however, the time allowed for registering potential associations and for testing alternative hypotheses is seldom very long, so Creature's resulting degree of confidence in the validity of such associations will rarely be significant. Thus "learning," whether behavioral or propositional in nature, remains at the level of "speculative conjecture about the putative success of certain behaviors," which seems to miss the fact that Creature can authentically feel it has achieved mastery over a particular new skill that it did not previously possess.

Ask can also posit that Creature learns by building and attempting to calibrate "probabilistic inference networks" around the complex phenomenon describing its own interaction with a domain of experience that it seeks to master by building networked arrangements of proximal and distal causes for the events it is trying to explain or understand and then seeking the most plausible explanations for the observed phenomenon on the basis of exhaustive (and computationally demanding) searches of the type that Ask is by now well equipped to model. Quite aside from the computational difficulty of this approach, Creature will run into the obvious problem that, the more complex the network of causal beliefs it uses to generate explanations, the less likely will be the resulting explanations, as probabilistic weights in belief networks are both subunitary and multiplicative for independent causal chains of events.

The pessimism of the analysis thus far belies experience. Creature can and does make bold new conjectures and try new behaviors, which it "hones" over time into a blueprint for more successful action, and this suggests that purely inductive strategies may not be the best solution search space for Ask's model of Creature's learning.

Creature learns by articulation and refutation: Faced with such difficulties, Ask attempts to formulate a model of learning that incorporates both the possibility of learning from prior experience and also a way of making inferences from prior experience to future performance that is not susceptible to the pitfalls of inductivism and justificationism.

Toward this end, he asks himself *What is the most* efficient *way of making a (fallible) decision as to whether an observed series of conjunctions of events represents an instance of an associative law?* He does not ask *How can I justify, by reliable methods, an inference of causality from a series of correlations?*—the question that previously led him (and Creature) down several unpromising paths. This question guides him to the realization that there is a fundamental asymmetry in the way that one tests for lawlikeness: It takes an infinite number of positive instances to justify the inference of a law from a series of conjunctions, whereas the observation of only one negative instance is enough to render the inference invalid. An inference of an observed conjunction to a law that expresses that conjunction is refuted by the observation of a single exception to that law. Ask would like to posit that learning takes place through the elimination of refuted guesses at the solution to the learning problem that Creature is attempting to solve. He follows Karl Popper for at least a few steps and posits that Creature learns by first articulating a model (a set of lawlike relationships among salient variables) of the situation he faces, deducing a set of observable implications of this model (jointly called *hypotheses*) and then looking for disconfirming evidence of these implications—rather than for confirming evidence or for a combination of confirming or disconfirming evidence. Finally, Creature eliminates the models that have been disconfirmed and retains only the models that have not been disconfirmed by the evidence statements it has collected [Popper, 1959; Popper, 1983]. The basic principle ("Creature proposes, experience disposes") of fallibilist inquiry supplies a logic of learning to which Ask can hold Creature by virtue of a principle of efficiency of learning.

What about validity? Will fallibilist experimentalism not founder on the same rocks as those that pierced the hull of inductivist experimentalism? Here, Ask takes two more steps with Popper and relinquishes the conflation of validity and justifiability as well as that of provability and truth. Putting behavior or conjecture *out there* for putative refutation and taking unrefuted conjecture and unthwarted behavior as tentatively true or tentatively successful is "foolish" only if one feels compelled to anchor conjecture in justification or proof and trial in past validation. In the unfolding model, Creature would no longer speak of being justified in its feeling of "having learned" by the lawlike nature of the regularities it uses to design its behavior; rather, it will speak of how the rules that form the building blocks of its behavior have *not been refuted*. It thereby loses the safeguard of "justification" and the affective shelter that justifications can provide. Creature will have gained, in exchange for this loss of affective security, a valid method for criticizing its beliefs and behaviors and for eliminating those that have been refuted either by evidence statements that it accepts as valid or by experiences that it perceives as veridical. Creature's belief in the "laws by which its world runs" is, in this model, only provisional and conjectural. However, reasons Ask, that is as well as Creature can hope to do once it has given up on believing in the path that would take it from justifiability to certainty to truth—something it needs to do given that it has no infallible foundations from which it can deduce its beliefs, which it therefore can never fully "prove" but only reject on the basis of observation statements that are themselves fallible. So, the move from a justificationist to a fallibilist logic of inquiry provides Ask with an "efficient" model of learning that simultaneously produces a more restricted form of validity through a different mechanism (attempted and failed refuta-tion) than that required by justificationism (repeated confirmation or proof on the basis of empirical propositions). The focus on refutation rather than confirmation also ameliorates, for Creature, the problems raised by confirma-tion paradoxes. "All swans are white" may be nonsensically confirmed by a sentence that reports the discovery of a non-white non-swan, but it cannot be disconfirmed by a sentence that reports anything other than the observation of a non-white swan.

Ask knows (Lakatos [1970]) that it is no simple matter to assert that an evidence statement conclusively refutes a hypothesis. For instance, Creature may be deceived or self-deceived or subject to some kind of perceptual illu-sion, and any of these conditions can influence the process by which it trans-forms raw perceptual data into evidence statements. This objection can be circumvented once Ask realizes that the processes by which evidence state-ments are produced can themselves be modeled and subjected to the same kind of fallibilist inquiry that regulates the process by which hypotheses are tested against evidence statements. An optical illusion can be modeled using the logic used to probe into any other phenomenon: via a model of the processes by which a "real" signal is morphed into an illusion that can be articulated and then itself tested against observation statements (arising from physiological experiments), which then can themselves be criticized using (recursively) the same logic of model articulation, testing, and selective elimination.

Ask is now ready to articulate a model of learning that closely tracks the "logic of scientific discovery" but without the pretense that this logic *must* supply a logic of inquiry by virtue of the success of the scientific enterprise to date. This is where Ask "falls off" the Popperian bandwagon, and what results is a "common person's" practical falsificationism backed by commonsense assumptions about the pragmatics of Creature's learning situation.

2. FALLIBILIST REPRESENTATIONALISM
VIA THE MODEL LEARN

Ask is interested in putting together a model of learning behavior that can be used to interpret, understand, and intervene in situations in which Creature *learns*—that is, produces novel, purposively designed behavior. The resulting LEARN model has several components that work together to produce the modeling effect Ask requires.

PROB: Learning is problem-driven. The outcome of a learning process for Creature is an acceptable solution to a problem that it has set for itself. This problem may be of the usual type ("how to get Y to happen," "how to get person X to take action Y," "how to get person X to hold belief Y") or it may be a purely *cognitive* problem. Examples of the latter include "how to reconcile logically incompatible theories that refer to 'the same' underlying phenomena" (e.g., general relativity theory versus quantum mechanics or neurophysiological versus computational-representational models of mental behavior) and "how to choose between 'rational' and 'quasi-rational' models for the choice behavior of a large ensemble of individuals (e.g., traders in a market) making interdependent choices." A problem circumscribes Creature's *learning project* in that it allows Ask to interpret Creature's behaviors as being purposively oriented toward solving it. The solution to a problem, then, is the end to which Creature produces its learning behavior. Thus, in order to ground its model of Creature's learning behavior, Ask first asks *What is the problem that Creature is trying to solve?* and then proceeds to interpret Creature's behavior in light of a (tentative) answer to this question.

Mod: Learning is model-based. A model is a collection of universal (law-like: applicable to a potentially infinite set of space-time locations) and particular (singular: specific to the time and place of the model's user) statements such that:

a. the universal statements are logically compatible (they do not contradict each other);

b. the universal statements are logically independent (none can be derived from any other); and

c. the particular statements are logically independent of the universal statements (i.e., the particular cannot be derived from the universal alone).

The model DEC, for instance, is made up of a set of universal statements (conditions on the kinds of choice functions that Creature may rationally exhibit) and a set of particular statements (the set of options that Creature is now choosing from). The universal statements of DEC—the axioms of rational choice theory—are logically independent of each other, and none of the universal statements can be used to derive any of the particular statements describing the menu of options from which Creature chooses. Universal terms and statements provide *bridges* by which Creature moves from particulars to particulars, and particular statements provide the (initial, final, and boundary) conditions of the model's applicability to Creature's particular predicament.

There are two senses in which Ask can hold Creature's learning behavior to be model-based. The first posits that Creature *represents* its learning predicament via a model whose variables, parameters, and so forth Creature is uncertain about or ignorant of. Learning consists of iteratively decreasing uncertainty about (a) whether the model's variables represent Creature's predicament in a way that allows Creature to specify truth conditions for propositions that follow from the model, (b) whether or not the combination of variables that are embodied in the model's propositions are the correct ones (structural uncertainty), and (c) the actual values of the model's variables and parameters (estimation uncertainty).

The second sense in which Creature's learning behavior is model-based is consistent with nonrepresentational models (e.g., KOMP) of Creature—and posits that Creature's learning behavior proceeds *as if* it is guided by the kind of explicit model-based learning just described *but need not be*. Ask uses a model to represent Creature's learning behavior as a convenient reification. A model functions as a regulative grammar for the interactions between Creature and the world, but Creature need not be conscious of the representation it uses or be able to explicitly state, at any point, which kind of uncertainty its behavior is currently aiming to decrease. Ask simply *interprets* Creature's learning behavior as being guided by a model that need not exist in Creature's mind at all—much as Creature might impute a complex feeling (e.g., shame) to a dog in a situation where a human might have experienced that feeling.

TEST: Models are learning instruments to the extent that they can be used to construct—by combinations of particular and universal statements—propositions that are *testable* against evidence statements, which means that their representational value and validity depend on the truth of the evidence statements that test them. For instance, using DEC and making some assumptions about Bob's menu of options, Creature can deduce that Bob's utility function ranks recreational drug A ahead of recreational drug B and thus that Bob, given the opportunity to choose either, will *not choose* drug B over drug A because—as a matter of universal principle—Bob-like creatures choose so as to maximize the utility function that is imputable to them on the basis of observations of their past choice behavior. Creature uses both the universal model DEC and the particular statements describing Bob's option set to construct hypotheses about Bob's behavior, which it can test by observing and recording an account of that behavior. It follows that the hypotheses resulting from Creature's learning model need to be expressed in a language that is commensurate with that model's language of universal and particular statements. The hypotheses need to share the same ontology, for instance, and need to adhere to the same underlying set of principles (first-order logic, say) by which propositions are constructed from variables, constants, sentences, and predicates.

REF: Learning is refutation-based. Ask will stipulate that Creature's tests be aimed at producing a refutation rather than a confirmation of its model. This stipulation requires Creature to create, for every model it uses, a class of falsifiers—of observation statements that, if true, would render one or more of the model's universal or particular statements false. For the previous example, Creature's hypothesis is not that Bob *will* choose drug A over drug B (by virtue of Bob's preferring drug A to drug B) but rather that Bob *will not* choose drug B (given that he has the option of choosing drug A). The idea behind this requirement is that, no matter how many times Bob chooses drug A over drug B, the lawlike statement *Bob prefers A to B (for all time)* cannot be conclusively verified, or proved. However, if Ask interprets the statement as a candidate for a law of Bob's behavior—in other words, a statement about his behavior that is *invariant* to changes in Bob's condition—then the statement can be refuted by a single instance of Bob's behavior. The refutation will be provisional, and its logical force will also be provisional: Creature may be misled into believing that Bob has chosen drug B over drug A when in fact Bob was unaware that drug A was an option. Nevertheless, the observation that provides the refutation can itself be analyzed and criticized using the same method that was used to produce it. It is appealing to Ask that model-based, refutation-driven testing is thus *recursively refinable*.

PUB: Not all refutations are equal. Those produced by *public* tests are stronger than those produced by private tests alone because the former are safeguarded by the perceptions of several different individuals; in fact, the *objectivity* of a test is an increasing function of the degree of interpersonal invariance in the testing process. This stipulation makes it more difficult for Creature to produce biased tests of its own models. It additionally requires that Creature anchor its observation statements in the range of statements that are ontologically and logically compatible with the linguistic practices of its peers. The stipulation thus restricts Creature from describing its observations in a "private" language that only Creature understands and that, if admitted, would make it possible for Creature to escape both the rules of grammar and the censure of others' observations as *tests of its tests of its model.* The "public-ness" requirement also makes it possible for others to carry out tests of Creature's model (and vice versa), increasing the rate at which learning can occur in a clump or community of Creatures who may be said to learn vicariously: "It has worked for *me*; will it work for *you*?"

PRED: Ask will rank *predictive* tests of a model higher than "postdictive" tests (i.e., tests based on explanation alone). Some have argued (see Friedman [1953]) that explanation seems to be no more *and no less* than prediction in reverse. But this view is false because, in an explanation problem, that which is to be explained (the *explanandum*) informs that which does the explaining (the model, or the *explanans*) and so assists Creature with its learning task in a way that is not possible with a prediction problem. *Explain the pattern of stock price fluctuations in industry X during the year Y* is a learning problem that is trivial relative to the problem *Predict the pattern of stock price fluctuations over the next N months* because knowledge of the pattern that has obtained informs Creature's choice of the possible models that could explain the pattern. In particular, this knowledge guides Creature's search toward models that are no more complex than the pattern itself (otherwise, they do not qualify as an explanation) and makes the problem of searching for the right model significantly easier than in the predictive case. Equating explanation with prediction ignores the "ontological" uncertainty associated with testing a model: Explaining the outcome of a naval battle between the Athenians and the

Spartans is different from predicting the outcome because, in the latter case, the "battle-ness" of the battle is not in question whereas, in the former case, "skirmishes," "debacles," and other pseudo-events must be "counted" within the space of possible events. Explanation does away with the uncertainty that surrounds (a) the representation of an event as the event it is (by processes, such as high-level vision, that are ignored by most postdictive models) and (b) the propositionalization of an event as an observation statement that can enter into logical relations with the hypotheses that follow deductively from Creature's model. Moreover, in a predictive learning situation, Creature cannot *select* the evidence statements that it will choose to consider as legitimate tests of its model on the basis of knowledge of the content of these statements, which is something Creature can routinely do when engaged in the business of "explaining things." Rather, Creature must stake its model on a prediction to which it has no ex ante access.

PARS: Ask's model of learning requires *parsimony*—that Creature prefer simpler models to more complicated ones in situations where several models are equally well corroborated. One reason for this is of the cognitive economy variety and dates back at least to William of Ockham. Another is that simplicity is desirable in a model because it makes refutation-oriented testing easier to carry out [Popper, 1959]: the simpler the model, the fewer degrees of freedom can be exploited by Creature to "repair" the model when it is refuted. Finally, a simpler model is easier to communicate than a more complex one. A model of a person's behavior that is based on beliefs and desires will, for this reason, be preferable to a model of behavior that is based on emotions, raw feelings, moods, conjectures, and higher-order epistemic states— provided that the former model can be used to model the same behaviors.

Ask knows that it is difficult to quantify a model's complexity. He therefore seeks to make matters as precise as his subject's nature permits by measuring the *complexity* of a model as its Kolmogorov complexity: the length of the minimal computer program that takes as input a set of particular statements (initial and boundary conditions) and outputs a set of predictions based on the model that the program encodes. The *Kolmogorov complexity* of such a program is its description length (in bits or other elemental alphabet units) [Li and Vitanyi, 1997]. The program that encodes Creature's predictive model for a set of evidence statements can be thought of as an encoder of the data that uses the model to generate the code words. A *minimal* encoder is one that provides a maximally efficient encoding and decoding of its target data. Therefore, informational economy (in the Kolmogorov sense) is desirable because it improves the efficiency of using the model to communicate with other Creatures about evidence statements that constitute their access to a "phenomenon."

Suppose that Creature uses a model to encode the data that corroborates it and also to communicate with others about that data. If it is a neurophysiologist, then Creature can speak to other neurophysiologists in terms of the "implication of the hippocampus in categorization tasks," which compresses the large body of speculative, calculative, and experimental work that has gone into distinguishing the hippocampus as an area of the brain, characterizing its response in certain contexts, and so forth. Creature can use the model, then, to map "natural language" onto "modeling language," which is the source of the codewords it uses to communicate with its professional brethren. If the model efficiently encodes the data, then (a) communication among Creatures that use the model is more efficient than between Creatures that do not and (b) the implication of refutations ("code violations," if Ask views the model as an encoder–decoder pair) are maximally detectable.

Whereas using a model as a communicative device is equivalent to using the coder and decoder that the model embeds in the transmitter (Creature) and receiver (some other Creature), *testing* a model is computationally isomorphic to attempting to decode a data set that has previously been encoded using the codewords of Creature's model. In such cases, it makes sense for Creature to choose the model with the minimal Kolmogorov complexity or the model that allows it to most quickly encode and decode its data set. This is something that Ask can measure via the time complexity $T(M, D)$ of the problem of using the model to generate the set of evidence statements, D, that the model, M, is supposed to predict. Ask can incorporate the requirement for the computational efficiency of encoding and decoding into his model of Creature's learning in one of three ways: as an additional objective, such that Creature attempts to jointly minimize the Kolmogorov complexity of its model and the time complexity of using the model as an encoder and decoder of data; as a constraint, such that Creature attempts to minimize the Kolmogorov complexity of the model M that can be used to generate a set of evidence statements D in at most $T^*(M, D)$ computational steps; or as a threshold, such that Creature's preferred model will be the one that minimizes the time complexity of generating a set of evidence statements subject to its Kolmogorov complexity being less than a prespecified amount. Ask can parlay these alternative formulations of Creature's model selection problem into a further elaboration of Creature's economics of mental behavior that includes both memory effects (via Kolmogorov complexity) and computational effects (via time complexity). Creature's optimal learning style will depend on its marginal costs and benefits of remembering and calculating in a particular context.

The Kolmogorov complexity of its model, like the "objectivity" of its beliefs, is a regulative goal that Creature can strive *toward* rather than aim *at*—for two reasons. First, the concept is definable only relative to a particular programming language or Turing Machine. Second, the Kolmogorov complexity of a model is not, itself, computable—which means that Creature can only tentatively surmise that it has arrived at the minimal representation of a phenomenon in the absence of evidence to the contrary.

EL: The *elimination* condition requires Creature to discard or modify models that have been refuted by accepted evidence statements. EL provides a basic engine of progress in Creature's learning. Whereas progress for the inductivist comes from increasing (through verification and confirmation) the probability that particular coincidences constitute instances of a law, progress within the model LEARN comes from the iterative but intelligent elimination of refuted models or of unrefuted models with higher Kolmogorov complexity than other unrefuted models. Ask will consider it to be genuine progress by Creature to find, by discovering *one* instance of Bob choosing B over A, that "Bob prefers A over B" is not a genuine law of Bob's choice behavior; whereas, for the inductivist, this discovery will be a setback in its quest to verify the lawlike statement "Bob prefers A over B."

MULT: What should Creature do if nothing works, if all the models it has tested have been refuted by evidence statements that have withstood further scrutiny and testing? Ask can see that, in such cases, Creature faces an unattractive choice between declaring to have "learned" that an invalid model is "useful" and facing a future that looks like a random collection of events or event sequences—in the sense that the Kolmogorov complexity of the most efficient model that describes these events is equal to the length of their straightforward listing or enumeration. Ask also recognizes that the value of models to Creature (in terms, e.g., of self-therapy, socialization, communicability) often transcends their empirical validity and so should be part of the nonepistemic utility that Creature finds in its models. In such cases, Ask would like to give Creature a pragmatic escape hatch through which it can retain useful fragments of refuted models as predictive crutches, nonepistemically valuable mental items, or performative scripts. Hence Creature will cultivate *multiple* models and submodels as solution-generating engines for the same problem and will also maintain an internal ecology of models to which it can apply a (potentially complicated) selection criterion that takes into account more than simply whether or not the models have been refuted.

3. LEARNING TO LEARN BY CHALLENGING LEARN

LEARN as a whole is meant to provide a (meta-)model of learning behavior: Creature learns when it instantiates LEARN-regulated behavior and not otherwise. LEARN-regulated Creatures learn; others do not. The implications of this stipulation may seem harsh and unreasonable (not least to Creature when Ask attempts to explain why it is not actually instantiating LEARNing behavior), so Ask will be interested in analyzing them further.

Is rote memorization a form of learning? It depends. Ask will hold that rote memorization of a text or a set of data—or the part of this process that is normally referred to as learning—is not learning but rather *inscription* or *transcription* because it does not involve any articulation, embodiment, or test of a model. However, the process by which Creature *figures out how to reliably recall* at will (i.e., remember) a piece of text or data is clearly a case of LEARN-guided behavior; Creature is "learning this text" because it is *learning to recall what it reads.*

Is routinization a form of learning? To Ask, this is not a sharply posed question. To be made precise, he will rephrase the question as *Is there anything about the process of routinization that LEARN would recognize as learning?* and then answer this question affirmatively insofar as routinization is the reduction to an intelligible set of replicable units of behavior (routines) of a complicated assembly of actions or behaviors, as Creature tries out different routines (embodied models) and rejects those that fail to satisfy a particular criterion (prediction, control). There is, then, *something* about routinization that is learning in the sense of LEARN, but typically it is not what one has in mind when speaking about the routine-based process by which one perfects a particular capability, which is an image of betterment by virtue of "mere" repetition. Repetition itself can also be understood as behavior in the realm of LEARN if each individual repetition increases the subsequent reliability with which a behavior is instantiated (or a model is recalled or used) or if the mental routine or algorithm associated with using the model to make a prediction becomes less psychically costly to Creature.

Is mimesis a form of learning? This, too, is an imprecisely phrased question and so, before answering it, Ask will rephrase it as follows: *Is there anything about the mimetic imprinting of a heretofore inaccessible behavior (or skill or representation) that requires something radically different from the conditions of LEARN for its realization?* By focusing on *successful* mimesis, Ask posits that the problem solved by Creature when it attempts to imitate its way to a new skill (or add a new behavior to its repertoire by "aping" someone else's behavior) is similar to the problem of "probing the unknown" that Ask used to motivate the derivation of the basic elements of LEARN in the first place. Creature does not know in advance whether or not it can imitate a successful behavior of another Creature—its success in no way guarantees its imitability. Furthermore, multiply linked sequences of "simple" behaviors are difficult to imitate, and the problem of learning "by trial and error" is still one that Creature must solve in order to successfully imitate a successful behavior.

Betting odds for fallibilists: Reconciling LEARN and BEL. Can one be, without contradiction, both a coherent bettor and a fallibilist learner? Ask would argue that Creature can bet coherently yet abstain from making inductive inferences about the lawlike regularities underlying the event sequence and associated propositional space on which it is betting. The apparent antagonism between LEARN and BEL can be resolved by realizing that the type of propositions whose truth value one bets on—say, $S = $ *the price of equity e will reach $p by 5 p.m. today* or $S = $ *Grenadine (a horse) will win her next three races*—are not about instantiations of *a* law (which derives—on the standard view—inductive support from individual events that confirm it). There is, in fact, no practical way that one can bet on the truth or falsity of a pure, single lawlike statement. One always bets on propositions that refer to *events* (or to sequences of events) that can be observed in practice (and not only in principle), and the "making true" of such propositions always entails the interplay of many other and different laws. Setting up a physics experiment that supposedly tests a single cause-and-effect relationship relies on the co-instantiation of many other laws—for instance, laws that govern construction and setup of the experimental apparatus. The propositions on whose truth value one bets refer, in fact, to the *simultaneous co-instantiation of many laws* that operate together on the right set of initial conditions to produce (or not) the event to which the proposition S refers and thus operate to make S true (or false). There is, moreover, an *infinite* number of possible laws that are co-instantiated by any one event. Ask can use Goodman's [1955] "grue–bleen" maneuver to create an infinite number of lawlike statements L_k—such as "emeralds are grue$_k$," where grue$_1$ is defined as "green before t_1 and blue thereafter," grue$_2$ as "green before t_2 and blue thereafter," grue$_3$ as "green before t_3 and blue thereafter," et cetera—and then argue that a singular proposition such as $S = $ *here is a green emerald* confirms all the L_k and is true if the conjunction of all of the laws in L_k is true.

Ask agrees that learning about a new law or lawlike relationship (for instance, the discovery of energy-bearing signals traveling faster than light or a proof of the conjecture that P = NP) *can* alter the betting odds Creature should be willing to take on a singular proposition (regarding, say, the value of a utility company or the value of a new Internet search engine). It is also the case that the truth of statements like $S = $ *law L is valid* may be directly relevant to how Creature constructs the space of propositions that are possibly true ("the state space"). For example, L could be a *causal law* that is constitutive of the *causal powers* that are the *essential properties* of an *object* that is necessary to the description of an *event* to which proposition S refers; thus, if L were not valid then S would be neither true nor false but instead *meaningless*. However, Ask does not wish to prescribe—beyond the "no Dutch book" conditions of BEL—how Creature's betting odds on a proposition relating to an event should change as a function of the discovery of a relevant new law or the discovery that a relevant regularity previously thought to be lawlike is an illusion or an artifact. Ask is reluctant to do so in part because LEARN and BEL are regulative models for fundamentally different ways of being of Creature, with different goals. Therefore, Ask interprets Creature's personal degrees of belief in terms of betting odds it would accept on propositions describing states of affairs rather than in terms of limiting frequencies for the lawlike relationships that populate Creature's models. These odds are *propensities* of Creature to behave in certain ways (make bets) in certain situations (given opportunities to bet) rather than epistemic scores for Creature's models.

LEARN-patterned behavior is aimed at purposefully minimizing the number of universal statements that are tested in order to make the event speak as closely as possible to the question *Has this universal statement been refuted?* Creature should reasonably aim for parsimony of lawlike statements in its models as a matter of experimental design and as a guide for gathering empirical data. This approach will allow Creature to scrutinize any one particular law more closely and unambiguously—and LEARNing's emphasis on seeking refutations of that law yields a more efficient scrutiny than does seeking confirmations. Even though Creature will never be able to scrutinize *only one* law in this way—for the same reason it cannot bet on the validity of a single law in isolation—its goal in LEARNing is very different from its goal in BETting. Not surprisingly, Ask will insist on different models for understanding Creature's learning and betting behaviors.

CHAPTER 6

COMMUNICATING
Turning Oral Noises into Speech Acts

Wherein Ask tackles the necessity for and the problem of communicating with Creature directly. He poses the problem of communication as a problem of interpreting Creature's oral behavior in ways that are consistent with the possibility of "having a dialogue with Creature," and he builds up a path to making sense of Creature's oral noises that allows him to interpret them as potentially meaningful utterances and as speech acts for which Creature can take or share responsibility. Ask then constructs a transcendentally justifiable set of discursive norms aimed at binding Creature to a logic of producing and responding to utterances and chains of utterances (arguments) that characterizes the kind of dialogue required for Ask to inquire into Creature's behavior in ways that are useful to both Ask and Creature.

BY NOW, a special feature of ascriptive science—one that distinguishes it from its descriptive and normative counterparts—may have dawned on the reader: Ask often needs to *talk* to and with Creature—for example, to set up the conditions that will allow Ask to test models of Creature's physical and mental behavior and to inform Creature of the model he uses to interpret its behaviors or, just as importantly, to extract information that will allow him to formulate a model of Creature in the first place. A maximization-based model of choice (DEC) can be tested only if Ask somehow knows the menu of choosable options from which Creature is making its choices. Likewise, a model of belief structure based on the logic of betting odds structured by the implicit or explicit threat of Dutch books (BET) can be fully formulated only if Ask knows the set of propositions on which Creature is making bets— the propositional "state space" on which degrees of belief are defined. These propositions are rarely, if ever, self-evident from Ask's raw perception of the content and context of Creature's behavior. Often it will be Ask himself who formulates the propositions in question and supplies them to Creature— indeed, this is necessary in situations where Ask offers Creature bets on the truth value of various combinations of propositions or *contracts* for the disclosure of personal degrees of belief based on optimal scoring rules. The use of COMP to examine Creature's mental behavior in general, and calculative reasoning proclivities in particular, require that Ask have some access to Creature's mental models: The *what* (Creature thinks of) is required for the study of the *how* (Creature thinks). Communication is also required if Ask is to fulfill his role as a true ascriptive scientist and (a) induce Creature to reflect on Ask's model-based findings regarding Creature's behavioral productions and (b) allow Creature the opportunity to produce new behaviors in response to being confronted with these results, which in turn will (c) allow Ask to ascribe more precise models to Creature's subsequent behavior and thus enhance the incisiveness and insight of his interpretations thereof.

What kind of structure should we impose on Ask's communicative interactions with Creature? Clearly, LEARN can be as much a model of Creature's interaction with the unknown as of Ask's own interactions with Creature, but it does not police the way in which Ask and Creature communicate with one another. Even though Ask may be a competent learner, there is no guarantee that either he or Creature will communicate with one another in a way that allows Ask to test his models and engage Creature in the analysis required to modify or reaffirm its commitment to its behavior. To move from a set of disparate conjectures about one another to a set of mutually shared conjectures and beliefs, Ask needs to exchange oral noises with Creature as well as to hold Creature *accountable* for various oral noises that it makes in order to formulate and test his models of Creature. In short,

Ask needs a constitutive framework for interpreting Creature's oral behavior as a set of speech acts.

Moreover, without a logic that structures their communicative interaction and to which Ask can bind Creature, there is no safeguard against moves and maneuvers by Creature that subvert or divert the dialogue between it and Ask—such as changing the sense in which words are used without notice or asserting mutually contradictory ensembles of propositions with no explanation of the discrepancy. Because ascriptive science—unlike "normal" social science—places its lead protagonist (Ask) in direct communicative contact with its object of study (Creature), ascriptive science remains *incomplete* if it does not furnish Ask with a *minimal logic of communication*; it is *toothless* if whatever logic of communication it furnishes Ask with cannot be used to bind Creature to a consistent, coherent, open, and responsive use of language. The consequence is the absence of a minimal mutually binding communicative logic: Even if *Ask* adheres to the communicative logic that he has articulated, he cannot presume that *Creature* will adhere (or can be persuaded to adhere) to that same logic. Since communicative success is a function of the *interaction* between Ask and Creature and not only of Ask's or Creature's separate actions, it follows that—in the absence of a binding framework for turning oral noises into speech acts that mutually bind the interlocutors—there are no grounds for Ask to assume that his communication with Creature will produce the results that ascriptive practice requires.

The situation for Ask is complicated by his lack of any a priori contractual or deontological claim on Creature, one that could bind Creature to attempt to produce oral behavior that corresponds to truthful and truthlike statements. Neither is Ask in a position of power or authority over Creature, which would allow Ask to command Creature to communicate in certain ways and not in others and to expect compliance by virtue of the coercive nature of their relationship. There is, accordingly, no immediately overwhelming incentive for Creature to be coherent, open, or responsive in its communicative strategy toward Ask. Moreover, there seems to be no implicit contract or principle by virtue of which Ask could call Creature to task for two-facedness, inadvertencies, slips of the tongue, inconsistencies, subversions, or other defensive maneuvers meant to obfuscate Ask's attempts to audit or otherwise understand Creature's oral noises. This difficulty can undermine the very project and possibility of ascriptive science.

What Ask requires in order to bind Creature to an enforceable and auditable framework for committing speech acts is, in fact, a set of several elements working together. First, he requires a logic of interpreting Creature's oral noises *as* speech acts. This requires, in turn, that Ask possess an interpretive framework for oral noises as intentional behaviors in addition to an interpretive framework for making oral noises count as speech acts within the dialogue he carries on with Creature. Second, Ask requires a framework for adjudicating the appropriateness or correctness of various speech acts, a framework that is not shaped by any subjective commitment that Ask may have and Creature may not share but rather is *transcendentally* justifiable— that is, justifiable to Creature by virtue of being that which it takes itself to be. These requirements provide Ask with a "road map" for constructing a model of communicative competence and discursive agency, which he will now follow.

1. PATHMARKS ALONG THE WAY TO A MODEL OF COMMUNICATIVE PERFORMANCE AND COMPETENCE

Donald Davidson and the Principle of Hermeneutic Charity.   Davidson [2001] posits a principle of charity as a foundation for the interpretation of the actions of human Creatures. This principle requires Ask to ascribe to Creature a set of beliefs and desires that make its action rationalizable via the application of a framework that closely resembles DEC, BEL, and BET. Applying the principle is simple enough in cases where Creature is indisputably conscious. Suppose it wants to leave a room but the door is closed. Creature gets up, walks toward the door, stops, and opens the door. The "charitable" interpretation is that, given what Creature wants (to leave the room) and what it truthfully and validly believes (that the door is closed), it performs the action (opening the door) that is consistent with its beliefs and its desires, thereby rationalizing the action. Had Creature harbored the belief that the door in question was just a carefully constructed hologram blocking its line of sight but not its egress from the room, then Creature would have been justified—by the same

principle of charity—in attempting to walk straight through the "door." Had
Creature also been a convinced skeptic who believes it is justified in believing
something (that there is a real, closed door blocking its way out of the room)
only if it is antecedently justified in believing that it is not dreaming (which it
is not), then Creature *may*, by the same charitable interpretation, try to walk
straight through the door—depending, perhaps, on its private cost–benefit
calculations of a successful versus a failed attempt and on the authenticity with
which it lives out its skeptical disposition. For Ask, the point is simple enough:
The charity principle is silent about *what* are the beliefs and desires that jointly
rationalize an action. Ask has other means of discovering these beliefs and
desires, of course, but if their discovery requires that he speak with Creature
beforehand, then he is faced with a problem of "circular search": Ask needs an
interpretive framework for these speech acts that depends on the characteristics that the speech acts in question will help him to discover.

It is even harder for Ask to rely on the principle of charity alone when it
comes to interpreting oral noises *qua* speech acts. Getting up and opening a
door is one thing, but how should Ask interpret a statement such as "I am
not here"—uttered by Creature in all seriousness? As a serious reference to
a dissociative mental disorder? As a reference to a liar-type sentence that undergirds Gödel's incompleteness proof for arithmetic? As a throwaway uttered
in jest at Ask's overzealous approach to formalizing models of behavior? As a
collection of random phonemes that "somehow" coalesced into an intelligible
sentence? The answer, obviously, depends partly on the beliefs and perceptions that Ask interprets Creature as having and partly on the level of computational potency and sophistication that he assumes Creature uses when
producing its oral behavior. Once again, these are characteristics that Ask is
able to probe. But if Ask must dialogue with Creature in advance of such inquiry, then he is once again constrained by his lack of knowledge about matters that he needs to resolve before addressing that very lack of knowledge. In
order to make progress, Ask needs more sophisticated approaches that address
speech acts in particular, not just any kind of behavior.

John Searle and the Epistemic Substructure of Speech Acts. Ask finds
some help toward this end in Searle's [1969] analysis of speech acts (such

as promising and predicating). If Creature promises Ask that it will perform action A by time t, then, according to Searle, Creature:

   a. *predicates* the action A "of itself" in the sense that "Creature's having done A" will be true at some $T < t$;

   b. assumes that Ask would prefer Creature doing A over Creature not doing A;

   c. assumes that it is not obvious to Ask that Creature will do A and therefore that Creature believes its utterance is informative;

   d. would not—and assumes that Ask does not think it would—do A otherwise (i.e., in the absence of a promise);

   e. *intends* to do A at the time it utters its promise;

   f. intends its utterance to count as the undertaking of an obligation to do A by time t; and

   g. believes that Ask knows (a)–(f) and that Creature knows that Ask knows this.

Observe that (a)–(g) sketch a minimal epistemic undergirding of the speech act that Ask would call a *promise*, and Searle's analysis offers a path to sketching the epistemic structure of other speech acts (such as predication and affirmation) on a case-by-case basis. Ask learns that his working model of Creature's attempts to communicate need not endow Creature with unrealistic levels of computational potency or sophistication, yet it should endow Creature with some level of interactive sophistication (depending on the speech act being analyzed). For instance, the *meaning* of a proposition uttered by Creature (i.e., the set of truth conditions for that proposition) is, at a minimum, something that Creature would know, would assume that Ask knows, and would assume that Ask knows Creature knows, for only then would Creature's utterance of that proposition count as a speech act in its communication with Ask.

At the same time, Ask still sees a new difficulty in his path to a framework for interpreting Creature's oral noises, which arises from having to interpret utterances expressing propositions that rely on implicit or hidden presuppositions that may be discoverable from the context or previous content of the conversation but are otherwise left unspecified. Suppose Creature says, "He just left" upon seeing Ask knock on his friend's locked office door; then, in the normal course of affairs, Ask will take the "he" to refer to the friend on whose door he is presently knocking. However, there is nothing in the epistemic structure of Creature's utterance that points Ask in the direction of such an interpretation, and the charity principle alone is far from providing Ask with the right interpretive schema. Something more is still needed.

Paul Grice and the Cooperation Principle. The "something more" may come in the form of Grice's [1989] cooperation principle, which enjoins Ask to interpret Creature's utterances as being (a) relevant to the context of the conversation and (b) informative to Ask within this context. By applying this principle to the utterance "He just left," Ask can infer that Creature is referring to the friend on whose door he is knocking. That is, the statement expressed by the utterance is (a) relevant to what Ask takes Creature to take Ask to be doing (looking for his friend) and (b) informative in that context. Ask notes, again, the level of interactive epistemic sophistication that even commonsense rules of interpersonal interpretation require of Creature and also notes the relative sophistication of the epistemic states that he must ascribe to Creature in order to make sense of its oral noises and interpret them as the utterance of propositions that bear meaning. For suppose now that, in uttering "He just left," Creature is referring to a conversation it had with Ask *previously* about the very same friend, and suppose Creature does not know that the office of that same friend is *not* behind the door on which Ask is knocking. Then, an infelicity results: Creature utters a meaningful statement; Ask takes it that Creature has uttered a meaningful statement; the statement, since it is informative and relevant, is "cooperative" by Grice's criterion; *but* the meanings that Creature and Ask assign to this sentence are quite different. Hence it is natural for Ask to try to ascertain: Who will take the responsibility for addressing and resolving such infelicities? The question is more general than it seems at first blush, and it relates to Searle's analysis of the "obligation" that Creature undertakes (and is understood by Ask to undertake) on account of uttering a promise. This question has the following general form: *When does an utterance become a speech act that generates an obligation to explicate or clarify it?* By what mechanism does an utterance convey the commitment of Creature to "make some proposition true"—or to rectify problems or infelicities that arise in the course of communication?

John Austin and the Performative Structure of Talk.   To solve this problem, Ask seeks to articulate conditions for turning utterances into speech acts,
where these are understood as commitments undertaken by Creature to make
true the propositions expressed by its utterances or to "make things right" in
the case of communicative infelicities or mishaps. Austin [1962] introduced
the distinction between *constative* utterances (e.g., "The sun is shining today"),
which can be "made true"—or false—by certain states of affairs (their truth
conditions), and *performative* sentences (e.g., "I hereby pronounce you man
and wife"), which are true by virtue of having been spoken by the speaker in
a particular context (a church or a town hall) following a certain set of rules
and in accordance with a certain sequence of events (upon the spouses having spoken matrimonial vows to one another). The "making true" function
of performative utterances can be extended, as Austin points out, to confer a
certain kind of responsibility upon the speaker of constative utterances by virtue of this speaker having uttered them. So Ask reasons that, when Creature
utters, "The sun is shining today," it is actually (but implicitly) making the
performative utterance "*I claim that* the sun is shining today." The "I claim"
is implicit in the fact that it is Creature (and not someone else) uttering the
sentence. Creature's performatively claiming that the proposition is true is
not a trivial matter. It is a claim to:

a. the *assertibility* of the proposition (it is well formed by the rules of the
    language in which it is expressed and has truth conditions that Ask
    can ascertain independently of Creature);

b. the *truth* of the proposition expressed by the utterance (i.e., the sun is
    actually shining); and

c. the *sincerity* of Creature in making the claim—that is, Creature *also*
    believes the sun is shining, perhaps in a way (it sees the sun shining)
    that is causally linked to its truth condition but not necessarily so
    (Creature is blind but has learned from someone else that it is a
    sunny day).

Ask is encouraged by the progress he has made in erecting a scaffolding for
the interpretation of Creature's oral noises, but he remains concerned about
convincing Creature to see things in the same way and thus to acknowledge
and feel the force of the commitments that Ask interprets it as undertaking

when it makes utterances. After all, what is radically different in the interpretation of an utterance versus some other behavior is that, in the former case, Ask and Creature must both interpret Creature's behavior in the same way; this is required in order for that behavior to make the same sense to Ask as it does to Creature and for their ensuing exchange of oral noises to qualify as a dialogue. What Ask is after, then, is some transcendentally justifiable "communicative ethics" that Creature will feel not only justified in following but actually *compelled* to follow.

Jürgen Habermas and Discourse Ethics. One move toward such a transcendental discourse ethics is made by Habermas [1987], who uses a maneuver similar to that used by Immanuel Kant in arriving at a "categorical imperative." Habermas's maneuver is to require that a genuine communicative act (a speech act) on the part of Creature represent a triple claim to truthlikeness (validity), truthfulness (sincerity), and appropriateness to the context of the conversation. The justification of this claim is by *reductio*: If all Creatures made oral noises that did *not* make good on such claims, then communication would be rendered devoid of any value because no one could reasonably take seriously what anyone else said. Ask follows Habermas's transcendentalization program insofar as it spells out the commitments that Creature would need to make by virtue of uttering well-formed propositions in the context of a conversation. Creature's utterance that "the sun is shining today" is interpreted by Ask, in accordance with Habermas's criteria for communicative action, as being a claim that the sun really is out (truthlikeness), that Creature truly believes the sun is out (truthfulness), and that Creature's utterance is not somehow "out of the blue"—that it is, for instance, relevant and informative to the interpersonal context that Ask and Creature find themselves in. But Ask is concerned (i) that there is no mechanism for effectively *monitoring* Creature's adherence to the triple commitment that its speech acts entail and also (ii) that there is no effective mechanism for *sanctioning* Creature's departure from this commitment on grounds that Creature itself already accepts. In particular, Creature may say something like, "What is a universal principle or universalization procedure to me?" and leave Ask with a justification problem that differs little from the one he was hoping to solve in the first place.

David Lewis's Scorekeeping in Language Games.   Ask will find some help in addressing his first concern from Lewis's [1979] notion of "scorekeeping in language games," which is based on viewing a conversation as a game between the discussants that unfolds according to a set of constitutive rules and a running score. For example, the 5-tuple "score" $S = (r, (h, i), b, s, o)$ encodes the state of play at any moment in a baseball game as the number of runs scored (r), the stage of the game (hth half, top or bottom, of the ith inning), the number of balls (b) and strikes (s) the pitcher has thrown to the batter, and the number of outs (o) of the hitting team; this encoding is uniquely determined by the rules of the game and the actions of players within the game. The rules of the game specify how its state changes as a function of the actions of the players, and these rules are thus *constitutive* of the game. A player cannot violate the rules without either changing the game's state in a predetermined way or performatively and de facto opting out of the game. If a hitter, for instance, walks to first base after receiving a ball from the pitcher, then the action is *legitimate* in the context of the game only if the ball count was just previously equal to 3; otherwise, the action vitiates the game itself because the rules by which its state changes *constitute* the game.

So, if Creature answers *The sun is shining today* to Ask's question *Why are you praying to this tree?* and proceeds to answer Ask's subsequent *What is the relevance of the sun's shining to your praying to the tree?* by *I do not want to walk far today*, then Ask can reasonably interpret Creature's oral noises as a departure from the language game that Ask and Creature must play when they are having a dialogue and therefore as an indication that Creature has "left the game." Ask immediately perceives that it is not easy, in general, to state conditions under which Creature's oral behavior transgresses the rules of such communicatively oriented language games. However, if such a set of rules could be specified to a sufficiently tight level, then it seems promising to pursue the basic approach of representing dialogues as certain types of language games and representing such language games via constitutive rule sets.

Robert Brandom and Deontological Scorekeeping.   Equally promising in Lewis's account is the notion of keeping the "score" in a language game. Creature's transgression of a set of communicative rules need not be immediately interpreted by Ask as meaning that Creature has definitively "checked out" of the project of using language to communicate. Instead, Creature may acknowledge incurring an obligation to clarify, explicate, or justify a speech act, an obligation that Ask can "redeem" at some point in the conversation. Ask may accept Creature's *I am praying to a tree because the sun is shining* provisionally—on the understanding that Creature will, when asked, explain the link between the two phrases (e.g., *Trees are sacred and we are in the midst of a drought*) that makes the first utterance relevant and informative to the latter. Brandom's [1994] notion of "deontological scorekeeping" is then useful as a *tracking* device that helps Ask to monitor the state of play of the language game that he and Creature are having. (It can also be used as a tracking device for debates, in which case the running score will indicate who is "winning the debate" at that time while the rules of the game specify the movement of the score as a function of what Ask and Creature say to one another.)

Karl Otto Apel and the A Priori of a Communication Community. Ask derives some comfort from the notion of a set of rules for language games that can be used to determine whether or not Creature buys into even basic preconditions for what it means to have a conversation. However, Ask is still concerned by the prospect of justifying these rules to Creature in a way that is not parochially dependent on Ask's own value system (or on the value system of Ask's own community) and by the related problem of devising sanctions for Creature's deviations from these rules that are *just* and not merely efficient. Apel [1980] offers a way of understanding the communicative and dialogical use of language that can be used to *bind* language users to a set of norms or principles. Apel argues that, when participating in a dialogue, Creature's failure to abide by (some rather far-reaching) injunctions that guide its use of language amount to a performative contradiction on its part. The simplest example of a performative contradiction is a situation in which Creature asserts $S = I$ *(here and now) do not exist*. The contradiction is performative rather than logical because it is necessary for Creature to exist here and now in order to be able to assert S—which, furthermore, Creature could not do if it (here and now) did not exist. The contradiction is not a logical one because Creature does not explicitly assert both $S = I$ *(here and now) do not exist* and $T = I$ *(here and now) exist*. Now, just as $S = I$ *(here and now) do not exist* is performatively self-contradictory, so is $U = I$ *(here and now) am not a participant in this dialogue* performatively self-contradictory if uttered as part of the dialogue or entailed by another utterance in the dialogue. This sets up the following possibility: If Ask can devise a logic of communication whereby each violation is equivalent to a performative contradiction on the part of the violator(s), then he will have established a communicative principle that Ask can use to call Creature to task in the same way he would call it to task for engaging in any other performative contradiction.

So what? Why can Creature not simply shrug and keep talking even after Ask points out that it is engaged in some performative contradiction? The question cuts to the power of any communicative principle Ask could use to *sanction* Creature's behavior. Apel's response is that violations of the logic of communication proscribe the violator from being a participant in the dialogue—indeed, in the community of communicators who attempt (through their use of language) to inform and understand one another. If Creature violates the norms of communication in ways that involve it in a performative contradiction, then Ask can—by virtue of these violations—stop treating Creature's verbal behavior as if it aims to "make sense"; he can instead treat its utterances as random collections of syllables. Having involved itself in such a contradiction, Creature opens itself up to the possibility that Ask can stop attempting to "communicate with its mind" and start merely "interacting with its brain" or other bodily parts. Because one *enters* a communicative community when using language in a way that does not involve performative contradictions and *leaves* that community upon committing such contradictions, Ask can sanction Creature's transgressions of communicative rules by ceasing to treat Creature's utterances as anything other than oral noises. The normative use of language—which Ask shall try to circumscribe by COMM, his model of communicative competence and agency—is then sanctioned by membership in (or exclusion from) a communicative community that includes all who are committed to the use of a language that is bound by a set of principles. The transcendental justification of these principles follows because committing speech acts *entails* an agreement to act in ways that are bound by them: In other words, by speaking (as opposed to merely making noises with its mouth) Creature is already committed to a set of rules.

Does the sanction "matter"? The result, for Creature, of opting out of a communicative community is that Creature cannot thereafter communicate with its members because none will be willing to listen with the intent of understanding what it is saying. Its utterances will be meaningless for the same reason that random collections of syllables (once they are understood as such) are meaningless: because no one will try to make sense of them by positing truth conditions for their propositional content.

2. DEONTOLOGICAL STRUCTURE OF THE COMMUNICATIVE USE OF LANGUAGE

With these stipulations in hand, Ask can proceed to an articulation of a model to guide its dialogical interaction with Creature—namely, COMM, which works as follows. For some injunction or principle to be part of COMM, its violation must involve the violator in a performative contradiction of the type *I (here and now) am not a participant in this dialogue* that can therefore be used to trigger disqualification of the speaker from the dialogue at hand. What safeguards COMM is the foundational presupposition that, in speaking, Creature is taking part in a dialogue—regardless of how explicit its agreement is to do so. The injunctions of COMM specify what it means for Creature to be part of the dialogue and provide Ask with an *audit mechanism* for Creature's communicative predicament or status. In particular, Creature's oral behaviors can be audited with respect to adherence to the rules of COMM by treating them as tokens of communicative competence and responsibility that Creature must redeem, when asked to do so, by showing that they indeed do not depart from the rules in question. Thus, the principles in question engender both a right of Ask to ask Creature questions that probe into the coherence and openness of its communication as well as an obligation of Creature to answer them.

> COMM. *Interpret Creature's oral behavior by taking it to instantiate a speech act that is bound by rules whose violation entails a performative contradiction on the part of Creature.*

COMM has several components, which can be grouped into four categories.

Commitments to Consistency. The first group of COMM's injunctions require Creature to be consistent in both a syntactic and semantic sense.

SYN-CON: No Creature may contradict itself (where Ask is also a Creature), and contradiction is interpreted in the logical sense: S "contradicts" R if S implies not-R (and vice versa). To see why self-contradiction as part of a dialogue entails a performative contradiction, consider what happens if Creature asserts both S and not-S without further justification (e.g., introduction of a new system of logic that explicitly accommodates mutually contradictory statements). By contributing the contradiction to the dialogue without additional explanation, Creature is subverting a basic premise: Statements are claims that can be validated or refuted by further discussion, because S has no value as a claim if it is admitted alongside not-S as part of the dialogue (and, conversely, neither has not-S any value if admitted alongside S). In such a case, no reply of Ask ("I agree" or "I disagree") will be able to function as a claim on Ask's own part, for saying "I agree" to a Creature that asserts S *and not-S* is no less vacuous than the assertion S *and not-S* itself. Creature can for its own part similarly not agree (or agree) with Ask's disagreement (or agreement) with S *and not-S*, and so forth. Thus, the unqualified and unexplained assertion of a contradiction negates the premise of a dialogue by making it impossible to interpret assertions as claims to truth. Therefore, asserting a contradiction involves the producer of this verbal behavior in a performative contradiction of the type *I (here and now) am not a participant in this dialogue* or *this (our interaction here and now) is not a dialogue.*

SEM-CON: The same word may not be used in different senses without due explanation. This requirement for semantic consistency is based on logic similar to that backing the requirement for syntactic consistency. If Creature uses the same word in different senses in the same dialogue without signaling the difference or providing further explanation, then its assertions cannot be audited *qua* claims and so any response that Ask ventures to give Creature can also not be audited *qua* claims (and so forth). In other words, absent a commitment to semantic consistency, there is an ambiguity in the substance of the claims that Creature is not committed to resolving—an ambiguity stemming from its lack of commitment to resolving problems that arise from changing the meaning of words "in mid-sentence." For this reason, failures of semantic consistency must also involve Creature in a performative contradiction.

Commitment to Sincerity.   The next requirement of COMM concerns the commitments to sincerity that safeguard assertions as claims to truthfulness of the speaker.

SIN: No Creature may assert that which it does not believe to be true. This "nothing but the truth" requirement arises because, in a dialogue, assertions are claims made by a speaker who thereby incurs an obligation to redeem them. Allowing Creature to make assertions corresponding to sentences it believes to be false while participating in a dialogue entails that Creature need not back its utterances with a commitment to their truthfulness. Accordingly, the results of any audit procedure carried out on these claims cannot be binding upon Creature or Ask: The speaker can just "walk away" from its commitment to redeem the claim to truthfulness implicit in a speech act. This state of affairs would negate any participant's role in the dialogue because its assertions would carry no discursive weight: Declaring S without a commitment to believing that S (rather than not-S) is true would land Creature in a performative contradiction similar in nature to that resulting from a violation of the requirement for logical and semantic consistency. Note that Creature has no obligation to tell "the whole truth," to not be self-deceived about the truth, or to utter *only* true propositions; such restrictions would require Ask to impute unrealistic qualities to Creature or to hold it up to unrealistic standards, such as logical and informational omniscience (in the case of holding it up to a commitment to "the whole truth," which would require Creature to state all of the logical consequences of what it knows to be true). Moreover, it is genuinely noncontradictory and "participative" for Creature to utter a false proposition ("today is Wednesday"), be cautioned by Ask that it is mistaken ("no, today is Tuesday"), and then change its original statement as a result of Ask's intervention.

Commitments to Responsiveness.   Ask recognizes that no speech act can be "complete" in the sense of giving, by itself, all the necessary safeguards and commitments that make it a speech act. Ask addresses this problem by replacing the requirement *make explicit the entire set of commitments and presuppositions that are implicit in a speech act* with the requirement that each interlocutor *be responsive to concerns that the other might have.* Two requirements fall into this category.

ANS: No Creature can refuse to answer questions, queries, or concerns raised by any other participant to the dialogue. The logic behind ANS is that such a refusal essentially disavows any proposition that (supposedly) backs an assertion, as the speaker is insulated from answering attempts to audit the assertion. Thus, asserting *S* but refusing to answer such questions as *Why S?* makes it impossible for Ask to audit Creature's commitment to *S*, thereby negating the role of assertions in a dialogue as tokens that must be redeemed upon request.

REL: The relevance of any new assertion to the dialogue's current state must be provided upon request. REL aims to protect against the introduction of irrelevant assertions by giving participants a right to question the material implication of any new assertion for the rest of the dialogue and an entitlement to an answer (which itself must fulfill the requirements that any other assertion satisfies to qualify as a speech act). Otherwise, Creature could introduce assertions (e.g., "grass is green," "it will rain tomorrow in Wichita") that are not connected in any way perceptible to Ask to the dialogue's current state but that do fully satisfy other requirements: they are assertible, syntactically and semantically consistent, and so forth. Suppose that Creature refuses to explain how these statements are related to either its own or Ask's previous assertions or queries. Then the commitment structure of the resulting communicative situation is equivalent to one in which Creature refuses to heed RESP after making an assertion that appears to violate SYN-CON—that is, Creature abdicates responsibility for helping Ask to make sense of its speech act in the context of the dialogue. This move engages Creature in a performative contradiction of its role in the dialogue in the same way that refusing to respond to Ask's query regarding its use of a word in a sentence does. Thus REL safeguards the integrity of a dialogue in the same way that SYN-CON and SEM-CON safeguard the integrity of an assertion, with relevance taking on the regulative function of consistency.

Commitment to Inclusiveness.   Ask is, finally, concerned with protecting certain questions or queries that serve to elucidate the commitments Creature makes when it speaks and also with protecting the roles of the speakers in the dialogue, whose identity and ability to speak and be heard is essential to the construal of such commitments (as a commitment is without fail "a commitment *to someone*"). For this reason, COMM incorporates an *inclusivity* requirement as follows.

INC: No Creature may be excluded or precluded from voicing its questions, concerns, or difficulties as a part of the dialogue. The injunction allows all who are capable of producing speech acts to take part in the dialogue and thus safeguards that no assertion may be excluded solely by virtue of its speaker's identity. The basic logic behind this injunction is that so barring certain speakers or subjects from the dialogue amounts to curtailing the opportunities for auditing the speaker's claims, which limits the power of the dialogue's participants to audit claims made as part of the dialogue. INC may look prima facie reasonable, but how does the exclusion of some speakers by virtue of their identity amount to a performative contradiction? Consider the situation where Creature says *No one shorter than six feet can participate in this dialogue*, an assertion admissible to a dialogue insofar as it functions as a claim and thus only insofar as it can be audited or challenged. Yet the claim excludes from its potential auditors and challengers the very ones most competent and motivated to do so. Thus, it preempts the most pertinent possible challenges to its validity. If COMM were to allow such moves, then a suitably minded Creature could iteratively preclude or exclude any possible challenges to its assertions by putting forth similar claims. This state of affairs would quickly render unauditable and vacuous any commitment that Creature incurs as a result of speaking, which in turn would render Creature's own position in the dialogue performatively self-contradictory.

3. DEPLOYING COMM: PRAGMATIC CONSIDERATIONS

COMM is a constitutive and regulative framework for *speech acts* committed by Ask or by Creature as part of a dialogue. It is a means by which both Ask and Creature can call one another to task for speech acts contradicting the basic assumption that they are participants in a dialogue and, by virtue of participating in this dialogue, are (implicitly but no less bindingly) committed to certain standards of coherence, responsiveness, sincerity, and inclusiveness. Thus COMM turns the *relational* space between Ask and Creature into a *communicative* space that is constituted by adherence to COMM.

How does a real Ask deploy COMM in conversation with a real Creature? This is, of course, the first and foremost problem that Ask must solve in order to launch any modeling exercise—no matter the end to which it will be put. It helps that COMM can itself be applied iteratively and recursively: Speech acts that make statements about other speech acts are themselves speech acts and so "fall under" the regulative grasp of COMM. The "trouble scenario" for COMM is one in which, for instance, Creature responds to one of Ask's probing questions (e.g., "Did you intend to stop thinking about this at this point or were you gripped by a sudden surge of fear that you might not get to the answer by the time it is due, which in turn caused you to stop thinking, as you had to attend to the fear?") in a way that is beyond reproach as regards content (e.g., "the latter") but is nevertheless communicatively of doubtful quality (because, say, the statement is accompanied by a wink or a snicker). In this case, Ask faces a problem for which COMM can offer only partial help: that of relating to the "entire" communicative act that Creature commits (which includes Creature's tone and facial expression) using a framework that necessarily can "really" regulate only the textual output of speech acts. Ask can relentlessly make use of COMM to turn what he perceives to be subversive but nonverbal behavior on the part of Creature into text ("when you snickered just now, was it because of the complexity of the question, because of the fact that you perceive the question to be irrelevant, or for some other reason altogether?"), but Creature will always have the option of exiting via the tacit dimension ("the latter"—it answers Ask's new question but with a new and even more caustic snicker). Such difficulties highlight why COMM, though a regulative framework, will never be or give rise to an *algorithm* for producing open, authentic communicative spaces. It can be used as a powerful principle in whose name Ask can call Creature to task and rebalance the dialogue. It can also be used as an audit tool for prospecting communicative spaces in general. However, COMM is not a substitute for the basic care that Ask must exercise when producing and accepting speech acts toward and from Creature.

A "CRUEL SCIENCE"
What Ask Is Up To

Wherein Ask reveals his identity(ies) and sheds further light on the nature of his inquiry.

WHERE ARE WE at this point? At a beginning, it is hoped, and not at an end: for ascriptive science is an activity—perhaps a way of life—rather than the kind of inert entity sometimes referred to as a "body of knowledge" (whatever that may mean). Ask, our ascriptive scientist, has fashioned himself a tool kit that includes not only ways of representing the thoughts and behaviors produced by Creature but also, and more importantly, moves and maneuvers that structure and regulate his interactions with and interventions upon Creature. Ask can use these tools to make sense of what Creature does or says and to figure out what Creature thinks on the basis of what he hears Creature say and/or sees Creature do; Ask can also use them when calling Creature into question for apparent deviations from logics of doing, thinking, and communicating, and he can learn from Creature's answers to such questions. Ask can ascribe to Creature desires (using DEC and INT), beliefs (using BEL and BET), and patterns of—including stopping rules for—thinking (using COMP, KOMP, and LEARN), and Ask can train his models on Creature's behavior by turning LEARN upon himself and then confronting Creature with his findings while relying on a communicative model (such as COMM) to regulate Creature's responsiveness to his queries. Ask can use DEC, BEL, COMP, KOMP, and LEARN to design experimental inquiries into Creature's behavior and thought, and he can deploy the arguments arising from the logics of utility pumps, Dutch books, and the pico-economics of thinking to reason with Creature regarding the all-things-considered desirability or optimality of Creature's behaviors and patterns of thinking. Thus, whatever information resides in these models—and they are informationally rich by virtue of being logically deep—is embodied in the kinds of inquiries and operations that Ask can effect upon Creature while making use of them.

The Ask–Creature relationship is itself interpretable in many different ways, each of which leads to a different version of ascriptive science. Four examples will serve here to make this idea more precise.

Ask/Creature = consultant or coach/client: In the most straightforward adaptation of the Ask–Creature relationship, Ask is Creature's consultant (or coach) and Creature is Ask's client. Their interests are prima facie aligned in the sense that both have a stake in raising Creature's "game" to a higher level and having Creature (at least more frequently) do what it has (all-things-considered and sound) reasons to do. However, Ask and Creature may not be aligned in terms of interacting authentically and openly about precise diagnoses of Creature's departures from optimal physical, verbal, or mental behavior that Ask makes in the course of his inquiry.

Ascriptive science in this case becomes a science of skillful and incisive coaching. Ask uses the basic models DEC, BEL, COMP, KOMP, and LEARN to organize his perceptions of Creature's observed behaviors and to "make sense" of that behavior as it unfolds; he uses the basic principles of RESP, BET, and RESP* to raise Creature's level of self-awareness about its own mental and physical behavior. Ask uses the normative underpinnings of DEC, BEL, COMP, KOMP, and LEARN to confront Creature with Ask's structured interpretations of its behavior that rest on auditable representations, about which Ask educates Creature.

In the course of such interactions, Creature may (and often does) become defensive when thus confronted. Creature may "disown" its own behaviors by explaining them away as caused by exogenous factors or random lapses that are not truly representative of its underlying ways of being. Yet the interactive aspect of ascriptive science affords Ask a much-needed lever in such cases, for he can ask Creature itself to specify the conditions under which it is willing to accept the validity of (or the truth conditions for) Ask's diagnostic inferences (e.g., "Under what conditions would you agree that you are a logical sloth relative to your own standards of logical depth or diligence? Under what conditions would you agree that you use self-regulation mechanisms that are suboptimal relative to your own standards for the behaviors that these mechanisms should produce?") and then proceed to seek evidence statements that are accepted by Creature as supportive of Ask's inferences.

Of course, Creature still has many potential "escape routes" from the task of squarely facing Ask's diagnostic analysis of its behaviors. However, COMM supplies Ask with a basic mechanism for regulating Creature's communicative behaviors by providing him with a set of regulative principles that transcend any particular and parochial set of value commitments. It matters not, from the perspective of COMM, if Creature is a Marxist or Hayekian processor of social information, or a utilitarian or deontological thinker in matters of value judgments; its participation in a dialogue with Ask a priori commits Creature to a set of rules of engagement that enjoin it to answer Ask's (relevant) queries regarding its behavior or state of mind and either accept Ask's ensuing arguments or state its disagreement with them and (upon Ask's queries) its reasons for that disagreement. Thus, ascriptive science can be understood as a structuration instrument for the kinds of diagnostic and prescriptive interventions that consultants are in the business of providing: It is a logic and a language, not merely an empirical science.

Ask/Creature = manager/employee (or employee/manager or worker/ coworker): Understood as a logic or blueprint for managing, ascriptive science is a logic of directive, informed, outcome-oriented inquiry and intervention. Understanding someone's behavior has sometimes been compared to winning a game of Twenty Questions, which aims at discovering the true but hidden value of some variable that lies between specified bounds, and is a task efficiently implemented by iteratively bisecting the intervals in which the questioner believes the value of the variable lies. In such games, inquiry appears as a form of interrogation—of trying to get information of a particular kind from a (possibly unwilling) informant or witness who is by default uncooperative in the sense that she does not volunteer information that is not asked for explicitly yet honest in the sense that she does not state falsehoods in answering direct queries. Ascriptive science, by contrast, posits a view of understanding in which the *interpretation* of the value of any particular variable is itself always in question and in which Ask is called upon to supply meaning to observed behavior.

Ask does so by (a) using schemata and logics for understanding behavior with powerful normative underpinnings that should be appealing to Creature and (b) designing experiments and interventions meant to educate Creature about its own cognitive, affective, and behavioral tendencies and also to induce Creature to change such tendencies in a manner consistent with its all-things-considered best interests. With the tool kit of ascriptive science, Ask can show Creature a detailed image of its own behavior and then ask: "Is this what you want? Is this how you want to be?"

But if he were to stop there, Ask would not be a manager but (perhaps) a mere guru or an applied ethicist. He needs to do more—and the "more" that he needs to do is enabled by the normative power of the basic models of behavior that he uses, by virtue of which he can truly say "here is why you do not really want to be this way" and be supported by the basic communicative framework of COMM. The fact that management, thus conceived, is a fundamentally communicative and interpretive process is a result of the ascriptive approach and one that is also at the foundation of action science, for if Creature "leaves the dialogue" then the basic levers of the action scientist have been severed.

Ask/Creature = pedagogue/student (or trainer/trainee): It may not have escaped the reader that ascriptive science has, at its core, a fundamentally educational or pedagogical intent. It can be deployed by Ask to teach Creature about better or worse ways of acting and thinking in various contexts through experiences that can be engineered by Ask through the judicious use of the basic models in his tool kit. Current approaches to teaching rational choice and rational belief theory are prescriptive in purpose and application. They are based on telling the student: "Here is how *most people* make judgments when they have different kinds of information (e.g., complete versus incomplete); here is how they *should* make such judgments; therefore, here is what *you* should do in order to advance beyond the lay person's less-than-perfect approach to acting and thinking and embody the *right way* to act and think.

The "right" way is, of course, supplied by a coarsely appropriated logic of scientific discovery that comprises an unexamined mixture of inductive logics, deductive rules, and optimization heuristics that are not necessarily internally consistent but are subject to challenges that have not yet been answered: Inductive inferences are not deductively justified; nor, for that matter, are the constitutive operators of deductive reasoning itself. Global optimization of the ways in which one does global optimization is not even considered as an object of study in the current literature, so *thinking strategically about thinking strategically* cannot be subjected to the kind of normative-descriptive analysis that thinking about doing has been (see Moldoveanu [2009]). Given this fragmented normative foundation, the prescriptive approach predictably often falls short of producing the desired results: Biases and fallacies of reasoning are notoriously incorrigible to the remedy of merely *informing* students about the right ways to think and choose [Dawes, 1998]. It may be that the "incorrigibles" are at least "reasonable" Creatures, in the sense that they *would* be responsive to the right external reasons for changing their way of being; but prescriptive science will never find this out nor zero in on "the right reasons for the right person at the right time."

To this conundrum, ascriptive science says: "Let them figure it out for themselves, and let education be the process by which they figure it out for themselves"—by the design of analytical, experimental, and most importantly, experiential pedagogical steps that allow Creature(s) to understand from their own experience why it is better to choose coherently than not (utility pumps), why it is better to bet coherently than not (Dutch books), and why it is better to think more deeply (in a logical and computational sense) in some situations than in others. To the instructor's inevitable anxiety about being deprived of a normative and "infallible" foundation for her teaching, ascriptive science answers with COMM: No matter what else the classroom is, it remains a communicative situation and process—one whose integrity can be safeguarded by a transcendental commitment to open and responsive argumentation, from which student Creatures can deviate only on pain of forgoing their participation in the dialogue.

Ask is Creature: Perhaps most significantly, ascriptive science can be understood as a science of purposive, intelligent, data-driven *self-inquiry* and *self-transformation*. If Ask and Creature are the same individual, then

the distoscopic move that Ask makes in identifying Creature as an "it"—and
in using the tools of rational choice and rational belief theory to model its
physical, verbal, and mental behaviors—will allow Ask-Creature to consider
itself as the subject of objective inquiry and thus to start on the path to ful-
filling Nietzsche's ideal of the Overman. *I am the kind of person who does X
or thinks Y under conditions Z* is transformed, in this interpretation, from a
mantric or self-therapeutic utterance into a testable hypothesis that admits
refutation supplied by the kinds of behaviors that Ask-Creature observes itself
engaging in.

It is not at all clear to the ascriptive scientist that every individual is a
self. A *self* is something to be achieved by doing the hard and humbling work
of self-experimentation, not something that one possesses solely by virtue of
being biologically human. The "self-management" tools and techniques supplied by the psychological sciences of self-regulation and self-control become,
within ascriptive science, personal technologies for the targeted transformation of some counterproductive behavior. Epistemic rationality is more than
something to talk about in the arid confines of academic classrooms; it is a
blueprint for a structured and more productive series of conversations with
oneself.

The rationality and reasonableness of an Ask-Creature nexus evolves as
a function of the rigor and detachment with which the self-modeling and
self-experimentation program is pursued. Better or worse self-transformation
programs can be identified on the basis of the results of their application. To
the extent that thought is a form of internal conversation between me-now
and me-later, COMM retains its value as a transcendental principle in this interpretation of the Ask-Creature nexus, a principle that regulates and polices
the process by which Ask-Creature produces linguistic mental behavior. This
process allows Ask-Creature to advance propositions about itself or the world
and to accept or reject alternative or contradictory propositions. Communicative ethics, then, becomes a logic of internal conversation and, accordingly,
of thinking.

BIBLIOGRAPHY

Ainslie, G. (1992). *Picoeconomics: The Strategic Interaction of Successive Motivational States within the Person.* New York: Cambridge University Press.

Ainslie, G. (2001). *Breakdown of Will.* Cambridge, U.K.: Cambridge University Press.

Albert, H. (1985). *Treatise on Critical Reason.* Princeton, NJ: Princeton University Press.

Apel, K. (1980). *Towards a Transformation of Philosophy* (G. Adey & D. Frisby, Trans.). London: Routledge.

Aragones, E., Postlewaite, A., Gilboa, I., & Schmeidler, D. (2003). Accuracy versus Simplicity: A Complex Trade-off. Unpublished manuscript, Department of Economics, Yale University, New Haven, CT.

Argyris, C. (1991). Teaching Smart People How to Learn. *Harvard Business Review,* May/June, 99–109.

Argyris, C. (1993). *On Organizational Learning.* Oxford: Blackwell.

Argyris, C. (1996). Unrecognised Defenses of Scholars: Impact of Theory and Research. *Organization Science, 7* (1), 79–89.

Armendt, B. (1980). Is There a Dutch Book Argument for Probability Kinematics? *Philosophy of Science, 47* (4), 583–588.

Austin, J. L. (1962). *How to Do Things with Words.* Cambridge, MA: Harvard University Press.

Bellman, R. (1957). *Dynamic Programming.* Princeton, NJ: Princeton University Press.

Bénabou, R., & Tirole, J. (2002). Self Confidence and Personal Motivation. *Quarterly Journal of Economics, 117* (3), 871–915.

Bernardo, J. M. (1979). Expected Information as Expected Utility. *Annals of Statistics, 7,* 686–690.

Boolos, J., & Jeffrey, R. (1993). *Computability and Logic.* New York: Cambridge University Press.

Brandenburger, A. (1992). Knowledge and Equilibrium in Games. *Journal of Economic Perspectives, 6* (4), 83–101.

Brandom, R. B. (1994). *Making It Explicit: Reasoning, Representing, and Discursive Commitment.* Cambridge, MA: Harvard University Press.

Brooks, R. (1991). Intelligence without Representation. *Artificial Intelligence, 47,* 139–159.

Bylander, T., Allemang, D., Tanner, M. C., & Josephson, J. (1991). The Computational Complexity of Abduction. *Artificial Intelligence, 49,* 25–60.

Casti, J. (1991). *Reality Rules: Picturing the World in Mathematics.* New York: Wiley.

Chen, X., & Deng, X. (2006). Settling the Complexity of Two-Player Nash Equilibrium. *Proceedings of the 47th Symposium on the Foundations of Computer Science,* pp. 261–271. Piscataway, NJ: IEEE Press.

Chwe, M. S. (1999). Structure and Strategy of Collective Action. *American Journal of Sociology, 105,* 128–156.

Conitzer, V., & Sandholm, T. (2003). Complexity Results about Nash Equilibria. *Proceedings of the 18th International Joint Conference on Artificial Intelligence,* pp. 765–771. San Francisco: Morgan Kaufmann.

Cook, S. (1971). The Complexity of Theorem Proving Procedures. *Proceedings of the 3rd Annual ACM Symposium on the Theory of Computing,* pp. 151–158. Shaker Heights, OH: Association for Computing Machinery.

Cooper, G. (1990). The Computational Complexity of Probabilistic Inference Using Bayesian Belief Networks. *Artificial Intelligence, 42,* 393–405.

Cormen, D., Leiserson, C., & Rivest, R. (1993). *An Introduction to Algorithms.* Cambridge, MA: MIT Press.

Cover, T., & Thomas, J. (1991). *Elements of Information Theory.* New York: Wiley.

Daskalakis, C., Goldberg, P., & Papadimitriou, C. (2009). The Complexity of Computing a Nash Equilibrium. *Communications of the ACM, 52* (2), 89–97.

Davidson, D. (2001). *Essays on Actions and Events.* Oxford: Oxford University Press.

Davidson, D. (2005). *Truth, Language, and History: Philosophical Essays.* Oxford: Oxford University Press.

Dawes, R. (1998). Behavioral Decision Theory. In D. Gilbert (Ed.), *Handbook of Social Psychology.* New York: Oxford University Press.

deCharms, R., Maeda, F., Glover, G., Ludlow, D., Pauly, J., Soneji, D., et al. (2005). Control over Brain Activation and Pain Learned by Using Real-Time Functional MRI. *Proceedings of the National Academy of Sciences USA, 102,* 18626–18631.

Elster, J. (1989). *Nuts and Bolts for the Social Sciences.* Cambridge, U.K.: Cambridge University Press.

Feyerabend, P. K. (1975). *Against Method.* London: Routledge.

Fogel, D. B. (1995). *Evolutionary Computation: Toward a New Philosophy of Machine Intelligence.* Piscataway, NJ: IEEE Press.

Fortnow, L. (2009). The Status of the P versus NP Problem. *Communications of the ACM, 52* (9), 78–86.

Friedman, M. (1953). *Essays in Positive Economics.* Chicago: University of Chicago Press.

Garey, M. R., & Johnson, D. S. (1979). *Computers and Intractability: A Guide to the Theory of NP Completeness.* San Francisco: Freeman.

Gershenfeld, N. (1998). *The Nature of Mathematical Modeling.* Cambridge, U.K.: Cambridge University Press.

Gigerenzer, G., & Goldstein, D. G. (1996). Mind as Computer: The Birth of a Metaphor. *Creativity Research Journal, 2/3,* 131–144.

Gigerenzer, G., Todd, P., & ABC Research Group. (1999). *Simple Heuristics That Make Us Smart.* New York: Oxford University Press.

Gilboa, I. (1991). Rationality and Ascriptive Science. Unpublished manuscript.

Gilboa, I. (2009). *Theory of Decision under Uncertainty.* New York: Cambridge University Press.

Gilboa, I., & Zemel, E. (1989). Nash and Correlated Equilibria: Some Complexity Considerations. *Games and Economic Behavior, 1* (1), 80–93.

Gödel, K. (1931). Über formal unentscheidbare Sätze der Principia Mathematica und verwandter Systeme, I. *Monatshefte für Mathematik und Physik, 38,* 173–198.

Goodman, N. (1955). *Fact, Fiction, and Forecast.* Cambridge, MA: Harvard University Press.

Gray, J. A. (1987). *The Neuropsychology of Anxiety.* Oxford: Oxford University Press.

Green, L., & Myerson, J. (2004). A Discounting Framework for Choice with Delayed and Probabilistic Rewards. *Psychological Bulletin, 130* (5), 769–792.

Grice, P. (1989). *Studies in the Way of Words.* Cambridge, MA: Harvard University Press.

Gul, F., & Pesendorfer, W. (2001). Temptation and Self-Control. *Econometrica, 69* (6), 1403–1435.

Gul, F., & Pesendorf, W. (2004). Self-Control and the Theory of Consumption. *Econometrica, 72* (1), 119–158.

Habermas, J. (1987). *The Theory of Communicative Action,* vol. II: *Lifeworld and System.* Boston: Beacon Press.

Hacking, I. (1983). *Representing and Intervening: Introductory Topics in the Philosophy of Natural Science.* Cambridge, U.K.: Cambridge University Press.

Heatherton, T. F., & Baumeister, R. F. (1996). Self-Regulation Failure: Past, Present, and Future. *Psychological Inquiry, 7,* 90–98.

Heidegger, M. (1927/1962). *Being and Time,* rev. ed. (J. Macquarrie & E. Robinson, Trans.). New York: Harper & Row.

Hempel, C. G. (1945). Studies in the Logic of Confirmation. *Mind, 54,* 1–26, 97–121.

Hromkovic, J. (2003). *Algorithmics for Hard Problems: Introduction to Combinatorial Optimization, Randomization, Approximation and Heuristics,* 2nd ed. Heidelberg: Springer.

Hume, D. (1748/1999). *An Enquiry Concerning Human Understanding.* New York: Oxford University Press.

Jaynes, E. T. (2003). *Probability Theory: The Logic of Science.* Cambridge, U.K.: Cambridge University Press.

Jeffrey, R. C. (1983). *The Logic of Decision,* 2nd ed. Chicago: University of Chicago Press.

Jensen, M. C., & Meckling, W. H. (1994). The Nature of Man. *Journal of Applied Corporate Finance, 7* (2), 4–19.

Kahneman, D., & Tversky, A. (1979). Prospect Theory: An Analysis of Decisions under Risk. *Econometrica, 47,* 313–327.

Karmarkar, N. (1984). A New Polynomial Time Algorithm for Linear Programming. *Proceedings of the 16th ACM Symposium on the Theory of Computing,* pp. 302–311. Shaker Heights, OH: Association for Computing Machinery.

Karp, R. M. (1972). Reducibility among Combinatorial Problems. In R. E. Miller & J. W. Thatcher (Eds.), *Complexity of Computer Computations.* New York: Plenum.

Kreps, D. (1979). A Representation Theorem for "Preference for Flexibility." *Econometrica, 47* (3), 565–577.

Kreps, D. (1988). *Notes on the Theory of Choice.* Boulder, CO: Westview.

Laibson, D. (1997). Golden Eggs and Hyperbolic Discounting. *Quarterly Journal of Economics, 112* (2), 443–477.

Lakatos, I. (1970). Falsification and the Methodology of Scientific Research Programmes. In I. Laka-
    tos & A. Musgrave (Eds.), *Criticism and the Growth of Knowledge.* Cambridge, U.K.: Cambridge
    University Press.
Lave, C. A., & March, J. G. (1975). *An Introduction to Models in the Social Sciences.* New York:
    Harper.
Lewis, D. (1979). Scorekeeping in a Language Game. *Journal of Philosophical Logic, 8,* 339–359.
Li, M., & Vitanyi, P. M. (1997). *An Introduction to Kolmogorov Complexity and Its Applications,*
    2nd ed. New York: Springer-Verlag.
Libet, B., Wright, E. J., Feinstein, B., & Pearl, D. K. (1979). Subjective Referral of the Timing for
    a Conscious Sensor Experience: A Functional Role for the Somatosensory Specific Projection
    System in Man. *Brain, 194,* 191–222.
Lin, S., & Kernighan, B. W. (1973). An Effective Heuristic Algorithm for the Traveling Salesman
    Problem. *Operations Research, 21,* 498–516.
Lo, A. (2004). The Adaptive Markets Hypothesis: Market Efficiency from an Evolutionary Perspec-
    tive. Unpublished manuscript.
Marr, D. (1982). *Vision.* San Francisco: Freeman.
Martello, S., & Toth, P. (1990). *Knapsack Problems: Algorithms and Computer Implementations.* Chich-
    ester, U.K.: Wiley.
Martignon, L., & Laskey, K. B. (1999). Bayesian Benchmarks for Fast and Frugal Heuristics. In
    G. Gigerenzer & P. M. Todd (Eds.), *Simple Heuristics That Make Us Smart.* New York: Oxford
    University Press.
Michalewicz, Z., & Fogel, D. (2004). *How to Solve It: Modern Heuristics.* Heidelberg: Springer.
Milgrom, P., & Roberts, J. (1990). Rationalizability, Learning and Equilibrium in Games with Strate-
    gic Complementarities. *Econometrica, 58* (6), 1255–1277.
Miller, D. (1994). *Critical Rationalism.* Chicago: Open Court.
Moldoveanu, M. C. (2009). Thinking Strategically about Thinking Strategically: The Computational
    Structure and Dynamics of Managerial Problem Selection and Formulation. *Strategic Manage-
    ment Journal, 30,* 737–763.
Moldoveanu, M. C., & Baum, J. A. (2008). The Epistemic Structure and Dynamics of Social
    Networks. Social Science Research Network Paper no. 88795.
Moldoveanu, M. C., & Langer, E. J. (2002). False Memories of the Future: A Critique of the
    Application of Probabilistic Reasoning to the Study of Cognitive Processes. *Psychological Review,
    109* (2), 358–375.
Newell, A. (1990). *Unified Theories of Cognition.* Cambridge, MA: Harvard University Press.
Newell, A., & Simon, H. A. (1972). *Human Problem Solving.* New York: Prentice Hall.
Nietzsche, F. (1892/2007). *Also Sprach Zarathustra* (in German). Middlesex, U.K.: Echo Library.
Nozick, R. (2001). *Invariances: The Structure of the Objective World.* Cambridge, MA: Harvard Uni-
    versity Press.
Papadimitriou, C. (1994). *Computational Complexity.* New York: Addison-Wesley.
Pearl, J. (1990). *Causality.* New York: Cambridge University Press.
Peirce, C. S. (1998). *The Essential Peirce.* Bloomington: University of Indiana Press.
Polanyi, M. (1958). *Personal Knowledge: Towards a Post-Critical Philosophy.* Chicago: University of
    Chicago Press.
Pólya, G. (1957). *How to Solve It,* 2nd ed. Garden City, NY: Doubleday.
Popper, K. R. (1959). *The Logic of Scientific Discovery.* London: Unwin Hyman.
Popper, K. R. (1961). *The Poverty of Historicism,* 2nd ed. London: Routledge.

Popper, K. R. (1963). *Conjectures and Refutations: The Growth of Scientific Knowledge*. London: Routledge.

Popper, K. R. (1983). *Realism and the Aim of Science*. London: Routledge.

Popper, K. R. (1999). *All Life Is Problem Solving*. London: Routledge.

Putnam, H. (1985). Reflexive Reflections. *Erkenntnis, 22* (1–3), 143–153.

Quine, W. V. (1951). *Ontological Relativity and Other Essays*. New York: Columbia University Press.

Rachlin, H. (2000). *The Science of Self-Control*. Cambridge, MA: Harvard University Press.

Ramsey, F. P. (1931). *The Foundations of Mathematics* (R. B. Braithwaite, Ed.). London: Routledge.

Rubinstein, A. (1986). Finite Automata Play a Repeated Prisoner's Dilemma Game. *Journal of Economic Theory, 46*, 145–153.

Rubinstein, A. (2001). A Theorist's View of Experiments. *American Economic Review, 45* (4), 615–628.

Russell, B. (1910). *Philosophical Essays*. London: Longmans.

Saloner, G. (1994). Game Theory and Strategic Management: Contributions, Applications and Limitations. In R. Rumelt, D. Schendel, & D. Teece (Eds.), *Fundamental Issues in Strategy: A Research Agenda*. Boston: Harvard Business School Press.

Samuelson, P. (1938). A Note on the Pure Theory of Consumers' Behavior. *Economica, 5* (17), 61–71.

Savage, L. J. (1954). *The Foundations of Statistics*. New York: Wiley.

Schelling, T. (1960). *The Strategy of Conflict*. Cambridge, MA: Harvard University Press.

Schelling, T. (Ed.). (1984). *Choice and Consequence*. Cambridge, MA: Harvard University Press.

Searle, J. (1969). *Speech Acts: An Essay in the Philosophy of Language*. Cambridge, U.K.: Cambridge University Press.

Searle, J. (2001). *Rationality in Action*. Cambridge, MA: MIT Press.

Sen, A. (1993). Internal Consistency of Choice. *Econometrica, 61* (3), 495–521.

Shannon, C. E., & Weaver, W. (1949). *The Mathematical Theory of Communication*. Urbana: University of Illinois Press.

Simon, H. A. (1973). The Structure of Ill-Structured Problems. *Artificial Intelligence, 4* (3), 181–202.

Simon, H. A. (1990). The Invariants of Human Behavior. *Annual Review of Psychology, 41* (1), 1–19.

Skyrms, B. (1986). *Choice and Chance*, 3rd ed. Belmont, CA: Wadsworth.

Sozou, P. D. (1998). On Hyperbolic Discounting and Uncertain Hazard Rates. *Proceedings of the Royal Society of London, Series B: Biological Sciences, 265*, 2015–2020.

Tarski, A. (1935). Der Wahrheitsbegriff in den formalisierten Sprachen. *Studia Philosophica, 1*, 261–405.

Thaler, R., & Sheffrin, S. M. (1981). An Economic Theory of Self-Control. *Journal of Political Economy, 89* (2), 392–406.

Turing, A. M. (1950). Computing Machinery and Intelligence. *Mind, 59*, 433–460.

Tversky, A., & Shafir, E. (1992). Choice under Conflict: The Dynamics of Deferred Decision. *Psychological Science, 3* (6), 358–361.

von Neumann, J., & Morgenstern, O. (1947). *Theory of Games and Economic Behaviour*, 2nd ed. Princeton, NJ: Princeton University Press.

Wang, L., Zhang, J., & Li, H. (2007). An Improved Genetic Algorithm for TSP. *Proceedings of the 6th International Conference on Machine Learning and Cybernetics*, pp. 136–140. Piscataway, NJ: IEEE.

Wegner, D. M. (1994). *White Bears and Other Unwanted Thoughts: Suppression, Obsession, and the Psychology of Mental Control*. New York: Guilford.

Wittgenstein, L. (1953). *Philosophical Investigations*. New York: Macmillan.

INDEX

Italic page numbers indicate material in tables or figures.

behavior: anti-, 71; ascriptive science approach
to study of, 45–50; automatisms, 27;
"everyday mental," 170–171; incorrigible,
56; itch-like, 64–66, 69, 75–76, 85;
learning, 222–223, 229–230; making
it count, 30; micro-, 215–216; must be
visible to be understood, 60; pain-like,
62, 65–66; prediction and production of,
16–18; privative descriptions of, 58; pulled
by incentives, 55, 59, 118; remedial, 53;
status-defensive, 42; stimulus–response
model of, 23; temporal, 52, 62–63, 75–76,
120–121; "unintentionally intentional,"
64; will-flipping, 54–58; willing versus
producing, 24
behavioral dispositions, interpretations of,
12–14
behavioral domains, 40
Being and Time (Heidegger), 10
being-in-the-world, 210–212
Bellman-type problem, 83–84
BEL model: architecture and justification of,
101–103; combined with BET, 251;
combined with DEC, 158, 165, 212;
Dutch books, 108–109, 125, 231; and
fiat strategy, 122; and learning to learn,
213–216, 251–252; and possibility
of auditing meaning, 117; reconciling
LEARN and, 230–232
benign, representational function of models
as, 4
Bernardo, J. M., 112
BET** (Talk the Walk variant), 99–100, 102
BET* (Walk the Talk variant), 99–100
BET model, 97–100, 158, 213, 232, 236,
251–252
betting: BEL and, 101–110; and belief, 14,
96–100; and "imbecility," 135–138;
and meaning, 114–118; and meaning
of sentences, 114–118; to measure
responsesiveness to syllogism, 210;
to measure uncertainty, 158; mental
kinematics of, 138–139; odds for
fallibilism, 230–232; and reasonableness,
126–128; scoring rules, 111–114; turning
logic into action, 117
betweenness axiom, 78–79

bias, 108, 160, 225, 255
binding, 32, 235, 243, 249
blinding effect, 56
Bob and recreational drug use, 224, 228
boredom and thrill seeking, 67
Boston street navigation problem, 172
boundedness of probabilities, 102–103
bounded rationality, 160, 201
bounds of applicability, 40
brains in a machine/brains in vats effect,
11, 62
branch-and-bound (BB) Heuristics, 188–190
Brandom, Robert, 242–243
breaking points, 171
bridges, 223
Brooks, Rodney, 211
browsing behavior, 180
brute force solutions, 159, 177–178, 181–184,
187, 191
budget, uncertainty, 120, 122, 123
build-up mechanism, 70
Buridan's ass choices, 32–33, 91

calculators, 7–9, 51
calibrating expectations, 36
Canadian navigation problem, 172, 187,
189–191
canonical algorithms, 159–164, 200
Carnap, Rudolf, 89
cataclysmic temptations, 79
causal reasoning, 177
Central Intelligence Agency interrogation
manuals, 61
certainty, 88, 150, 220
charity, principle of hermeneutic, 236–237
choice(s): ascriptive science of, 27–29; decision
science modeling of, 29; exploring
contradictory, 34, 46–47; inferring
preferences from, 22; order of, 29; in slow
motion, 24–27
cigarette addiction, 59, 76, 78–81
CLIQUE problems (CP), 184–185, 190
closure, deferral of, 123–124
code violations, 227
codewords, 95–96, 227
Cognition predicting Affect, 118–120, 126
cognitive indifference, zone of, 160